KILLINGS ON ROUTE 66

Ronald E Bowers

Former Senior Prosecutor
Los Angeles County District Attorney's Office

Some names and locations have been changed to protect the privacy of individuals connected with this story. Certain events have been inferred from the facts of these cases.

Ronald E. Bowers, Publisher
losangelestruecrime@aol.com

ISBN 978-1-7326655-2-1

First release October 2015

INTRODUCTION

When I, the author, meet visitors or tourists and they learn that I live in the Los Angeles area, I am often asked if I live near old Route 66. I am amazed how many people have some type of fascination with this old historical road. Since I grew up next to Route 66, I fail to understand the allure of this antiquated dilapidated highway. To me, it was always just another road, like any other.

Over the years, I have attempted to learn what has given such notoriety to this highway. Why does this American highway receive worldwide attention? Some suggest it is because of the song "Get Your Kicks on Route 66," which was composed by Bobby Troup in 1946. Others believe it is a result of the TV series titled ***Route 66*** that was a huge hit between 1960 and 1964. Either way, this particular road has been well etched in the psyche of many Americans, who have a warm and fond memory of Route 66 even though they may never have driven on it.

Old Route 66
From Chicago to Los Angeles

While growing older, I have learned certain trivia about Route 66. It formally was created in November 1926 and stretched from Chicago, Illinois, all across the midsection of the USA to end in Santa Monica, California. It covered 2,448 miles, crossing through eight states. In June 1985, it was phased out and replaced by the Interstate Highway System. Over its 60-year history, Route 66 has been considered 'America's Main Street.' During the 1930s, it played a role in the mass migration of thousands of destitute people during the Depression who were traveling west in hopes of finding a better life.

My family roots extend deep into Route 66, since I grew up in the City of Glendora, California, 30 miles east of Downtown Los Angeles. I remember during the 1940s through the 1960s a steady flow of cars and trucks rambling down the main artery of our community. Many of the travelers stopped at our local motels to rest up before making the last day's travel to their new paradise (Los Angeles). During those years, I was a budding teenage entrepreneur looking for ways of making money. On many occasions, I set up a fruit stand next to the curb of Route 66 and sold fresh oranges to the weary travelers. They were amazed to see all the orange trees dotted with large oranges hanging from the branches. These new immigrants thought they had truly arrived in the 'World of Milk and Honey.'

I sold those travelers lug boxes of shiny oranges for 50 cents a box. What they didn't know was that these oranges had been blown off the trees during the wind storms. The orange-packing houses wouldn't permit those fallen oranges to be included in their produce line. What the local ranch kids did after school was take a wagon or wheelbarrow down the rows of orange trees picking up all the fallen fruit. There wasn't anything wrong with the oranges a little wiping with a tattered rag wouldn't do to make them sparkle like new. It was a win-win situation for the buyers, who got cheap fruit, and the kids, like me, who made some spending money.

Granted, I didn't make enough money to put myself through college, but it was a learning experience. As a result, I have a fondness for old Route 66 for delivering all those customers to my fruit stand. Years later, when I returned home during college vacations, I began to notice how Route 66 was changing. The heavy traffic turned to a trickle. Many of the motels and coffee shops were being shuttered closed. Then one day in 1985, the Route 66 signs came down without any fanfare. The new Interstate

Highway System gradually replaced Route 66, which became an old relic from bygone days. Many of the old communities that the route passed through felt a nostalgia for all the activity and excitement that they had enjoyed from being a part of the pioneer spirit this old road represented. Many years later, some of the cities, like my hometown of Glendora, reinstated the name 'Historical Route 66' to the original path of the highway crossing through our town.

Back in 1966, I graduated from the USC Law School, and upon passing the state bar exam, I decided to work for the Los Angeles County District Attorney's Office to gain litigation experience. To my surprise, I enjoyed the excitement and fast pace of trying cases so much that I stayed with the DA's Office for over 40 years. During my lengthy career as a prosecutor, I worked on thousands of cases, many of which were homicides. Since I had grown up on Route 66, I was especially familiar with the exact route it traveled through Los Angeles County. When I received a new homicide case, often I would recognize the crime scene as being on or near old Route 66. Needless to say, the homicide detectives didn't care that the murder had occurred next to a historic old road, since their focus was on solving the case for court.

However, I made mental notes to myself of all those homicides involving Route 66. After many years of informally tracking such cases, I thought I saw some type of pattern to those murders occurring on the old highway. I was always so busy with my own caseload that I never had time to analyze those Route 66 cases. However, after I retired, I started to review those old Route 66 cases and found some fascinating results.

This book is a result of my effort to make sense out of all those homicide cases occurring along the old route of Highway 66. Initially I examine the type of murder and why and how it occurred. Next, I review the police investigation and how the detectives were able to solve the case. This is followed by a discussion of the courtroom process with its high-stakes drama and the jurors' ultimate decision in each case. Finally, we review what impact this particular case had on the community and criminal justice system.

For convenience, this book starts at the very end of this legendary highway and works its way eastward to Barstow's Route 66 Museum. So our story begins on the Santa Monica Pier, which is considered the terminus of old Route 66. This first homicide case involves a mass shoot-out on the pier. Few remember when two mass killers came to the pier and were spotted by the police, which set off a huge shoot-out in which a number of civilians and officers were unfortunately shot. This True Crime case gives you, the reader, an opportunity to learn how to avoid being the next victim of these remorseless killers.

After we conclude our review of the pier shoot-out, we merely go a few feet to visit our next Route 66 True Crime homicide. This case was given the nickname 'German Tourist Murder,' since it involved several vacationers from Germany who were walking along the beach area when they were confronted by a group of young robbers. We examine why this crime escalated into a murder.

After that case, we leave the pier and merely travel three blocks to one of the most tragic crimes of all time. This is the infamous case involving the deaths of ten people who just happened to be visiting the Santa Monica Third Street Farmers' Market. You as the reader will be introduced to the 86-year-old driver who plowed into all these shoppers in his old Buick LeSabre. The chilling facts of the case will subject you, the reader, to figure out what would be Justice in such a tragedy.

After struggling with this heartbreaking case, we head eastbound on Santa Monica Boulevard, retracing old Route 66. After a couple of miles, we pass under the new 405 Freeway. Before reaching Westwood Boulevard, we turn right for a block and pass by an apartment house where a murder occurred that changed our use of DNA evidence in homicide cases. This is a fascinating case, since a LAPD Sgt. declared the female victim had died of natural causes. You, the reader, will learn how a bureaucrat from the Coroner's Office wouldn't release the body to the family for cremation because the investigator's report inadvertently was missing a signature. As a result, another investigator was sent out to sign the report. He just happened to look at the victim's body at the mortuary and noticed red marks on the neck which hadn't been noticed before. Upon a further examination, they found that the victim had been strangled and raped.

After we finish reviewing this rape-murder, we again take Santa Monica Boulevard (old Route 66) and continue through Beverly Hills and then to West Hollywood. Turning off several blocks on Rangle Street, we come to the site of the dreadful death of Dominique Dunne, who was the daughter of writer Dominick Dunne. She was found strangled to death in a neighbor's backyard. The impact of this homicide case changed the public's perception as to how they view murder cases. As a result of the trial of his daughter's case, Dominick Dunne became so disillusioned with the Criminal Justice System that he became a legendary True Crime writer who crusaded for the victims' side.

Leaving West Hollywood, we enter the Hollywood district and travel for a couple of miles until we come upon the Paramount Studios lot on Santa Monica Boulevard. There, we learn about a murderer who was standing near the studio gate after committing the most monstrous double murder in Tinseltown. How does a human cut off someone's head and carry it around like a trinket? This double murder was so bloody that you will want to wash your hands to make sure none of the blood and gore accidentally splashed on you.

Finally, we leave the Hollywood area, hoping to regain our sanity by traveling old Route 66 in the direction of the Downtown Los Angeles area. We leave Santa Monica Boulevard and turn onto Sunset Boulevard. After a mile or two, we come to the Echo Park district, with its huge, flowery lily pond. There, we can't help but notice the colossal Angelus Temple, which rises up to the heavens trying to impress anyone who passes by in its gigantic dome. Even though we have been concentrating on homicide cases, we can't help but wonder if today's new tools of forensics could put to rest the mysterious kidnapping of the church's founder, Aimee Semple McPherson.

She disappeared in 1924 from Venice Beach, where she went swimming. Instead of drowning, Aimee reappeared a month later in Mexico. She claimed she had been kidnapped by three people, who were never caught. The news media, though, made it appear that she had absconded to have a clandestine affair in Carmel, California with a church employee who was a married man. This became an international scandal which resulted in charges against Sister Aimee McPherson for committing a public fraud. Like in the Clinton–Lewinski scandal, where forensics showed Bill's DNA on Monica's blue dress, could Aimee's old dresses reveal some DNA clues regarding a secret rendezvous in Carmel?

Then, we continue on old Route 66 until we see the sign pointing to Dodger Stadium, and we veer left into the parking lot. Here we examine a shooting that occurred after a baseball game which was solved in the most astounding way. After we review the evidence of that case, we fast forward to 2008, when we encounter a similar case which pitted the City of San Francisco against Los Angeles for having hooligans attack Giants fans in the Dodgers' parking lot.

After leaving Dodger Stadium, we continue on Route 66, which is now named Cesar Chavez Boulevard. We proceed for one long block, then turn left on to a side street and proceed to an alley which has been given the name the 'Killing Field of Los Angeles.' Here Dr. Haing Ngor, who survived the killing fields in Cambodia, was gunned down in the carport of his apartment. Earlier, he had been recognized for his acting role, winning an Academy Award.

From that sad case, we fast forward up Figurreo the old Route 66, to Colorado Boulevard, passing through Pasadena and drive all the way to my hometown of Glendora. There we will stop at the 20th Century Motor Lodge, which was one of the busiest motels during the bustling days of Route 66. There we will discuss a shooting of a police officer and of a young mother, who was shot six times. After unraveling that case, we come to the east end of Los Angeles County, and Route 66 takes off for a long run through San Bernardino County.

In the high desert near Barstow, Route 66 reappears in the form of the National Trails Highway. This road follows the path of the old highway when it was decommissioned as a national highway. As we head for Daggett, we pass over a culvert which once contained the body of a young lady who was murdered in the Hollywood Hills. Luckily, a desert flash flood dislodged the body from the drain, allowing the case to be solved.

We pass through the city of Daggett, which is the closest thing to a live ghost town, with its several dozen residents. From there, we slowly drive along a straight two-lane highway which is only marginally maintained. All that can be seen is raw unadulterated desert. Most people are bored after the first mile, but the diehard Rout 66 enthusiast will continue for miles seeing nothing, just to experience the true feelings of the old Route 66. There are only abandoned service stations, motels, coffee shops, grocery stores, and just nothing for many miles until the old Route 66 disappears at a T intersection out in the middle of the desert to nowhere.

CONTENTS

SERIAL KILLERS TAKE OVER THE SANTA MONICA PIER

People vs. Amezcua & Flores

CHAPTER 1. A GREAT PLACE TO VISIT

What a delightful evening, standing on the iconic Santa Monica Pier. After spending a pleasant evening walking around the pier with all its 'sideshow' attractions, the time passes into the early-morning hours of the Fourth of July. Several hours later, beach goers would be swarming the beach to find the ideal spot in the sand to celebrate the holiday. Music would be gently filling the air with songs like ***This Land is Your Land*** by Los Lobos with Jerry Garcia or, as evening befalls the beach, a stirring rendition of the ***Battle Hyman of the Republic***. This patriotic day would be capped off by a colorful fireworks display illuminating the skies over the serene Santa Monica Bay.

End of Old Route 66

(July 4 , 2000)

Santa Monica Pier Shoot-Out

All that would soon happen, but first the remaining pier visitors wanted to savor the remaining quiet moments before the hordes arrived. Couples standing along the pier railing were gazing out over the tranquility of the ocean. They observed a slender haze lingering on the horizon, muting the lights from passing distant ships. As they turned their heads to the coastline, their eyes were mesmerized by all the lights from the city and, at the end of the pier, the kaleidoscope of colors from the Ferris wheel. Turning further to the left, one's eyes became fixed on Venice Beach, with its twinkling lights, curving into the South Bay communities. As one's eyes followed the shoreline, the outline of the affluent Palos Verdes peninsula could be seen in the foggy distance.

The weather was ideal, with a slight breeze blowing the ocean scent from the waves below the boardwalk. One's ears were bathed in the roar of the waves crashing below. This romantic site had to make an impression on the people still lingering on the pier. No one was consciously mulling over in their minds the fact that the Santa Monica Pier was claimed to be the end of Route 66, which commenced in Chicago, Illinois. At one time, Route 66 was one of the beloved roads of America that many traveled through the Midwest in order to arrive at a new home in sunny Southern California. When the traveler reached the pier, they thought they had arrived at their 'Garden of Eden.'

This early-morning hour was being enjoyed by all, not because of the significance of the historic location but because everyone's senses were in harmony in their minds. Many were cherishing the moment. One could still hear the sound of laughter and the clatter from the arcade games. Couples were strolling alone, hand in hand, and even some hugging and kissing. For some, this was a romantic time and place, and they were having their private moments. Loving couples had the feeling their lives were in tune and they were on the same page as their partners.

This moment in time seemed almost perfect, and things couldn't be better. Then the piercing sound of gunshots interrupted this pleasurable moment. At first people disregarded the gunfire as a possible early fireworks demonstration. But the continued sound of gunfire reinforced everyone's suspicion that something sinister was happening and they were in the middle of it. At first one's concern was finding cover. However, one recognized quickly that the sound of gunfire was coming from several directions. Where do you find safe cover when shots are ringing out all around you? You can't find cover until you know the source of the gunfire. After each new shot, the panicked crowd listened intently to determine its origins.

Everyone on the pier kept their heads down and tried to find shelter behind any type of large object. Some tried to dart between structures, but most hunkered down to await some direction from authorities. Police officers could be seen running down the pier, taking refuge behind telephone booths and parked cars. Soon the shooting focused around the Penny Arcade building, which was in the center of the pier. Those people who were further out on the pier had nowhere to go but to flatten themselves against the splintery wooden boardwalk.

Thus began the nightmarish 'Fourth of July Shoot-Out on the Santa Monica Pier' that lasted for hours and ended with a number of civilians and officers shot. At the time, the question on everyone's mind was, "How do we survive?" Why were killers with their AK-47s wandering the Santa Monica Pier this particular night?

Earlier that evening, the killers arrived in their car crammed with weapons and a vast supply of ammunition. They passed under the iconic Santa Monica Pier sign stating "SANTA MONICA YACHT HARBOR; SPORT FISHING & BOATING; Cafes." It gives the appearance of a neon sign from the 1950s. It doesn't project the significance that is historically contained on this pier. If this sign could talk, it would have tall tales to tell about celebrities coming and going. Today there isn't any 'Yacht Harbor' as written on the sign, since all the boats have been moved south to the Marina Del Rey. The fishing boats are gone, and the only fishing left is a few diehards who want to try their luck fishing from on top of the pier.

To many people, the sign signifies the end of Route 66. A plaque on the pier designates that this is the official end of the famous Route 66 which started in Chicago. Only the Route 66 aficionados and map lovers would appreciate the history of the Santa Monica Pier.

Dozens of movies have been made featuring the pier, and by now, millions of tourists have strolled the pier wondering what is so significant about this location. It is a tiny Coney Island and Atlantic City Boardwalk which lacks the character that the tourists expect.

As one walks down the pier's wooden planks, one is transported back in time. The first building one passes is the aging wooden building that houses the old carousel. From the open windows and doors, one can hear the carousel music tooting the ever-present rhythm as the painted horses prance up and down. This is a mandatory stop for families with young children. All kids have a childlike fascination with riding the wooden horses. Everyone can recall their first ride. At first, every kid fears falling off the horse. But there is the feeling that one can do it if mom or dad stands nearby for moral and physical support.

The ride starts slowly, and the first thought is that this isn't so bad. But then the carousel picks up speed, and the child begins to move up and down while the carousel continues to spin, and at that point many a child has second thoughts. The organ music seems to heighten the excitement, and one wonders how much longer the ride will last. Finally, the wooden horses come to a full stop. The young child anxiously waits for the attendant to undo the safety belt so he or she can dismount gracefully. The youngster doesn't want anyone to know how scared he or she was. When asked whether he or she liked the ride, the answer is a brisk, "It was okay."

So carousels evoke special memories for the young and old. In today's world, a carousel would seem so tame compared to all the amusement rides that have been created over the years. At the far end of the pier, one can find other rides, which include a Ferris wheel that affords the riders a spectacular view of the entire coastline. At night, the large Ferris wheel is all lit up with colorful flashing lights that make the pier stand out against the backdrop of the dark ocean. The carousel and Ferris wheel may seem too subdued for today's young people, who want more thrill in their rides. To cater to that crowd, a small roller coaster was installed. The pier may not have the scariest amusement rides, but the setting couldn't be better.

Other people find their enjoyment by visiting the Play Arcade on the pier. Originally, it was called the 'Penny Arcade,' when it was filled with the old pinball machines. But with the advent of the modern video games, the price of playing far exceeded a penny. Kids flock to the Play Arcade. Just walking by, one can't miss the dizzying sound of dozens of video games all at the same time screaming out circus tunes.

What's wonderful about the pier is there is something for everyone. If thrill rides and arcade games aren't your taste, you can merely stroll the boardwalk, taking in all the fresh air with the pounding surf beneath your feet. The pier is inspirational to some, and to others it is merely an exciting place to hang out. On a night in July, this could be the coolest place to literally and figuratively 'chill out.' In the summer, many people migrate to the beach to get away from the sweltering heat of the valleys.

One can say that the people congregating on the pier are like a melting pot of all cultures. Of course, there are the foreign tourists who have seen postcards of the pier, and they want to feel and experience firsthand what it is all about. And there are American tourists who have seen the pier in various movies over the years. The older generation will remember the movie ***The Hustler***, with actors Paul Newman and Jackie Gleason. There were memorable scenes that were filmed in and around the carousel building.

Aside from the tourists who visit, there are the locals who just like to be a part of the beach scene. It is so peaceful, and there isn't any admission to walk around the pier. That means there are no barriers as to who can and cannot visit the pier. Since it is so accessible and free, there are times that less desirable people tend to congregate there. The City of Santa Monica prides itself on being one of the most liberal and progressive cities in the country. It doesn't want to say no to anyone. The city fathers have a softer and gentler policy regarding the homeless. They don't want anyone to feel unwelcome in their fair city.

Because of the city's liberal attitude, the pier became a magnet for gangster types to hang out. This has led to gang fights and knifings. The city's reaction was to create a police annex station on the pier. That provided the police a visible presence on the pier, and the idea was that it would deter gangsters from acting up while visiting the pier.

CHAPTER 2. WELL-ARMED VISITORS

For those on the pier that early morning of the Fourth of July, their Perfect Moment had quickly evaporated into a Panic Survival Mode. How did this all come about? To learn the answer, we turn back the clock to 1:00 a.m., when a person on the pier received a page on his pager. (For those who don't remember pagers, they were used to inform the receiver that they needed to phone someone by listing the phone number to call. They were used before the advent of cell phones.) This person's name was **Joseph Flores**. He was visiting the pier with his very close friend **Oswaldo Amezcua**. What they had in common was that they were both members of the 'East Side Bolen Parque' gang of Baldwin Park. They and fellow gang members had driven some 40 miles to see if they could pick up some chicks on the pier.

Flores looked at his pager and didn't recognize the number. But he was curious if it was from one of his girlfriends. Since he didn't have a cell phone, he looked around and found two pay phones in the middle of the pier. He walked over to one of the pay phones and dialed the number. To his delight, the phone was answered by a girlfriend by the name of Carina. He and Carina had spent some exciting times together about a week earlier. He liked Carina and was pleased to hear from her. For the next few minutes, he continued to engage her in lightweight chitchat.

What Flores didn't realize was that Carina had paged him the number of a private line from the San Bernardino Sheriff's Office. While he was talking to Carina, homicide detectives were tracing the call to see where Flores was calling from. The detectives were able to quickly determine that he was calling from a pay phone on the Santa Monica Pier.

One of the homicide detectives on another phone called the Santa Monica Police Department and contacted their watch commander. Within seconds, the Santa Monica dispatcher was radioing to all officers that there were two suspects on the pier who were wanted for triple murders and the shooting of a deputy sheriff. All this information was relayed to the Santa Monica Pier police annex, which was within 100 feet of the pay phones. At the same time, several officers were patrolling in their police cars near the pier. All these officers started to converge on the pay phones on the pier.

Most of the time, it takes a long time for a police department to mobilize. But in this situation the stars, the planets and moons must have been in the perfect alignment. All of a sudden, officers seemed to come out of the woodwork. The officers gathered and they approached the area of the pay phones. They had a general description of two male Hispanic gangster types—one short and the other one taller. As the officers reached the pay phones, they didn't see anyone standing around.

The officers as a group started walking westbound on the pier, past the phones. Immediately, they saw two gangster types walking toward them. One of them looked up and saw the officers approaching, and he promptly made an about-face and started to return to the Arcade building. The other person, who was **Joseph Flores,** put his head down and continued toward the officers in an attempt to walk past them. The officers broke rank and approached him in different directions.

Flores started running. By this time, several officers had reached him. He tried to break away. He kept putting his hands behind him as though he was trying to retrieve something from the back of his pants. Before he could remove anything, the officers had him face down on the coarse boardwalk. He continued to struggle, but the group of officers was able to prevent him from retrieving a TEC-9 semiautomatic weapon he had stashed in the back of his pants. From his left pants pocket, the officers recovered a fully loaded magazine clip. Later, they discovered he had a Colt .25 semiautomatic handgun in his front pants pocket.

Fortunately for the officers and the general public, Flores was quickly subdued and wasn't able to use his arsenal of weapons. If he had been able to reach his TEC-

9, there would have been many people on the pier who would have been killed or injured. However, the capture of the other gangster, **Oswaldo Amezcua**, didn't go as well. He was able to escape into the interior of the Arcade building, with all its hiding places behind bulky video games.

Amezcua immediately forcefully grabbed a female bystander as a hostage. He grasped her by his left hand and held his 9 mm Ruger semiautomatic next to her head. With the hostage in tow, he went to the doorway of the Arcade. There he started looking for the officers. When he saw one, he fired at the officer. The police were at a disadvantage in that they didn't dare fire back since he was holding the hostage between him and the officers. Also, the police didn't know how many gang members were actually on the pier, especially in the arcade.

The police assessed their position and realized that they had an extremely dangerous situation. There was an armed man who was holding a hostage and firing indiscriminately from the Arcade. The officers didn't have time to evaluate all the options. The first thought of the police was to surround the Arcade building so the suspect couldn't escape. As a result, several officers went to the rear of the building. Officer Coria was one of the officers who ran to the rear. There were numerous rear doors and windows. She was trying to find a safe place to take cover and at the same time trying to view the rear doors.

Officer Coria couldn't see where the shooter was in the Arcade building. As she looked for cover, she heard another gunshot that sounded louder than the others. Immediately, she felt excruciating pain in her arm; at the same time, the limb went numb. Later, she learned a bullet had shattered her arm bone. She keeled over on her knees, realizing she was out of action.

At about the same time, Officer Wong was running by the south doors, chasing another gang member who was climbing a chain-link fence. While Officer Wong was pursuing someone else, Amezcua, still inside the Arcade, took aim and shot him in the right hip. He immediately went down. Since he was still in the line of fire, fellow officers reached out and grabbed his limbs and pulled him to safety. Within the first five minutes, the police were taking major hits. The police couldn't assess exactly where the shots were coming from. Ironically, the police had the feeling that they were the objects of target practice for those in the Arcade. Just as the police thought they had gained control, there was another piercing shot from the Arcade's window, which hit Officer Hirt in the left calf. He grabbed his injured leg and started to limp away from the field of combat. Bullets continued to fly from the Arcade as the officers tried desperately to contain the situation.

CHAPTER 3. KIDNAPPING AND STANDOFF

While the shooting of the officers was occurring, Amezcua had taken 15 civilian hostages and barricaded himself with the captives in the center of the Arcade. Amezcua ordered some of the hostages to move some of the video game machines in order to form a fortified area where he could take cover with the hostages. Then the shooting subsided and the standoff began. The police had surrounded the entire building. Thus began the containment period. The SWAT officers had been awakened at their homes. Within the hour, they started arriving at the pier to relieve the first responding officers. The suspect Amezcua wasn't going anywhere. The police now had time on their side.

Amezcua started yelling out demands. The Police Hostage Negotiation team was able to send in a telephone that Amezcua could use to make his demands. One of his requests was to be able to hear from his cohort Flores, who had already been captured. The negotiators agreed to tape a statement from Flores so that Amezcua could hear that he was okay.

Flores was at the hospital receiving treatment for some dog bites and bruises he had incurred when he was arrested. As promised, the police did obtain a taped statement from Flores. By this time the sun was coming up, and Amezcua was getting tired of having to hold all the hostages by his lonesome self. After a five-hour standoff, Amezcua, agreed to give up without harming any of the hostages.

Amezcua was taken into custody, and his 9 mm Ruger was seized on the floor where he had fortified himself. The standoff at the Santa Monica Pier was over.

In the end, no one was killed. There were three officers injured and one civilian had been shot in the leg. It was interesting that the suspects had never committed any previous crimes in Santa Monica. All of their murders and other violent acts had occurred miles away in other cities. However, it was the City of Santa Monica who ended up having to pay the price of having their officers injured in the shootout.

At a later date, the investigators spoke to the two defendants. They didn't have any objection to talking to the investigators without an attorney. When asked about the shooting on the pier, they said the following:

Amezcua:

"I'll tell you one thing, I would make suggestions if police officers at the Santa Monica Pier were very lucky. I had a fully automatic AK-47 with a 20-round clip drum..."

As it turned out, the Santa Monica Pier situation could have been much worse. If the two suspects could have reached their car in the parking lot, the causality count could have been staggering. If they could have used the AK-47 with all the ammunition they had in the trunk, the result of the Pier Standoff would have looked more like a massacre. The pier would have forever lost its innocence and turned into a memorial for those who lost their lives there on July 4, 2000.

CHAPTER 4. WHO WERE THESE GANGSTERS?

Many people don't want to learn or know anything about gang violence, since they have it all figured out in their minds. They have compartmentalized gangsters as people who don't affect them. The belief is that gangsters do drive-by shootings as a part of their turf warfare. In other words, the public feels safe from gang violence, since they aren't in a rival gang and they don't travel through gang territory. The rationale is that if gangsters want to shoot at each other, then that's okay.

The public is totally naïve about urban gang violence. Here we are talking about the public visiting one of the most recognizable areas in the world, the Santa Monica Pier, and members of the public were subjected to gang violence. Anyone living or passing through an urban area NEEDS TO KNOW more about gangs and their activities, since their violent tentacles touch all of us.

Now would be a good time to introduce the reader to the two suspects in this case and try to learn something about gang violence. The more dominant gangster in our story is **Oswaldo Amezcua**, better known to his friends and foes as the **'Wizard.'** His companion was **Joseph Flores,** who went by the moniker of **'Jo-Jo.'** They were both proud members of the **'East Side Bolen Parque'** Hispanic street gang. The two were quite a team in that the 'Wizard' was about six feet tall and rather muscular. His partner Flores was short and skinny. Some people called them the 'Mutt and Jeff' team of criminals. But there wasn't anything funny about the manner in which they created a path of death and destruction wherever they went. As gang members, their mission was to protect their gang territory. They wanted everyone who lived in their territory to respect them and their gang.

After the Santa Monica Pier standoff, the homicide investigators had their work cut out for them. They had recovered three weapons from the suspects, the 9 mm Ruger used by Amezcua and the TEC-9 and Colt .25 taken from Flores. Immediately, the investigators had these weapons tested to see if any of the slugs or shell casings recovered from earlier murder crime scenes could be matched to those weapons. Also, the investigators had the opportunity to show witnesses photo lineups with the booking photos of these suspects.

The investigators knew that many people would be afraid of identifying either of them because witnesses feared retaliation from the other members of the 'East Side Bolen Parque' gang. No one wanted to be labeled a snitch, especially if they had to continue to live in the gang-infested neighborhood. Neither suspect possessed a car. In order for them to get around, they had to rely on others to give them rides or they had to borrow someone's car. Fortunately for the suspects, they knew two young women, one by the name of Katrina and the other named Carina, who did the driving when they went on their shooting sprees. These ladies could be considered accomplices. If they were willing to testify against Amezcua and Flores, they could be highly beneficial for the prosecution. But even if they agreed to cooperate, the prosecution needed to be able to corroborate their statements.

At the time of the suspects' arrest on the Santa Monica Pier, there were only three murders that the suspects could be connected to. Criminal charges were filed against the two suspects, and later there was a preliminary court hearing in which a judge found there was sufficient evidence to hold them for trial on those three murders. But after considerable investigation, these defendants were both linked to two additional murders. That required a Grand Jury hearing in order to add those previous murders to the original complaint. The prosecution wanted to consolidate everything into one trial. There could have been even more murders that they were involved in, but the prosecution had to draw the line in order to get the case to trial.

It was decided to prosecute the trail of violence that these two defendants had committed from April 11th to their arrest on July 4th, which lasted less than three months. During this period, these two individuals had murdered five people in cold blood and committed attempted murder on ten other people. The crime scenes covered two counties and a distance of over a hundred miles.

CHAPTER 5. KILLING SPREE

To better understand how gang violence can be harmful to all of us, let's start with the first homicide committed by these two gangsters and review these killings in chronological order. It was April 11th, 2000, when this murder spree began during the early-morning hours in the City of Baldwin Park. This was a heavily populated Hispanic suburban community east of Los Angeles. It was not uncommon to have gang rivalry simmering on the surface of everyday life. One of the prominent gangs in town was the 'East Side Bolen Parque.' It had its homeboys who were called the 'soldiers,' who went around the neighborhood making sure that no other gang violated its territory. A gang that wanted to be respected had to be vigilant at all times, since it was common for other gang members to try to sneak into the other's turf.

That meant that at all times of the day and night, enforcers had to cruise the part of town which they claimed as their territory. On that April morning, these two gangsters were doing their job for the gang by cruising Los Angeles Street in Baldwin Park, which was in their gang's territory. Since it was still early, there weren't too many people out and about. The blue-collar workers and their kids who were enrolled in school were deep in sleep at 12:34 a.m. Still open in town were several bars and a local Circle K mini-mart which never closed.

These two gangsters, while cruising by the Circle K, had noticed two guys who went in the store. They waited until they left the store to see if they recognized them. The two young men got on a bicycle and started riding down Los Angeles

Street. John Diaz sat on the handlebars, while his brother Paul did the hard work of pedaling. The beach cruiser bike they were on was a little difficult to get going, but once they had some momentum it was a breeze, since all the streets were flat. They had gone to the Circle K to get some chips and goodies. Life wasn't too bad for them at that moment in time. It was fun biking through the streets after midnight when there weren't any cars to get in their way.

The bicyclists could see an SUV was a short distance behind them. The SUV was driving rather slowly for traffic. They didn't pay much attention to it. When the guys reached Merced Street, they made a left turn to go back to their house. When they made the turn, they noticed that the SUV turned as though following them. This concerned the boys, and they wondered if it was someone they knew. The windows of the SUV had a dark tint, making it difficult to recognize the occupants.

Then the SUV went past them and they were relieved. Their main concern at the moment was not falling off the bike as they rode down the street. Then all of a sudden, the SUV made a U-turn in front of them and returned past them, going in the opposite direction. This seemed suspicious, but the SUV drove by slowly. Again, the young men thought it must be someone who was lost or unfamiliar with the area. Their thoughts were on the snacks that they had just bought.

Out of the corner of their eyes, they could see the headlights of the SUV coming back down the street toward them. They glanced back and could see that the same SUV had made another U-turn. The car was parallel to them, and the passenger yelled, *"Where are you from?"* Before they could answer, they heard shots coming from the direction of the car. John Diaz, who was on the handlebars, fell forward off the bike as his brother Paul tried in vain to steady the bike. The next thing Paul realized was that he had lost control of the bike, and it fell over.

The first bullet had hit John Diaz in the upper torso, causing him to fall into a neighbor's driveway. As the passenger exited the SUV, Diaz realized that he had to get away. Although he had been wounded, he desperately tried with his last burst of energy to crawl away. He was no longer able to control his legs. He sat up on his rear and tried to push himself away from the shooter, who was still pointing the gun at him. As he struggled to get away, the shooter continued to shoot him and struck him in his buttocks.

By this time there had been five or six shots fired, and the porch lights in the neighborhood were being flipped on as weary residents were reacting to all the noise. The shooter jumped back into the car. He and the driver sped away into the darkness. By now John Diaz was lying and dying on the front lawn of a house two doors from where he lived. His half-brother Paul had not been hit by the volley of shots. He had managed to run between two cars in the driveway and tried his best to be inconspicuous. For whatever reason, the shooter didn't seem to be interested in shooting at him.

After the SUV had fled the scene, Paul ran over to his half-brother to see how he was doing. He could see that he was breathing but seemed to be bleeding. Paul was torn as to what to do. His brother wasn't able to respond to him and there was no one around to help. All he could think about was running to his house two doors down.

When he got home, he had his relatives call 9-1-1 to get paramedics to respond. Within minutes, there were police cars converging on the scene. There had been a police unit at the Circle K mini-mart. The officer was writing a report and had noticed both young men go into the market and after several minutes return to their bike and leave the parking lot. The officer didn't pay any attention to them in that they weren't violating any laws and seemed peaceful. It was only several minutes after they had left that the officer heard gunfire coming from the direction the two young men had gone.

That officer and many others tried to make sense out of the situation. The paramedics worked on John Diaz to see what his condition was. They transported him to the local hospital, where he was pronounced dead.

The homicide detectives were called at home and asked to respond to the crime scene. Within an hour, they had arrived and were starting the investigation. Initially they talked to the half-brother of the victim, Paul. He was confused as to what had happened. He and his half-brother hadn't been doing anything wrong. They hadn't gotten into a fight or done anything to anyone. He couldn't figure out why someone would come along and shoot at both of them for no reason.

Paul could not understand why his half-brother John Diaz was a target. However, the reason would later be determined with the help of the tattoo on the victim's knee. It stated the word "Monrovia," which was the name of another gang whose territory was a short distance away. John Diaz was known as 'VAGO,' from a rival gang. The punishment for another gangster entering the 'East Side Bolen Parque' territory was the 'Death Penalty.' There was no trial by jury or opportunities for innumerable appeals. The punishment was executed swiftly to act as a deterrent for any other gang rival from entering their turf.

In this Diaz killing, it was Amezcua the 'Wizard' who was the driver of someone else's vehicle. His pal 'Jo-Jo' Flores didn't like to drive. 'Jo-Jo' would rather ride 'shotgun' and be the man with the gun. 'Jo-Jo' may have been short in stature, but his 9 mm semiautomatic made him very tall in the eyes of his victims. Both suspects kept a cache of weapons always at their disposal.

Much later in the case, both suspects were willing to talk to the detectives about their involvement in the shootings. It seemed that they were proud of the havoc that they had successfully created in their killing spree. They wanted to brag and take credit for their accomplishments. There was no remorse on their part. They lived by another standard of values, different from the rest of society.

Amezcua stated:

"I'm driving... It was a truck...like a 4Runner type."

"We got him in the butt, hard..."

Flores had no hesitation in describing what happened that night when he shot John Diaz.

Flores stated:

"Okay, he was coming from the direction of Circle K. He was on a handlebar of a bicycle, and his gang name is V-A-G-O, Vago, and he's from a gang called Monrovia.

"We came from Merced, bam. They across the street. I mean he was right there. Went all the way straight, threw a bitch (meaning making a U-turn) Threw a bitch (making another U-turn)... and came back around, boom, that's when I caught him by the pole (meaning a power pole next to the driveway).

"I popped him twice. He fell off the handlebars, the bike rolled over, boom. This dude standing closest to me. The other one's by—there's that little driveway right there, bam, and the one (referring to John Diaz) tried to crawl with his hands like—he was like on his—on his butt with his feet on the ground and his hands on—in back of him, and he was trying crawl back to me pow, pow, pow, put the rest to him.

"Dude (referring to Paul) can identify me. No problem, you know. Younger dude, believe it might be his brother or his friend.

"A 9 mm pistol was used, was not a revolver. It was a click, right... A semi. Uh, I believe you should find five cases, right, there should be five cases, but one might not have landed there, but there's five bullet impacts."

By examining this first shooting, you receive a good understanding of the thought process of real gangsters. Virtually never do you, the reader, ever have an opportunity to hear directly from a gangster as he explains in his own words why he did what he did.

CHAPTER 6. ANOTHER KILLING

Four weeks after the Diaz murder, there was another shooting, on May 5, 2000, in the City of Baldwin Park. This case was slightly different in that it involved a drive-by shooting of someone inside a car. Yet this incident reveals more details of the reasoning of gangsters. The victim, Arturo Madrigal, had grown up in a gang-infested area. He had taken on the appearance of a gangster by dressing in baggy pants and sweatshirts. He easily became involved in the drug scene and occasionally used marijuana and sometimes methamphetamine. He had lost his job because of his drug use and tried to take on the role of a 'middleman' in drug transactions.

His behavior had become so extreme that his folks had kicked him out of their house. A couple of months earlier, he was at a party where he was shot in the arm and leg. This was a wakeup call for him to straighten out his life or he would likely end up just another cold body in the morgue. He began spending most of his time with his friend Fernando, who permitted him on numerous occasions to spend the night at his house.

It was hard for Madrigal to turn his life around, especially since he didn't have a car to get to a job. His folks had an old Blazer that still ran fairly well, although it had a few dents in it. They were willing to give Madrigal the old Blazer if it would help him find a job. Around 9:00 p.m., he went over to his folks' house. His stepmother signed over the 'pink slip' for the Blazer to Madrigal. There wasn't much said, just making sure that the paperwork was in order so Madrigal could officially be the owner of the old SUV. He was there with his friend Fernando. They both were excited about the possibility of having a car for transportation.

His parents thought of this as an opportunity to help Madrigal grow up and get a job. Madrigal might have seen it a little differently. He talked to his younger brother before he left his folks' house. He told his brother that he and Fernando were going to immediately drive around town to pick up some girls. At that moment in time, the parents were hopeful, and the guys were happy since they now had a 'chick vehicle' (or maybe an old Blazer does qualify as a chick vehicle).

Madrigal headed over to meet some girls to show off his new car. He spent ten minutes trying to impress the girls. He told the girls he would be back to pick them up but he had to go over to Fernando's house in Baldwin Park. He drove directly to Fernando's and turned the corner to park next to the curb. To his surprise, another car pulled up alongside on his left. The passenger of the other car leaned out of the window and yelled, *"Where are you vatos from?"* Madrigal was worldly enough to know what to say in order to stay alive. He turned and said in a strong, firm voice, "We are from nowhere." That should have been the 'password' to saving their lives.

The people in the other car were **Amezcua,** the driver, and **Flores,** the passenger. Immediately, Flores shot Madrigal three times with his 9 mm. These shots proved to be fatal. Fernando, who was on the other side of Madrigal, ducked down, trying to find cover. As the shots continued to fly through the old Blazer, he kept trying to push himself as far as he could under the dashboard.

When Amezcua and Flores described this shooting to the police, they explained the shooting in the following manner:

Flores: *"You'll find a blue Blazer, right?"*

Amezcua: *"No primer, it's like a primer—old—older model Blazer... had a shell."*

Flores: *"Right when he stopped at the corner, he pulled over at the corner. We're going down south, making a left on the same street that he just turned on."*

Amezcua: *"I'm driving the car... I'm driving a light bluish car."*

Flores: *"I'm the shooter... He stopped, we stopped, and I go boom! Domed him (meaning shooting Madrigal in the head). There was two to three shots. There was two to three shots. I believe one in the face, one in the neck."*

Flores: *"I tell you, I like 9 mm... This one is a 9 mm, I believe, which would be a Smith and Wesson. Tight with 9. That's why I like 9s."*

After the shooting, Amezcua and Flores sped away. Fernando didn't know if it was a safe time to pry himself out from under the dashboard. He could hear his friend Madrigal in intense pain as though he were dying. Finally, he couldn't hear the other car, so he sat back up and could see Madrigal was seriously wounded. He ran into his house to have someone call the paramedics.

As people came out of their houses on this Friday night to see what had happened, all they could see was this old Blazer with the engine still running and the car in drive. Fortunately, Madrigal's foot was still on the brake. As people approached, all they could see was blood gushing from a hole in his head. At the same time, there was blood trickling out of his noise and ears. Aside from the blood rushing down his face, there was no other movement from his limp body seated in the driver's seat of his newly acquired old Blazer.

CHAPTER 7. HEADING FOR THE HIGH DESERT

Some people believe that gangsters only operate in and around their gang territory. This next murder case to be discussed occurred almost a hundred miles from the gang's turf. As a matter of fact, it occurred in an entirely different county. Further, this case shows that it is nearly impossible for a gangster to change his ways and leave the gang. This case illustrates how once you are in a gang, there is no escape out except in a casket.

It was almost a month after the Madrigal shooting. Around 4:00 a.m. in the early morning of Wednesday, June 7, 2000, Paul Ponce was at home with his friend Katherine. After meeting her, he had decided that the gang life wasn't for him any longer. For years he had been an active gang member of the 'East Side Bolen Parque' gang. Over time, he was taking on different values and realized there was more to life than 'Gang Banging.' Paul is a good illustration of how difficult it is to get out of the gang lifestyle.

He had moved to the high desert of Victorville to distance himself from his old gang buddies. He had settled into a pleasant blue-collar neighborhood where everyone worked for a living and took pride in the appearance of their houses and yards. He was adapting to his new life. On that early morning, Ponce was at home with his companion, Katherine. Ponce received a phone call and told Katherine that 'Jo-Jo' was coming over. She had known 'Jo-Jo' to be Joseph Flores.

Katherine didn't think anything was wrong, and she continued to do the laundry in the garage. She had gone in and out of the door to the garage several times. Then she heard a knock on the front door, and it sounded to her that Ponce opened the front door. Within seconds, there was the sound of gunshots. She didn't know what to make of it. She was scared to death that the shooter or shooters were going to find her in the garage. After hearing several more shots, she heard the parties leave by the front door. When she got up enough nerve, she looked inside the house and could see Paul Ponce, her boyfriend, lying dead on the living room floor.

The police were called, and the homicide investigators were able to recover several 9 mm shell casings and also several .22 cal. shells. The San Bernardino Sheriff's Office was unable to match these shells to any known weapons. Not until the arrests at the Santa Monica Pier and the recovery of those weapons did the investigators receive a match on the 9 mm. The .22 cal. shell casing was connected to another shooting in which the 9 mm and a .22 cal. were used. Since two weapons had been fired, it could be inferred that there were two shooters. Those might be the same people who had used those weapons together in the other shooting.

Later, both Amezcua and Flores freely admitted that they had been the only ones who had used these weapons that they possessed. From those statements, one could infer that they were the ones who used the weapons in the Ponce shooting.

The neighbors in this Victorville residential area tried to be helpful. The best description they gave was that a small vehicle drove up to Ponce's house and two or three people got out and knocked on the door. After the shooting, these same individuals left, driving off into the darkness without their headlights on. It all happened so quickly, as though it were a professional hit. The shooting was to send a message to anyone thinking of leaving the gang. In other words, there was no way out of the 'East Side Bolen Parque' gang unless one wanted to spend eternity pushing up daisies.

CHAPTER 8. SLAUGHTER

Up to this point, you have seen the two killers commit the murders basically by themselves. However, these killers were able to talk young women into chauffeuring them around in order to conduct the shootings. In this next case, they called upon a Katrina to provide transportation for them. Katrina was nice enough to give a lift to Flores and drive him to Hemet so he could visit with his mother. Later, she drove both Flores and Amezcua back to Baldwin Park in a Toyota Cressida that had been stolen earlier. The suspects had spent several days traveling around and wanted to freshen up themselvews, so they stopped at fellow gang member Luis Reyes's house. There they took showers. After that, they were planning to drop off Katrina at her mother's house in Baldwin Park.

It was the early afternoon on June 19, 2000. Since all three guys were from the 'East Side Bolen Parque' gang, they wanted to cruise their old turf to see what was going on. So they had Katrina drive the stolen Cressida while Flores was the passenger, looking at all the people on the street. Amezcua rode with their fellow gang member Luis Reyes, who drove his new Chevy Monte Carlo.

Katrina was driving toward her mom's apartment, going down Ledford Street near Molina Street. They noticed a group of males sitting on a short block wall along the sidewalk in the front of a house. Flores asked Katrina if she knew who these guys were as she slowly drove by. She indicated that she didn't recognize any of them. She asked Flores if he wanted her to make a U-turn to come back. He indicated that she should turn around so he could get a better look at who these guys were.

At the same time, Luis Reyes with Amezcua had circled the block and was directly behind her. Flores got out of the Cressida and said to Amezcua, "Well, well, well, what do we have here?" Immediately, Amezcua shouted at the group of guys, *"Where are you from?"* Someone on the wall said, "We're from nowhere."

Tensions seemed to quickly escalate. It was like the showdown at the OK Corral. But in this case, only one side was armed. The guys sitting on the wall realized that they were sitting ducks, and they began to nervously look for cover. They soon realized that there was no place to run for refuge. The guys on the wall could see Flores throw a gun to Katrina to use. Then Flores picked up a large AK-47. At the same time, Amezcua took aim with his trusty 9 mm.

Within seconds, Flores let loose with the AK-47 and bullets went flying in all directions. People were being hit left and right. One of the residents, George Flores, no relation to 'Jo-Jo' Flores, was shot several times. Since the victim was trying to get away, he was shot fatally in the back. He fell to the ground next to a shiny, well-polished black Camaro in the driveway.

Several of the other guys had been able to run to the front door and were desperately trying to get inside. At the same time, Flores and Amezcua were firing at these guys huddled near the front door. The suspects continued to shoot. There were women and children inside the house who were seeing bullets whiz by their heads. Everyone inside dove for the floor and tried to protect the children from being hit.

The people inside were familiar with this type of indiscriminate shooting. It hadn't been too long before when one of the residents had been killed in the same front yard. It was hard to understand how the same front yard could twice be turned into a killing field. Both killings had been committed by the 'East Side Bolen Parque' gang. After they had created complete havoc and a reign of terror, the shooters jumped into their cars and sped off.

During the shooting, Katrina held the gun that Flores had given her, but she didn't fire it. This shooting in Baldwin Park would seem like enough excitement for one day. However, after the shooting, they all decided it was time to get out of Baldwin Park. Katrina didn't go to her mom's as planned, but continued to drive the stolen Cressida eastbound on the I-10 Freeway with Flores as her passenger. Following her was Luis Reyes driving his Monte Carlo with Amezcua as his passenger.

Katrina was driving the Cressida and all seemed well. However, as she was driving through the City of Ontario, she noticed the engine developing problems. She didn't know what was wrong, but she was losing power. As a result, she decided to pull off of the freeway at the Guasti Road exit. This is an area that seems rural. It was the site of one of the oldest wineries in California. As a matter of fact, the Guasti Road she turned off on was named after the family that had established the famous Guasti Winery. The acres of vineyards were yanked out in the name of suburban development. On the other side of the road was the huge Ontario Airport. Although there wasn't much traffic on this side road, one was relatively close to civilization.

CHAPTER 9. UNBELIEVABLE KILLING

Some people like to emphasize that gangs stand for honor and trust. Conversely, it may be hard to explain how the next killing fits into the gangsters' code of conduct. Amezcua, Flores and Reyes were long-time gang members of the 'East Side Bolen Parque' gang. They had just participated in a bloody massacre in their gang territory, all for the prestige of their gang. They were as close as blood brothers could be. They would all be willing to give their lives for the sake of their gang.

Katrina pulled the disabled Cressida to a stop on the dirt shoulder of Guasti Road. Luis Reyes in his Monte Carlo with Amezcua pulled up alongside her disabled car. Flores told Katrina to get all her stuff out of the broken-down car and place it in the Monte Carlo. Without warning, she heard gunfire coming from the Monte Carlo next to her. After about a dozen gunshots, she turned and looked at the Monte Carlo and saw Amezcua shooting his fellow gang member Luis Reyes from point-blank range.

One could say that Reyes looked like Swiss cheese, since he had been shot so many times. His body lay twisted halfway out of the driver's seat. Flores immediately yelled at Amezcua and asked him why he had had to kill Reyes at this location. It seemed like Flores wasn't upset about the shooting but that it had been done in such a public place. Amezcua said it had to be done, and Flores didn't want to argue with Amezcua as to when it was the appropriate time to kill their friend.

Without any fanfare, the two of them pulled Reyes's body out of his Monte Carlo and dumped it on the side of the shoulder of the road. Flores directed Katrina to get into the driver's seat of the Monte Carlo and start driving. Even Katrina was slightly shocked at the execution of one of their closest gang members. Katrina's immediate attention was on having to sit in the driver's seat where, minutes before, Luis Reyes's body had been blown to pieces while seated there. Blood and flesh were all over the driver's compartment. Katrina slid into the driver's seat, partly due to all the bodily fluids saturating the cushioned seats. Amezcua stayed in the passenger seat, and 'Jo-Jo' squeezed into the back seat of the Monte Carlo.

She started the engine and put the car in drive. The Monte Carlo has a powerful engine, but the car stalled as she pressed hard on the accelerator. She was having trouble pulling back onto the road. Then she realized that their gang brother's body was caught under the vehicle. At that point, either Amezcua or Flores told her to drive over Reyes's body. She revved up the engine and pulled the shifter into drive. As the tires were spinning, she was able to pull over Luis Reyes's lifeless body, which was still oozing blood. Then they proceeded to Hemet, where Flores had an opportunity to have a pleasant visit with his family. They remained in Hemet for several days, after which Flores took Katrina to her sister's place to stay.

Apparently the word on the street was that Luis Reyes had provided information to the Baldwin Park police. Both 'Whizard' Amezcua and 'Jo-Jo' Flores thought that Reyes had become a snitch. For a gang member, being an informant was a death sentence. They had to deal with this problem immediately by setting an example so that others in the gang would be deterred from assisting the police.

CHAPTER 10. SHOOTING AT THE DEPUTY SHERIFF

Katrina liked Flores, but she felt it was time to distance herself from him, since she didn't want to be arrested for their gang violence. Flores fancied himself as a 'ladies' man.' He was continually trying to impress any woman he came into contact with. Several weekends earlier, he had been at a nightclub and caught the eye of another young lady, by the name of Carina. (This name was similar to his other girlfriend, Katrina. With such similar names, he had to think twice which one he was talking to.) Flores and Carina had exchanged phone numbers. She had two kids and worked at K-Mart. Gangs weren't her thing, and she was glad that she lived a long way from the gang-infested area of Baldwin Park. She was financially struggling to make it. Visiting nightclubs wasn't a common occurrence for her, but occasionally she hoped to add some excitement and romance to her life.

On June 25, 2000, Amezcua and Flores only transportation was Luis Reyes's Monte Carlo. It was six days since they had killed Reyes and confiscated his car. They were becoming concerned that the police might be on the lookout for Reyes's Monte Carlo. Flores remembered meeting Carina and that she had a relatively new Honda Civic. He called her up to see if she would like to go out 'clubbing.'

On Saturday evening around 10:00 p.m., Flores and Amezcua drove the Monte Carlo over to Carina's place. Everyone was in a happy mood, looking forward to an enjoyable and cool evening of entertainment. For whatever reason, the three of them left in two cars. Carina drove her Honda Civic, with Flores as the passenger. Amezcua drove the Monte Carlo of their fellow gangster he had killed. Initially they drove both cars to the local 7-11 mini-market to purchase some sodas and gasoline for the Monte Carlo.

As they filled up the gas tank of the Monte Carlo, Reserve Deputy Putney was patrolling in the area. He had just cleared a 'Disturbance Party' radio call. He was an experienced volunteer deputy who once or twice a week helped out doing patrol work for the San Bernardino Sheriff's Office. Deputy Putney wasn't doing this police work for the money, since he wasn't being paid. He just enjoyed doing something for his community to make it a safer place.

It was getting late for a Saturday evening, and he was patrolling north on Cedar Avenue in the Fontana area. He observed a Monte Carlo pulling out of the driveway of the 7-11 mini-mart at a high rate of speed. This caught his attention. He didn't think much of it but decided to call in the license plate number, 3SKX537. In the meantime, the Monte Carlo continued toward the I-10 Freeway. While both vehicles approached the intersection, the signal turned red and they all had to stop at the signal, waiting for it to turn green. At this point, Deputy Putney didn't know anything about the status of the car. Then the signal changed to green and the Monte Carlo proceeded to enter the freeway on-ramp. Deputy Putney had to decide whether to continue to follow the car or let it go. If there were any traffic violation after he entered the freeway, it would be within the jurisdiction of the California Highway Patrol and not the responsibility of the Sheriff's Department.

At that precise moment, the dispatcher called back and confirmed that the Monte Carlo was wanted and the parties involved were Armed and Dangerous. Deputy Putney immediately turned the steering wheel so he could continue to follow the Monte Carlo onto the freeway. The deputy had a situation in which he was in a 'one-man unit,' and he was a reserve deputy. He knew he shouldn't do anything until he had backup. He decided not to turn on his emergency lights in hopes that the driver of the stolen car wouldn't try to evade him.

It quickly became apparent that the driver realized he was being followed by law enforcement. The driver of the Monte Carlo started speeding up and weaving in and out of lanes. The evasive driving was making it difficult for the deputy to follow the fleeing car. Deputy Putney tried his best to follow the Monte Carlo while he waited for backup. Then all of a sudden, the Monte Carlo swerved abruptly to the right and cut off a truck. The driver was able to regain control and pulled off on the 'Sierra' off-ramp.

This all occurred so fast Deputy Putney wasn't able to follow the Monte Carlo off the freeway. He immediately notified the dispatcher that he had lost the car. This seemed to be enough excitement for a reserve deputy to have in one night of patrolling. But the excitement was just about to begin. There was a car ahead of him in the left-hand lane. He could see a person in a Honda Civic leaning out of the passenger-door window. This was Flores in Carina's car. While leaning out of the window, he was pointing a handgun at Deputy Putney. With all the training he had received as a reserve deputy sheriff, there was nothing that prepared him to know what to do in such a situation. Before the deputy could react, he saw the muzzle flash from the gun and heard bullets striking the police unit. Bullets were flying and hitting the front of the unit, with one striking the radiator.

This was the worst nightmare for any deputy, especially when in a one-man unit. The chase of the Monte Carlo had caused the deputy to be driving at a high rate of speed. As the bullets pelted the driver's side of the police unit, Deputy Putney gripped the steering wheel to maintain control. As the slugs began to strike at his driver's door, he wanted to duck below the dashboard, but he realized that would cause the unit to crash into other vehicles on the freeway.

The deputy's next thought was to return fire. However, that idea was impossible, since he was buckled in his seat and there was no quick way to un-holster his gun to fire back. Deputy Putney was learning the meaning of the phrase being a 'sitting duck.'

In total, 'Jo-Jo' Flores had been able to shoot 15 rounds at the deputy. Fortunately for Deputy Putney, none of the bullets struck him. Possibly he was spared when the shooter blew out the front left tire of the police unit. When the tire went flat, the police unit dipped down, and it started losing speed while the Honda with Flores in it pulled away from the disabled police unit. Deputy Putney was able to steer the police unit to the right shoulder of the freeway.

Undoubtedly Deputy Putney must have been wondering whether it was truly worth being a volunteer deputy. His reflections were quite different from what was going on in Carina's little Honda Civic. During the shooting, Carina was yelling at

Flores to stop the shooting and even tried to pull him back into her car. He kept shooting and told her to keep on driving. After they had gone a short distance, she pulled over at a Target store parking lot and demanded that 'Jo-Jo' get out of her car. She yelled at him as to how he could allow her to get involved in a shooting of a Sheriff's deputy. She said that she had two daughters to raise and couldn't afford being involved in such criminal activities.

Flores the gang banger became contrite and got out of her car. He tried to apologize for involving her in the shooting, but he realized that nothing he said was going to calm her down. So he walked away from the car and Carina immediately drove back to her home. There she appeared distraught, but didn't want to talk about what had happened. The next morning, she got up and didn't know what she should do. She was afraid that the Sheriff's deputy or someone else might have gotten her license plate number and authorities would come looking for her car. She didn't know what she should do.

Now Amezcua and Flores realized that they had a real serious problem. Amezcua was still driving the Monte Carlo. They knew that law enforcement was looking for this vehicle for two reasons. First, it had been taken in the murder of Luis Reyes in Ontario, and secondly, it had been used in shooting at Deputy Putney. The question was how to get rid of the Monte Carlo. Since they had been driving the car for almost a week, they knew their fingerprints were all over the vehicle.

The only smart thing to do was to torch the Monte Carlo so their fingerprints wouldn't be able to be found on the vehicle. Flores went over to his mother's place in Hemet and got his mother's assistance in buying a large can of gasoline. Then they all drove to a very isolated area of San Jacinto at 3:45 a.m. There they poured the gasoline all over the Monte Carlo and they lit it on fire. It ignited quickly, and Amezcua and Flores were pleased that their connection to the Monte Carlo had gone up in smoke.

By now it was late in the month of June. Law enforcement had a number of unsolved crimes. They had an arson case involving a Monte Carlo. Also they had the murder of Luis Reyes, who was missing his Monte Carlo. At the same time, Deputy Putney had gone in pursuit of the same Monte Carlo. All these crimes seemed to be tied together. However, the shooting at Deputy Putney didn't sit well with law enforcement, since it doesn't take lightly shooting at any officer or deputy. This was especially true when there was nothing that the deputy had done to provoke the situation. And law enforcement can't afford a situation in which a reserve deputy is shot at when he isn't even being paid to assume the risk of being a peace officer. The end result was law enforcement was going to track down whoever possessed or used the Monte Carlo.

CHAPTER 11. THE WEAK LINK

Law enforcement wasn't coming up with any practical leads to find the suspect or suspects. At the same time, Carina was becoming more concerned that her car would be tied to the shooting of Deputy Putney. Carina was the type of person who wanted other people's advice as to what she should do. She asked several of her K-Mart co-employees what she should do. She explained that she hadn't known that Flores had a weapon when he was in her car. She kept minimizing her role in the shooting. Her co-workers, who had never been involved in such matters, weren't able to give her much in the way of advice.

Even though she hadn't received any useful advice, she had set things in motion that would be the undoing of one of the biggest crime sprees to ever hit Southern California. One of her trusted friends had passed on her information to authorities. Her co-worker told investigators that if they wanted to obtain information about Deputy Putney's shooting, they should contact Carina.

When the investigators received the information, they were thankful but didn't know if Carina would be willing to talk. On July 1, 2000, they called her in and talked to her. She didn't provide much information at first. They received permission to search her Honda Civic. They didn't find any shell casings or any evidence that would tie her to the shooting of Deputy Putney. However, the investigators found a photo of a male Hispanic in the glove box of her Honda.

On July 3, the investigators confronted her with the photo of the male in her glove box. At this point she admitted that it was her boyfriend, Jose Flores. She explained the entire situation in which she was driving her Honda and Flores was with her on the night of the shooting. She said that Amezcua was driving the Monte Carlo when he pulled out of the driveway of the 7-11 mini-mart. She noticed that the Sheriff's unit pulled in behind the Monte Carlo. When they were waiting at the signal to the freeway on-ramp, Flores said that Amezcua had to have been very nervous, since he was hauling a lot of weapons in a bag in the Monte Carlo. She explained that at that point she had been directly behind the Sheriff's vehicle.

Carina pleaded that she hadn't known that Flores, one, had a gun, and two, would shoot at the deputy. The investigators wanted to see how sincere Carina was in proving her innocent involvement in what had happened. They asked how Flores could be contacted or found. She said that she didn't know, but she had his pager number. The investigators had her call the pager from one of the Sheriff's station's private lines.

To everyone's surprise, within several minutes, that private line received a phone call. The investigators traced where the phone call was coming from. That's when law enforcement realized that Flores was on the Santa Monica Pier in the early-morning hours of July 4th. As a result of that phone call, the reign of terror by Amezcua and Flores would finally be over.

CHAPTER 12. WHO SHOULD PROSECUTE SUCH A CASE?

Now that law enforcement had caught and arrested the 'Whizard' and 'Jo-Jo,' the ball was passed to the prosecutors to make decisions as to how to file charges against both of them. Since these two defendants had committed so many crimes in both Los Angeles and San Bernardino counties, the initial decision was whether to file one gigantic case including all the crimes in one county or file charges only in the county where the crimes actually occurred. The basic rule of jurisdiction and venue is that a person accused of a crime should be prosecuted in the county where the crime occurred. This rule works well in most situations, such as in a robbery, since all the acts of the robbery occur in one location (one county). However, in other crimes, such as kidnapping, the initial act of kidnapping may take place in one county but the victim may be transported into another county.

Even in a murder case, it isn't always clear where the murder occurred. The initial violence may occur in one county and eventually the body may be discovered in another county. In such a situation, law enforcement may not know for certain where the actual killing occurred. However, in the crimes committed by Amezcua and Flores, all the facts regarding each murder clearly occurred in only one county, in that the victims all were shot and died in one place each.

The Santa Monica Pier shootout all occurred in one place, that being Los Angeles County, therefore it would be prosecuted by the Los Angeles DA. Likewise, the three murders that occurred in Baldwin Park (Los Angeles County) would go to the LA DA's Office. As to the two other murders and the shooting at Deputy Putney that occurred in San Bernardino County, those cases could be prosecuted by the San Bernardino County District Attorney's Office.

First the investigators had to decide in which county to file the charges. One could say that the San Bernardino Sheriff's Department was in the lead, since they had two murders and one attempted murder, compared to Los Angeles County, which had only one murder and a number of attempted murders regarding the shooting at the Santa Monica Pier.

In order to decide who should prosecute Amezcua and Flores, there were several practical facts. It was Los Angeles County who had custody of these defendants. Also, the Santa Monica Pier shootout was considered highly serious, since a number of Santa Monica Police officers had been shot and seriously wounded. Therefore, the Los Angeles DA had the upper hand, since they wanted to prosecute them first before turning the two defendants over to the San Bernardino County DA.

It is advantageous for one prosecutor to bring all the cases at once. Conversely, the Defense position is that they would rather have the cases all tried separately. The advantage to the Defense is that the jury won't hear about all the other crimes that the defendant has been charged with. The Defense claims that the defendant is prejudiced when all the crimes are prosecuted together. As a result, the jurors quickly learn that the defendant has been involved in numerous crimes, and he or she may not appear as innocent as the Defense would like him or her to appear.

In some jurisdictions, the various District Attorneys might fight over who should have the opportunity to prosecute such murderers. Since the position of District Attorney is a political position, there might be a desire to gain publicity from such a newsworthy case. But in Southern California, there are more than enough murderers to go around. Seldom will a DA want more murder cases to gain notoriety.

The question is whether a DA can prosecute murder cases that occurred in another county. California has had numerous serial and mass murderers who freely crossed over county lines to commit their crimes. The legislature recognized the need to centralize prosecutions. It amended the state statutes so that one county District Attorney can prosecute a defendant who has committed other murders in other counties. The only constraint is that all the murders or crimes have to be connected in some manner. In other words, the criminal justice system realized that it is more efficient to try all the matters at one time in one place. This prevents numerous separate trials that could consume considerable court time in all the various counties where the offenses have occurred.

So when Amezcua and Flores were arrested, the Santa Monica Police detectives took the case to the Los Angeles County DA's Office Crimes Against Peace Officers Division. The case was assigned to prosecutor Darren Levine, who worked closely with the Santa Monica Police Department regarding the attempted murders involving their officers at the hands of Amezcua. The San Bernardino Sheriff's detectives accompanied the Santa Monica Police when the case was submitted to prosecutor Levine. The prosecutor recognized the complexity of all the charges that should be brought against the two defendants. It was decided that the Los Angeles DA's Office would be willing to consolidate all the crimes that were committed in both counties into one complaint. The San Bernardino DA's Office had no objection, since they had their hands full already with dozens of homicide cases involving other defendants. In this way, all the murders and attempted murders could be tried in one court at one time.

The U.S. Constitution requires that all accused have the right to a Speedy Trial. That has been interpreted to mean that an arrested person must be brought to court immediately and told of any charges filed against him. Generally, the courts have permitted the police to have up to 48 hours to file charges and bring the arrestee to court. As laudatory as this Constitutional right may seem, it does cause an inordinate number of problems in serial and multiple murder cases. This case was a perfect example of what happens when the detectives are forced to file charges within 48 hours, before they have any chance to investigate all the crimes the suspect is accused of.

Since we have already discussed the various crimes that the defendants were involved in, you, the reader, know more than what the investigators knew on July 4th, 2000, when both were arrested on the pier. Originally, the investigators knew about the shooting at Deputy Putney in San Bernardino County through the statements of Carina. Also, the San Bernardino Sheriff detectives learned information that the two suspects were involved in the murders of Reyes in Ontario and Ponce in Victorville, both of which occurred in San Bernardino County. In the beginning, the Los Angeles Sheriff detectives knew of only one murder in Los Angeles County, and that was the one in which Flores used an AK-47 to shoot George Flores on Ledford Street in Baldwin Park.

In order to prevent the suspects from being released, the prosecutor Darren Levine filed all the attempted murder charges that occurred on the Santa Monica Pier against defendant Amezcua. Included in that Complaint document was the Baldwin Park murder that occurred on Ledford Street involving George Flores. Also included were the two San Bernardino murders that the investigators had connected to the two defendants, plus the attempted murder of Deputy Putney.

The end result was that prosecutor Levine filed 41 counts in the Criminal Complaint against Amezcua and Flores. As complex as this charging document was, it was filed in time, before the arrestees would be scheduled for release. The prosecutor recognized that the Complaint document wasn't perfect, but it set out the initial charges, and most importantly it was filed in a timely manner. He knew that he would have plenty of time before trial to sort everything out.

CHAPTER 13. DEFENDANTS THINK DIFFERENTLY

Any criminal felony case that contains more than ten counts will be more challenging to prosecute, since there are more facts and issues that the jurors will have to deal with. Often jurors have more difficulty comprehending all the legal issues and remembering all the relevant facts in complex cases. In the Amezcua and Flores case, the jurors would be faced with 41 counts. The prosecutor knew from the start that this would be a nightmare of a case to present to a jury. The other problem faced by the prosecutors in these multi-count cases is the inherent witness problems.

After filing the case, the initial task was preparing for the Preliminary Hearing, when the prosecutor has to call witnesses to prove all the counts in the Complaint. At these Hearings, the prosecutor does all the 'heavy lifting,' since the Defense attorney usually doesn't call any witnesses. In a complex case such as this one, it can be a logistical nightmare to have all these witnesses come to court to testify. However, prosecutor Levine, with the cooperation of all the various investigators, was able to prove up all the counts in the Complaint. As difficult as this task was, it was nothing compared to all the factual and legal challenges the prosecutor would face in steering this case through the Criminal Justice System over the next four years.

The two defendants, 'Whizard' and 'Jo-Jo,' were hard-core gang members of the 'East Side Bolen Parque' gang in Baldwin Park. By their very nature, they looked at life and the court system completely differently from the rest of society. They didn't believe that they had to abide by the law of the land. They had their own set of rules they lived by. To their way of thinking, the gang was the center of their life. They believed in total loyalty to the gang. In their minds, the laws of the state didn't apply to them. If someone disrespected their gang and its territory, that was reason enough to kill them.

The same was true with the court system. Their feeling was that if they were caught then they would go to state prison, which is a 'second home' for gang members. They had little concern for the rules and procedures of the courts. Since they had been caught, their main concern was where to serve their time in state prison. They didn't want to be sent to Pelican Bay State Prison in Northern California, which is considered the 'Super Max' prison. At that institution, they would not be able to enjoy the freedoms and be able to easily mix with their fellow gang members.

They would rather have been sent to San Quentin, which is considered by gangsters a more prestigious place to be sent. The best way to be assured lodging at San Quentin is by receiving the Death Penalty. In order to navigate their way into San Quentin, they began firing their court-appointed attorneys, who desperately wanted to save these defendants from the Death Penalty.

The DA's Office has a lengthy procedure in determining whether it should seek the Death Penalty in various cases that are eligible for such punishment. Prosecutor Levine had handled numerous Capital cases and was thoroughly familiar with the standards that must be complied with. Never had prosecutor Levine ever had a case that was more worthy of the Death Penalty than this one. In this case, the defendants had killed so many people and attempted to murder Deputy Putney, as well as all the people shot on the Santa Monica Pier.

Those who oppose the Death Penalty most likely would find these two defendants come close to deserving the ultimate penalty even though morally these people oppose it. However, there was another consideration that might tip the scale for death. While Amezcua and Flores were in custody awaiting trial, they committed another violent offense, which illustrates how dangerous they were even in custody.

On November 2, 2001, the two of them were in the Los Angeles County Jail and waiting in a line with one Steve Mattson. Even though the defendants' hands were shackled, they both were able to pull their hands free. They both pulled out separate shanks (homemade knives) and stabbed their fellow inmate numerous times.

Although the victim of the stabbing recovered, he suffered massive stab wounds. This wasn't the first time that Amezcua and Flores had been caught with shanks. Earlier in the year, on January 29, 2001, a shank was found in Amezcua's jail cell. Several months later, Flores was likewise found with a shank in his jail cell on April 30, 2001.

The opponents of Capital Punishment like to claim that Life in prison is sufficient, since the murderers won't be able to harm anyone when locked up. However, that argument overlooks the lives of guards and fellow inmates. When considering only logic and not morality, the Amezcua and Flores case makes a compelling argument for the continuanace of the Death Penalty.

CHAPTER 14. RIGHT TO REPRESENT ONESELF

Amezcua and Flores had been given all the rights of the accused by both receiving their own free attorneys to represent them. However, after going through several different free attorneys, both defendants requested that their court-appointed attorneys be removed, since they both wanted to represent themselves in the court proceedings. The judge tried to explain to them the dangers they faced representing themselves. There is an old saying, "a person who represents himself has a fool for a client." This certainly applied in this case. Neither defendant was capable enough to represent himself, but they had an absolute right to do so according to the appellate courts. In the case of ***Faretta v. California***, 422 U.S. 806 (1975), the Supreme Court of the United States held that criminal defendants have a Constitutional right to refuse counsel and represent themselves in state criminal proceedings.

This becomes a 'Catch 22' for the trial judge. The appellate courts are so concerned that the defendants receive a fair trial that they will often reverse a case on the basis that the 'Pro Per' defendant didn't do a very effective job in representing himself. Conversely, the appellate courts will reverse a case if a judge appoints an attorney to represent a defendant over the objection of the defendant on the basis that a defendant was denied his Constitutional right of representing himself.

For over a year, the defendants represented themselves in all the court proceedings. This made it difficult for the prosecutor, since he can't ethically talk to a defendant without the permission of the defendant's attorney. But when the defendant is representing himself, the prosecutor has no choice but to talk directly to the defendant about court proceedings and witness issues. Without a doubt, this is an awkward situation for any prosecutor.

One day when the defendants were in court, they indicated that they wanted to talk to prosecutor Levine. The prosecutor wasn't sure what the specifics were the two defendants wanted to talk about. Technically, Darren Levine could talk to them, since they were representing themselves. However, prosecutor Levine was only too well aware how devious and conniving they were.

Prosecutors learn early in their careers to always have someone else present when talking to a defendant and even a witness. The reason is that these parties later will deny what they told the prosecutor. Why this is such a problem is that if the witness changes his or her statement on the witness stand, it might require the attorney to take the witness stand to testify what was stated earlier. Ethically, that attorney can't argue his or her credibility before the jury.

Prosecutor Levine knew better than to talk to Amezcua and Flores alone. He immediately arranged to have one of the investigators present with a tape recorder. Then, prosecutor Levine sat down with both 'Wizard' and 'Jo-Jo,' plus the investigator. The investigator automatically advised the two defendants of their Miranda Rights and asked if they understood their rights and wanted to waive them and talk to the prosecutor.

At first it was slightly awkward, since the prosecutor and investigator didn't know why the defendants wanted to talk to the prosecutor. So the prosecutor tried to break the ice by beginning to ask the defendants questions about the charges. Then the defendants started talking about two earlier murders. They admitted being involved in the killing of a person who was riding double on a bicycle on Merced Street in Baldwin Park. The investigators were familiar with it, but didn't have any evidence connecting these two to that murder. The other was the killing of Arturo Madrigal on Rexford Street in Baldwin Park. Flores indicated that he 'domed' him, meaning shot him in the forehead.

All of a sudden, one of the most complicated cases became even more convoluted. Prosecutor Levine appreciated learning about these additional homicides. But the question that went through his mind was why these two gangsters were telling him this very incriminating information. He continued to listen to them providing details that only the killers would know. Then it dawned on prosecutor Levine that these defendants wanted to brag about the crimes they had committed. It was like they were trying to compete with all the other gangsters and wanted the world to know that they were 'the Baddest Gangsters in Town.'

They were willing to admit to all the murders and crimes of violence that they had committed and seemed to take pride in all of their antisocial accomplishments. Apparently, in their minds, the more murders they were convicted of, the higher status they would have in the 'prison gangs.'

After prosecutor Levine and the investigator had this revealing conversation for over an hour with 'Wizard' and 'Jo-Jo,' it was time to consider what to do with all this information. At this stage in the case, the Criminal Complaint consisted of 41 counts, and the defendants had been held to answer for all of those charges. The question became how to add these two new murders, which in reality had occurred before all of the other crimes and charges.

Prosecutor Levine was a well-experienced prosecutor, and he knew that if he could quickly have a Grand Jury hearing on these two new murders, he could consolidate them with the original Complaint. Immediately, he obtained a Grand Jury hearing date. Within weeks, he had received an Indictment on the two new murders and had the original court permit him to join all the murders in the one case. Now, the original Complaint (Information) consisted of the first 41 counts. Then the new murders were added counts 42 to 47.

This added another layer of confusion for the jury to sort out all these various murders, since now they weren't in chronological order.

CHAPTER 15. READY FOR TRIAL

The Amezcua and Flores case continued to slowly proceed through the judicial process. The judge came to the realization that as long as the defendants represented themselves, there was no way to speed up this monstrous case that everyone was growing tired of. After many months, the judge came to the conclusion something needed to be done to move the case to trial. He ruled that the defendants could continue to represent themselves; however, he appointed two separate attorneys whose job was to make sure the defendants' rights were protected, but they would not call witnesses to testify on the defendants' behalf.

This was a thorny situation but appeared to meet the requirements of protecting the defendants' rights as well as assuring that the defendants received a fair trial. Because these new attorneys didn't know the facts of the case, the case had to be put over for almost a year for them to read the thousands of pages of police reports and transcripts. Once they understood the complex facts, they could advise the defendants what objections they should make in regards to the prosecution's evidence.

Over the four years this case churned through the courts, the prosecution had prepared it for trial many times. However, the prosecutor Levine had many other cases that were assigned to him for trial. When the Defense attorney eventually said that they were ready, the prosecutor was engaged in another trial. Since all defendants have a right to a Speedy Trial, the prosecution had to quickly pull everything together in order to comply with the defendants' right to a Speedy Trial.

The DA's Office immediately provided prosecutor Levine several law clerks to assist him in determining what witnesses still existed four years after the crimes. Some witnesses had disappeared, and some investigators had retired or been transferred to different assignments. All of these factors again added layers of difficulty to the case. The Defense knows that if they delay a case long enough, the prosecution's case will become weaker, as witnesses aren't available or the witnesses' memories become so blurred and confused that the jurors may interpret this to mean those witnesses aren't believable, and therefore that becomes reasonable doubt in the minds of some jurors.

The DA law clerks were able to synthesize the thousands of pages of police reports into an outline for each available witness. This effort accomplished two objectives. One, it allowed the prosecutor to have an outline that referred to the specific reports that could be used in refreshing the witnesses' memory if that became necessary. The other objective was that these law clerks assigned to this case had an unbelievable opportunity to work on one of the most complex serial homicide cases handled by the Los Angeles District Attorney's Office.

Darren Levine recognized that the 47-count case was too confusing for jurors to get a handle on. He decided to break the case down into three parts. The first would pertain to all the murders and the attempted murder that occurred in Los Angeles and San Bernardino Counties prior to July 4th. Part 2 would deal with the 27 counts that occurred on the Santa Monica Pier. Finally, Part 3 would refer to the incidents that occurred while the defendants were in custody. Dividing this huge case into three parts helped the jurors to separate the evidence into three separate components.

The case took many weeks to try, because there were so many witnesses to testify to all the various crimes. The jurors listened to all the evidence and came back with a guilty verdict on all counts. Since the DA's Office was seeking the Death Penalty for both defendants, the prosecution put on evidence about their years of criminal activity, especially with their gang. The jurors had to consider if the aggravating factors substantially outweighed the mitigating factors. The jurors all agreed that both the 'Wizard' and 'Jo-Jo' should receive the Death Penalty.

At the time of sentencing, the judge imposed the Death Penalty and instructed that the defendants be transported to San Quentin to be housed on Death Row. The prosecution was gratified that the jury found them both guilty and imposed the Death Penalty. Both defendants were elated that they got to go to San Quentin and not Pelican Bay 'Super Max.' They had arrived at the pinnacle of success for a gangster by having their own cell on Death Row.

It is strange that all human beings have different values. The real question is whether 'Wizard' and 'Jo-Jo' qualified as 'human beings,' especially since they disregarded the human life of all those around them.

As to an epilogue on the three Santa Monica Police Officers who were shot. They all returned to duty but Officer Coria's injury was more sever so she eventually had to retire. Sgt. Hirt later left SMPD and transferred over to DOJ where he retired.

THE SHOT HEARD AROUND THE WORLD AFFECTING TOURISM

People vs. Roshana, Carpenter, Tyrina, Santos

CHAPTER 16. LOOKING FOR FOREIGNERS

Our next Route 66 case doesn't require us to travel more than one block southeast of the Santa Monica Pier. Our first case was complex because the crime scenes were spread over two counties; however, this second case will seem like a 'piece of cake.' It encompasses only one location, consisting of a simple attempted robbery of several German tourists which ultimately resulted in the murder of one of them.

The basic objective of a robbery is to find someone who has cash or something of value. Tourists make attractive targets for being robbed, because they generally carry a large amount of cash and offer little or no resistance. The perfect robbery victim is a 'foreign tourist.' The great benefit of robbing foreign tourists is that even if the robber is caught, there is no realistic way of him ever being convicted of the robbery charge. (This case occurred before Conditional Examines were widely accepted in criminal trials.)

Graphics Page

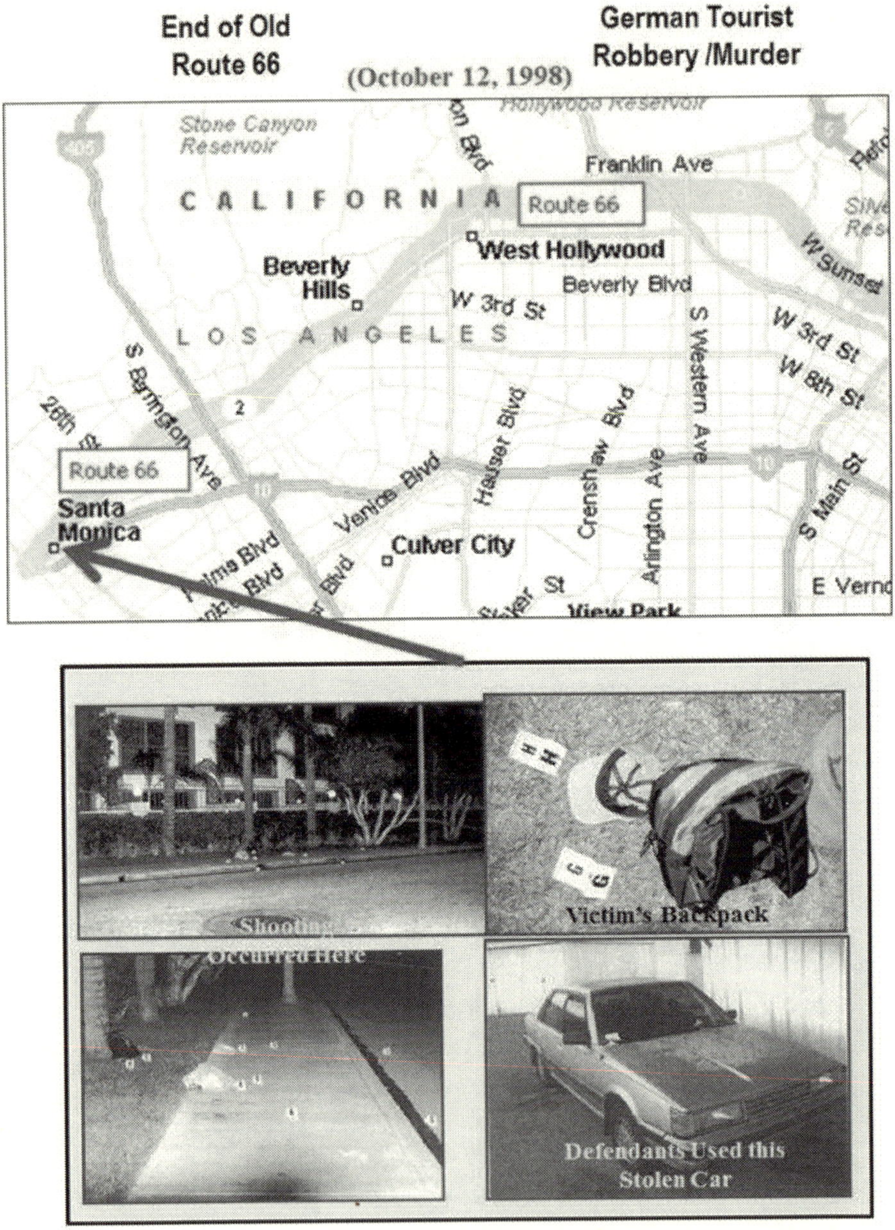

Robbers of foreign tourists are protected by the U.S. Constitution. Robbers are more than aware that they have an absolute right to be confronted in court by foreign tourist victims. Since most foreign tourists are visiting the country for only a couple of days, they are long gone to their home in a foreign country before the robbery case is ready for trial. However, at the time of the trial, if the foreign tourist isn't physically present in court to testify, then the case is dismissed for lack of a victim. (This was true in this case before Conditional Examines were applicable.)

Robbing a foreign tourist is the easiest crime to commit. All the robber need do is be able to spot a foreign tourist. Years ago, it was much easier to recognize a foreign tourist, since they were the ones with the large SLR cameras hanging around their necks. With digital cameras becoming smaller, this profiling trait isn't as noticeable. Nowadays, the criminals need to rely more on the manner in which foreigners' dress, their hair styles and types of glasses worn. Even the way foreigners walk and talk can be a revealing factor.

In order for robbers to be successful, they need to go to areas where tourists congregate. Tourist attractions as well as hotels and restaurants are the best places to find potential victims. Also, people driving rental cars are likely to be tourists. The car rental companies for years had a practice of placing decals and used license plate holders advertising that the car was a rental vehicle. The criminals liked this practice, since it made it easy for them to identify a visiting tourist.

Many states have enacted new laws that prevent rental car companies from putting anything on their vehicles to make them appear as rental cars. This has made rental cars a little less conspicuous, but robbers have learned that most rental cars fit a certain profile. Usually rental cars are four-door vehicles with standard features. Rental vehicles stand out in the parking lots because they are new 'Plain Jane' cars recently washed. Most experienced crooks can still distinguish a rental car a block away.

The City of Santa Monica is a perfect place to find tourists. Aside from all the hotels, the city has an endless supply of restaurants which cater to the tourists. So often couples will have a fine dinner along the Third Street Promenade and afterwards will walk off their meal by strolling along the cliffs overlooking the beach. The Santa Monica Pier is like a magnet attracting foreign tourists from all over the world.

On October 12, 1998, around 8:25 p.m., it was a pleasant, balmy evening in Santa Monica. The sunset overlooking the Pacific Ocean had been magnificent. As darkness filled in the indigo night sky, the stars were reflecting off of the placid ocean surface. Two German couples in their late 40s had finished up a delicious dinner at one of the trendy bistros. For some unknown reason, Germans love to travel to America to see its natural beauty, especially visiting the National Parks such as Yosemite, the Grand Canyon and even Yellowstone. One would think they would have an abundance of natural beauty in their own country. Particularly the Bavarian area of Germany has incredible scenery, but apparently some Germans somehow think the grass is greener in the USA.

Very often, German tourists when visiting America want to include Hollywood and Santa Monica as places to see. This tradition may be a result of all the movies and TV programs they have been exposed to over the years. Somehow, they are fascinated to see where the so-called 'rich and famous' live and play on the Westside of Los Angeles. This is especially true of the city of Santa Monica that overlooks the Pacific Ocean. These two German couples had traveled throughout the States and had arranged to stay at a budget hotel across from the fashionable Loews Hotel.

These couples were spending their last night before returning to Germany. They went to a fine restaurant to celebrate the ending of a wonderful trip throughout America. They had nothing but enjoyable memories of their travels. Knowing that the next day they would be sitting for 12 hours on a plane, they decided to take a walk along the beach front. It was 9:25 in the evening, and the beach's madding crowd had faded away. Although the temperature at the beach was usually mild, this night had a cool ocean breeze.

These four individuals had grown up in Germany, where crime is a rare event. They all felt totally comfortable walking in public, even after dark. To them, nothing could be safer than strolling along the beach-front property. This was America, '***the land of the free and the home of the brave.***' None of their travel brochures or tourist magazines had prepared them for what they were about to encounter.

German blind trust and American dark side were about to clash. As the four Germans were walking and talking, they were totally oblivious to four youthful robbers who were cruising around looking for someone to rob. Roshana (17) was slowly driving as the two guys with her were sizing up potential targets. Her boyfriend, Paul Carpenter (20), was seated up front with her. In the rear seat was Tyrina (17) with her friend Lamont Santos (20), who had his gun at the ready. Generally, the mere showing of the gun would make any tourists submit to the robber's request. One of the guys told Roshana to slow down so they could check out the two couples who were leisurely walking down the sidewalk.

One of the guys said that this foursome looked promising. Then someone said "stop," and Roshana pulled the car over to the curb. The two guys jumped out of the car with Tyrina following. They quickly approached the two couples from behind, hoping to surprise them. The next few seconds would change everyone's lives. There would be a collision between the lives of these four Germans and the lives of four African American youths that would create an international incident.

CHAPTER 17. ROBBERY TURNS INTO MURDER

The street that the two German couples were walking on was named Appian Way, a well-lighted area. As a matter of fact, the crime occurred almost under a street light. This should have been a simple robbery that shouldn't have taken any more than 30 seconds. But something went terribly, horribly wrong. Maybe there was a misunderstanding due to a language barrier. Maybe the couples were in disbelief and didn't know how to react.

Foreign victims of robberies may often respond slowly, since they may not understand what the robber really is saying and trying to do. If a robber says "Stick 'em up," few foreigners would understand what that meant or what they were supposed to do. Some robbers may interpret the slow reaction by the victim as a sign of being uncooperative. This may cause the robber to elevate the situation by pulling out a weapon to threaten the victim into complying with the requests to hand over the money.

The other possibility of what went wrong is the victims may have been caught totally by surprise. The couple in front was Horst Fietze, who was 50 years old, walking side by side with his wife, Astrid Fietze. As they walked, they were intermittently conversing with the other German couple behind them, consisting of Gisela and Jurgen. The group didn't notice a slow-moving blue Toyota pulling up behind them. When the car stopped, three occupants jumped out and approached the two couples. Gisela was first to react by shouting out in her broken English, "German, German. No money, no money." Suspect Paul Carpenter (20) tried to push

Jurgen to the side to separate him from the front couple. Instantly, Lamont Santos approached the other male, Horst Fietze, and tried to grab some type of handbag he had in his hand. It wasn't clear whether Santos was trying to take Astrid's handbag or Horst's backpack. The robbers were trying to get the victims to hand over anything of value.

Horst's wife Astrid turned to the three robbers and said, "No money." Everyone looked surprised as to what to do next. Astrid repeated, "No money." In order to protect his wife, Horst stepped in between his wife, Astrid, and the suspect Santos. That was when robber Lamont Santos pulled out a gun and started holding it in a threatening manner. By this time, Lamont was standing in front of Horst, and he pointed the gun at Horst's chest. At that moment in time, there were three robbers and four victims frozen in fear, not knowing how to respond and what to do. The one female robber pushed the other German lady, Gisele, back out of the way.

Somehow Horst may have tried to push the gun away from his chest. He may have thought he could defuse the situation by getting the gun put to the side so no one would get hurt. The robbers were grabbing at the victims' pockets, trying to pull out valuables. Horst wasn't the type who wanted to be a hero or foil a robbery attempt. However, he was unfamiliar with how to react to an American robbery.

All we know for certain is that there was a struggle over the gun and it went off. Mr. Fietze was shot in the chest and started to slump to the sidewalk. There is no way to look into Lamont Santos's mind to see exactly what he was thinking when he pulled the trigger. Did Santos intend to shot Horst Fietze, or was it an accidental discharge of the weapon? It is hard to know, and there are various versions of the facts. What is known is that Horst was shot not just once but three times, which discredits the claim of accident.

As Horst Fietze staggered to the sidewalk, the three robbers ran to the car, which had pulled up directly next to them. When all three were in the car, Roshana, the driver, sped away. Everyone in the car was frustrated that they didn't get anything for all their efforts. Everyone had heard the shooting, but the four of them didn't know what injures had been created by the shooting. As far as they knew, they had attempted to rob some tourists, but they had no idea if they had injured or killed anyone. To the four of them, it was not a prosperous night, only a disappointing night.

However, one can only surmise the terror that went through the minds of these four German tourists. They weren't doing anything wrong or risky. They weren't purposely going through a gang-infested neighborhood. There are places in Los Angeles and in most urban communities where no one goes after dark. But this was Santa Monica, a popular tourist attraction where the community takes great pride in the safety of their city.

The Santa Monica Police immediately responded, and the injured German tourist was whisked away to one of the finest emergency rooms. Initially, it was unknown how seriously Horst was injured. A heroic effort was made to save his life, but unfortunately, the bullet had entered his upper chest and caused considerable internal damage, resulting in death.

CHAPTER 18. IMPACT OF SHOOTING

What may have been most surprising was the fact that Lamont Santos, the man with the gun, had no conception what his actions would result in. It was as if this shooting on the streets of Santa Monica were being heard around the world. The crime took on worldwide significance. The news media created a colossal story out of this crime. The German press questioned how safe it was to travel in America, where there were roaming gangsters preying on tourists. Five years earlier, a similar shooting of a German tourist in Miami had set off a firestorm in which the German government put out a strongly worded advisement for German tourists not to visit the City of Miami.

The City of Santa Monica was petrified of having a similar boycott by German tourists. Of the 2.3 million tourists who visit their city annually, German tourists make up 15% of the visitors. The fact that the shooting occurred on a public street next to a luxury hotel turned off many potential tourists. The feeling by foreign tourists was why take a chance going to Santa Monica when there are so many other places one can visit without being a victim.

What about the impact this case had on the four young people who committed the crime? They were without a doubt four young inner-city kids who were unsophisticated as to the outside world. They as a group had congregated at a Santa Monica park and wanted to get high on drugs. They didn't have any money, so they decided to 'jack' someone in the area so they could get the money to buy drugs.

They were able to secure a stolen car to use to commit their robberies. This would ensure that they wouldn't get caught. Their expectation wasn't to harm anyone but merely to persuade people to hand over some cash so they could purchase some drugs. Naturally, foreign tourists would be the best types to rob. When they spotted the two German couples walking down the sidewalk, this gave them the perfect situation they were looking for. They believed that only a little force would be needed to persuade these strolling tourists to hand over their cash.

The use of the guns was merely to be persuasive, not to harm anyone. Never in their wildest plans were the guns to be used to shoot someone. They were shocked as to how much attention this little 'attempted robbery gone bad' had created. The media reaction to this incident had become so intense that these suspects became so scared that they decided to leave the State of California. One moved to Oklahoma, and another disappeared to South Carolina. Even one of the robbers left for Jamaica in hopes of not being discovered and arrested. They thought if they ran far enough the whole thing would go away. What they didn't realize was the firestorm they had created was bigger than they could ever have imagined.

CHAPTER 19. SOLVING THE CASE

With the descriptions given by the victims, the detectives went to work looking for the four suspects. They reviewed security cameras at the hotels and restaurants along the Appian Way. At a location a block away, they found a security camera that had good photos of the suspects when they were cruising around looking for victims. Also, at the same time, the stolen car that had been used in the robbery was recovered. The CSI technicians examined the vehicle for latent prints and found several useable ones. The police have learned that one of the best places to find a fingerprint in a stolen car is on the rearview mirror. When a person gets into a car for the first time, they automatically reach up and adjust the rearview mirror. In the process, they leave a nice thumbprint on the surface of the mirror. This is exactly what Roshana did, and this is where her latent print was found.

She was a juvenile in the 11th grade in high school. The detectives were tipped off that she had left the area to live with relatives out of the state. The detectives followed up on the information and located her in Oklahoma, where they met with her. They advised her of her Miranda Rights. She showed no reluctance to talk to the police, because she didn't think she was responsible for the incident, since she was merely the driver. Even though she wasn't one of the three who had jumped out of the car to rob the German visitors, under the law she was still criminally liable for the acts of the others.

Next the detectives received information that another female suspect was located locally. They were able to track her down and subsequently arrested Tyrina, who admitted to her role in the robbery. She explained everyone's role in the incident. She wanted the detectives to know that she hadn't had a gun like the two males.

Finally, the detectives were told that Lamont Santos was living with his aunt in South Carolina. The detectives called him by phone and talked to him, but he denied any involvement. Eventually the detectives went to South Carolina and met with him. They didn't arrest him and didn't advise him of his Miranda Rights. They only stated that they wanted to know his story as to what happened. He continued to deny his role in the shooting. The detectives still didn't arrest him but merely had him listen to tape recordings of his relatives. In those recordings, his relatives spelled out how he had described the shooting. The detectives indicated that they wanted to be fair to him and find out what his explanation was.

After Santos had listened to what his relatives had said, he meekly admitted his role in the incident. He tried to minimalize his involvement. He explained he had been involved in the attempted robbery but he wanted them to know that the gun had gone off accidentally.

None of the suspects seemed to understand California criminal law. They totally didn't comprehend the legal concepts of **Aiding and Abetting** and the **Felony Murder Rule**. The theory of the **Aiding and Abetting** concept is that the law can't always determine the level of involvement each person has in carrying out a crime. In the eyes of justice, everyone is equally liable no matter what role they played, as long as they aided in some way or encouraged the commission of the crime.

The other legal concept they were unaware of was the **Felony Murder Rule**. If someone sets out to commit a felony such as robbery and in the course of the robbery someone is killed—in this case, it was one of the victims of this robber—as a result, all the robbers are guilty of **First Degree Murder**. That is true even if the robber had no intention of killing anyone during the robbery. When one combines the **Felony Murder Rule** with the **Aiding and Abetting** rule, these defendants were in serious trouble with the law.

CHAPTER 20. COURTS SEEKING JUSTICE

I, the author, did considerable work on this case during the preparation stage. I personally knew many of the court personnel handling this unusual case. This relationship gave me a different prospective on how this case was ultimately handled. I have had dealings with Det. John Henry when I worked with him on the ***Victor Paleologus*** case, which was the basis for my book ***Meet Me For Murder***. I learned that Det. Henry had a unique approach when dealing with criminals. He used a softer and gentler method when questioning them. I wasn't surprised how well he was able to get all three of the suspects to open up and talk to him. He convinces the suspects that he only wants to be fair with them and hear their side of the story. Undoubtedly, most crooks will think that they can talk their way out of any situation.

What the suspects don't understand is that when Det. Henry talks to them he has all of his 'ducks in order,' so when a suspect gives him a bogus story, the detective turns on his tape recorder from other witnesses who totally debunk the fabricated version. Henry's response is, "Well, what is your response to the statement made by this other witness?" This method of interviewing suspects is so disarming. In this case, he convinced Lamont Santos to totally admit to his involvement, with only the caveat that the gun may have gone off accidentally.

Det. Henry's low-key technique provided the prosecutors with strong evidence for trial. The DA's Office assigned the case to one of the 'top guns' in the Major

Crimes Division. Tony Manzella was the one selected. Tony and I started together in the DA's Office in 1967 and were 'old-school prosecutors.' We both watched the old-time great attorneys like J. Miller Leavy and Joseph Busch in trial. These incredible attorneys were more than merely brilliant in that they knew how to keep the jurors engaged in the case. Watching those greats was a learning experience for Tony and myself which we never forgot.

Tony Manzella was smarter than I was, since he left the DA's Office after about ten years and joined a prominent civil law firm. There Tony became their chief litigation attorney and as a result made tons of money. Tony stayed with the law firm for years, and when he retired, he made a deal with the DA's Office to come back as a prosecutor doing major cases at a fraction of what he had earned in civil law. His only condition was that he wanted to bring with him his legal assistant Ruth. Because the DA's Office is a civil service operation, it couldn't hire her as a paralegal.

Since Tony really missed the excitement of criminal trials, he agreed to pay Ruth's salary out of his own pocket. Few prosecutors if any could afford to do that. With that problem resolved, Tony and Ruth quickly took on some of the biggest and most complex cases in the DA's Office. Tony always wore an impeccable black suit with a vest containing his pocket watch. Ruth was tall and had a professional assurance about her. She wore her hair up and dressed in a woman's business suit. When the two of them walked into the courtroom, everyone took notice of this dynamic duo.

Tony was a stickler for being prepared. When he addressed the judge, he had his Points and Authority in hand and used them if anyone disputed his position. The judges and Defense attorneys quickly learned not to take Tony on unless they wanted a legal fight. For many years, Tony had been a part-time law professor. As a result, he had taught many of the judges he appeared before, and many of the Defense attorneys had been his students.

When Tony and Ruth became more immersed in the so-called 'German Tourist' case, there were only three of the suspects to prosecute, since suspect Paul Carpenter had not been apprehended. They realized that the biggest issue they were going to have to deal with was not the lack of evidence but the logistics of trying the case. Tony sized up the case and had great sympathy for Astrid Fietze, the victim's wife, who lived on the other side of the world in Germany. She was trying to get on with her life without her husband Horst. Tony realized that all of the defendants had made statements incriminating their co-defendants. As a result, if Tony wanted to use those statements, he would have to try each defendant separately. That meant that the three German witnesses would have to travel back and forth numerous times to testify in each separate trial.

Tony was trying to find a solution to this logistic nightmare. There was always the possibility that the German victims/witnesses might become upset with all the appearances they had to make and therefore refuse to cooperate. Tony knew he needed their cooperation. He drew upon his civil law firm experience and recognized that maybe there was some way to negotiate an agreement where all sides had something to gain.

Tony negotiated with the Defense attorneys that the prosecution would agree to reduce the maximum sentences that each of the defendants would receive. The only thing the Defense would give up was the right to **jury trial**. The idea was to have a judge hold a **court trial** and determine the defendants' guilt, and if convicted, they would be eligible for the lighter sentence.

The Defense attorneys explained the offer to the defendants, who could see the advantage to them. All three of them agreed to it. In a court trial, the prosecution would be able to use all the defendants' incriminating statements. The end result was the prosecution only had to bring the three Germans over for this one trial. The next question was what judge the Defense attorneys and the prosecutor could agree on to hear the case.

CHAPTER 21. TIME FOR TRIAL

After both sides had vetted the names of various judges, there was a mutual agreement to ask Judge Lance Ito if he would agree to conduct the **court trial** in this case. He had become a household name during the ill-famed O. J. Simpson case. I remember when Lance Ito worked in the DA's Office as a prosecutor. What I remember most about Lance was that he had the messiest office of all the prosecutors. His office was always cluttered with boxes of old cases and stacks of tattered newspapers turning yellow around the edges. When DA files entered his office, it was like they were entering a gigantic black hole, since they were seldom ever seen again. When Lance became a judge, there was hope that many of the missing DA files would be rediscovered tucked away in some corner of his old office.

The non-jury trial before Judge Ito took five days. Tony, the prosecutor, called Astrid Fietze to testify to what had happened. Since she didn't speak much English, a translator was used. She testified that she and her husband Horst were walking down the sidewalk with their friends. She explained how the robbers approached them and she heard Gisela shout, "German, no money." Her husband turned but didn't touch any of the suspects. The robbers were trying to grab for a handbag. She saw the one male place a gun against her husband's chest. Moments later, a shot rang out, and then several more shots. Her husband fell to the sidewalk, and the robbers ran to a car and they all drove away.

Judge Ito listened to all the German witnesses and the statements that the defendants had made to the detectives. Also, the fingerprint evidence was introduced to prove that the two young females had been in the stolen car. From all this testimony, the judge could easily see that Roshana was the least culpable of all the robbers. She was the youngest and was the least involved, and she had no prior criminal record. Further, she hadn't any involvement with gangs, as the other three robbers had. Her main connection to this group of robbers was that she was dating Paul Carpenter, who was one of the robbers.

The judge found Roshana guilty of **Second Degree Murder**. This was a giant stretch of the legal principles to find her guilty of Second Degree Murder. If one followed the rules of law, Roshana could only be found guilty of **First Degree Murder**. Obviously, the judge didn't want her to be stuck with the more serious charge. At time of sentencing, the judge further reduced the case to a mere **Voluntary Manslaughter**. As a result, she was sentenced to only 13 years in prison. And in weighing all the factors, it was understandable why the judge would want to give her a reduced sentence. Justice may have been served by reducing the charges, but the law was clearly not followed to the exact letter.

Tyrina, whose involvement was trying to separate Gisela from the others, was more involved in the robbery than Roshana. Again, the judge found her guilty of **Second Degree Murder**. Somehow, he didn't follow the Felony Murder Rule and seemed more interested in making her sentence more proportional to her involvement. Her case was not further reduced, and she ended up with a sentence of 16 years to Life in state prison. Tyrina wasn't pleased with that result and smashed her head on the counsel table, claiming that her life was in essence over by such a long sentence. The irony was that she could have received a sentence of **Life in Prison Without the Possibility of Parole**.

Lamont Santos, who had the gun, received the harshest sentence. The judge sentenced him to 35 years to **Life in Prison With the Possibility of Parole**. This was a strange sentence, since if a Special Circumstances of Robbery Murder was found true, as it was, the sentence should have been **Life Prison Without the Possibility of Parole.** In other words, all three defendants could have received much harsher sentences if they hadn't agreed to have a **court trial** before a judge like Lance Ito.

CHAPTER 22. FINAL CONCLUSION

Paul Carpenter was able to elude the police for over a decade. *America's Most Wanted* did several TV episodes on the fugitive Paul Carpenter. In 2007, they re-aired the program, and this time they mentioned that there was a $20,000 reward for the arrest and prosecution of Carpenter. That all helped but the real break occurred when the SMPD detectives talked to Carpenter's girlfriend in prison. She indicated that she had planned to meet him in Jamaica. Also the detectives had checked out Carpenter's mother and found that she had traveled to Jamaica shortly after the shooting. All that information was turned over to the FBI which started checking out his whereabouts in Jamaica. It wasn't long before the FBI was able to track down Paul Carpenter working under an assumed name at a BMW dealership in Kingston, Jamaica.

By then he was 35 and was well thought of by his employer and had a three-year-old son whom he was trying to raise on his own. Everyone who had contact with him during those ten years never saw him display any violent tendencies. They were shocked to learn he was a suspect in a murder case. When he was brought back to Los Angeles, he was prosecuted by another colleague of mine, Bobby Grace, since Tony Manzella had finally retired for good. From then on, Tony spent his time sailing his new yacht.

Prosecutor Grace was hoping for a plea of guilty and an acceptance of a similar sentence to what Tyrina had received. However, Carpenter's case was slightly different in that he had carried a gun in the robbery, although he hadn't fired it. He was the one who had tried to separate Jurgen from the others during the attempted robbery. Carpenter wasn't going to agree to anything. This defendant demanded a **jury trial**, and the prosecutor, Bobby Grace, had to see if he could locate all the witnesses after a lapse of 13 years. He was able to gain the cooperation of Astrid Fietze, the wife of the victim, and have her return to Los Angeles to testify for a second time.

It took considerable work and time to resurrect the case, but it was done. The jury deliberated only a day and a half and came back with a verdict of **First Degree Murder** and finding the Special Circumstance of Robbery Murder to be true. He received a sentence of 35 years to Life and was given credit for the three years he had been in custody before trial.

After the final sentencing, the news media asked prosecutor Bobby Grace about his assessment of the case. He stated the following: "We depend upon a sense of confidence that we can walk our streets safely. This was probably one of the first events that kind of broke or shattered that sense of calm, or that sense of serenity, in Santa Monica." The city fathers wanted to return to the calm days when they were used to having only one homicide for that entire year. Unfortunately, 1998 was the year when the homicide rate went above six deaths. The city recognized it needed to target gang violence if it wanted to continue to attract tourists from all over the world.

This case shocked the City of Santa Monica to the core. The shooting death of Horst Fietze was a tragic loss of a human life. He was born in 1948, which was three years after the devastating defeat of Germany in World War II. He lived in Lobau, Germany, which was near the Polish border. He grew up in East Germany, which was a Communist puppet state of the Soviet Union. During those years, life was extremely harsh, stark for anyone having to live in East Germany. In 1961, I, the author traveled throughout East Germany. I remember crossing from the Allied section of Berlin into the Soviet section of Berlin without any difficulty. However, after August 13, 1961, I remember having to use 'Checkpoint Charlie' in order to enter into the eastern sector of Berlin. At first, East Berlin was surrounded by barbwire fencing to keep the East Germans from escaping to freedom by crossing over into West Berlin. Later, a more secure block wall was built which made it much more difficult to escape.

What's interesting is that Horst Fietze was 13 years old when the wall went up and 41 years old on November 9, 1989, when the world saw the Berlin Wall come tumbling down while U.S.S.R. President Gorbachev did nothing. During part of this time, Horst had to serve in the East German army. It was only nine years after the wall came down that Horst and his wife wanted to visit America to see for themselves what a truly free society was like. For years, Horst worked as a building maintenance worker and tried to save up his money. In October 1998, he had saved enough to be able to afford a trip to the USA with his friends. They first landed in New York and spent three weeks crossing the country, ending up their glorious trip in Santa Monica.

October 12, 1998, was the conclusion of a dream vacation to America by four former **East Germans**. What a contrast to the four young American suspects, who had never had to endure the hardships the victims had lived through. Why would these Americans wander the streets looking for someone to prey on? The defendants weren't hardened criminals or sophisticated killers. Their lack of good judgment and imprudent behavior cost them the best years of their lives as they waste away in a state prison.

After learning the facts and consequences of this truly sad case, one wants to believe this tragedy has been somehow a learning experience to someone. Unfortunately, there is no silver lining in this case. No matter how you analyze this case, everyone came out a LOSER.

BIGGEST KILLING OF PEDESTRIANS IN USA

People vs. George Weller

CHAPTER 23. THIRD STREET FARMERS' MARKET MASSACRE

As we resume our trip along old Route 66, we turn around and bid farewell to the Santa Monica Pier area. We now have mixed emotions about the pier after reviewing the July 4th shootout and the German Tourist murder. We head one block over to Santa Monica Boulevard and travel two blocks to the Third Street Promenade. When we look to the left, our mind becomes overcome with the most horrific event to consume the City of Santa Monica. It occurred on July 16, 2003, around 1:45 p.m. Up until then, it was a perfect day that everyone was enjoying. For a summer day at the beach, it couldn't have been better. It was a Wednesday afternoon, and still people were strolling through the local Farmers' Market.

Graphics Page

Car Killing 10 visitors and injured 63

Knocked over Stands

Where Car Came to Rest on Arizona Ave.

Driver George Weller (86)

Since it is one of the largest Farmers' Markets on the Westside of LA, it attracts shoppers from far and wide to squeeze the tomatoes and sniff the strawberries to be sure they are getting the freshest produce. Third Street is always closed to traffic, and on the day of the Farmers' Market, other streets are closed so the merchants can set up their booths and spread out their wares. Beside the farm produce, many of the stalls have hobby crafts for sale. Aside from the fresh sea breeze, there is the strong aroma from the freshly baked goods. Other senses join the mix with homemade salsa and the cinnamon smell of churros. Throughout the entire Farmers' Market is the sound of undiscovered musicians playing their instruments. Occasionally, these minstrels make an attempt to sing, which can range from great to those who aren't ready for prime time.

Even though the serious shoppers have come and gone during the morning hours, this is the time, in the early afternoon, when the bargain hunters arrive, hoping to find the merchants tired and wanting to get rid of their leftover merchandise. At this time, merchants and shoppers are negotiating over watermelons and cantaloupes. But the best buys are on the produce that has a short shelf life, since the merchants' choice is to take the few cents for it or know that within an hour the item will be tossed in the trash dumpster.

George Russell Weller, who was 86, was on a mission to go to the post office for his wife. Finding a parking space wasn't easy on Wednesday because of the Farmers' Market. After completing his business at the post office, he pulled back onto the street to go home. There was a Mercedes in front of him who had stopped to permit some pedestrians to cross over to the Farmers' Market. The pedestrians were taking their time, and Mr. Weller was becoming impatient, wondering why they couldn't cross faster.

Mr. Weller turned the wheels of his Buick LeSabre to go around the Mercedes. In the process, he nicked the back of the Mercedes. Although it was a minor accident, it turned into the most horrific tragedy of all time. Mr. Weller's car careened into one of the entrances to the Farmer's Market, knocking down the large wooden barricades which blocked the entrance to the market. The engine revved louder and the car appeared to pick up speed. The car remained in the pathway filled with shoppers. It mowed them down like an out-of-control bulldozer. At no time did the car veer into the shopping stands or parked cars but remained racing down the center of the street.

The path of destruction took a mere 20 seconds. As Mr. Weller's car entered the Farmers' Market, it struck Leroy Lattier, 55, a homeless man standing at the entrance. Leroy was shuffling along minding his own business and seemed almost invisible as many of the shoppers were in the process of filing out the entrance. The Buick started to accelerate as it hit Leroy dead center with such force as to knock him out of his shoes, propelling his body in the air like a rag doll sailing over the roof of the car and coming down smack dab on the hard asphalt of the street. The result to Leroy was instant death.

As the car flashed forward through the crowd of shoppers, it next came into contact with Diana and Kevin McCarthy, 41 and 50, who were visiting from New York. They were playing the role of tourists who were thoroughly enjoying themselves milling around all the sales booths. They weren't in any rush and hadn't come with the purpose of buying anything. Without any notice, the car struck them with such force there was no way they could have done anything to save their lives from being snuffed out before they could enjoy their long-earned retirement.

The path of destruction didn't discriminate by age as it picked its next victim to be Cindy Valladares, who was a mere three-year-old baby. She was pure innocence in that she was being carried by her mother. They were visiting her father, who was working at the market. The force of the car hitting her mother caused her to lose her grip on her as she was literally torn out of her mother's arms. Her small body went flying through the air, striking everything in her path. When she finally landed on the ground, her life was quietly and quickly snuffed out.

Similar carnage occurred next as the car sped down the closed street filled with bargain hunters. This time it was Molok Ghoulian, 62, who was carrying a child, Brendon Esfahani, seven months old. They were the next fatalities. The intensity of the impact caused Ghoulian's skin to be literally torn from her body. As much as she tried to shield the seven-month-old, the impact of the car traveling at an estimated 60 mph was too great a force for her hands to cling to the baby.

As the car struck more victims, the speed of the car didn't diminish but only seemed to gain speed. People from behind noticed no sign of the brake lights going on. People on the side glanced over and saw an elderly man behind the wheel with an intense gaze. He seemed to have his hands firmly on the steering wheel at the 10 o'clock and 2 o'clock position. At that point the car's airbag activated, but the driver continued to be fixed on what was in front of him.

At about that time, Theresa Breglia, 50, from the Bronx was struck, and Lynne Weaver, age 47, was hit with such force that her brain was separated from her spinal column, which caused instant death. The impact of both of them didn't slow the old Buick as it proceeded to near the end of Arizona Street.

Next was Gloria Gonzalez, 35, who had come from Venice Beach a mile away to find some good homegrown produce. Since the human carnage had been occurring for 20 seconds, undoubtedly, she had heard the death-defying screams from the other victims. She had turned to see what was happening, and before she could react, she was hit so hard she was knocked completely out of her shoes.

When was all this carnage going to end? Movsha Hoffman, 78, with his wife, had come on a bus to buy some fruits and vegetables. They were headed back to the bus stop to go back home. They had heard the screaming, but at their age, Hoffman wasn't mobile enough to change course. He remained frozen in the path of the car while his wife was able to move to the side. When Hoffman was struck, his body flew into the air, landing on the hood of the car. The Buick all of a sudden slowed to a crawl, since a body had gotten wedged under the front of the car.

From the entrance to the Farmers' Market, the car had traveled nearly a 1000 feet almost straight down Arizona Street in the process of killing **ten** human beings and seriously injuring **63**. This was the worst incident of pedestrian killing in the country's history.

CHAPTER 24. WHAT DO WE DO NEXT?

When the dust settled, the immediate reaction was to determine which victims needed prompt attention. The crime scene was so chaotic it was hard for law enforcement to know where to start. Since there were so many seriously injured, the focus had to be on them first. Some attention was directed to where the car had come to a stop. Officers wanted to assess the condition of the driver of the car causing all this destruction.

The driver, Mr. Weller, was shaken up and removed from his car. Some witnesses who confronted him indicated that he said, "When you saw me, why didn't you get out of my way?" Eventually he was taken to the police station, where detectives would interview him to find out what had happened. Mr. Weller stated the following:

"But, God almighty, those poor people, poor, poor, tragic people. I have the feeling that they were just down there for the value of the thing in the first place, because the prices were good. And what a tragic ending to their outing, and I contributed to it, which is just almost more than I can figure out.

"When I finally came to a rest—my God, what have I done? And right to this moment I can't tell you. From the moment that car accelerated, to the best of my knowledge, I tried everything that you do to an automobile and tried to put on the foot brake. I tried to take my foot off of the gas. I tried to take the control knob and jam it into park. Everything, anything that I thought would stop the action of the car. I tried in that block, unsuccessfully, maybe, maybe not. Because it did come to a stop. I don't know what caused that."

During the interview he talked about his military service during WWII as well as his bout with cancer and the condition of his ill wife. At the end of the interview, the detective, Sal Lucio, thanked Mr. Weller for cooperating and told him he was not under arrest. Weller said, "I'm in big trouble with my heart and soul. That you can't fix."

Shortly thereafter, he obtained two attorneys who acted as his spokesmen from that point on. They claimed he was taking medicine which may have caused him to have a mini heart attack. Earlier, he had had a hip replacement which left him with limited mobility and the need to use a cane. Later, he had implanted a pacemaker, but it had had to be removed because of an infection.

His driving experience went back a long way to when he had learned to drive in a 'Model T Ford.' Throughout his life he had an impeccable driving record until recently, when he had had some minor violations. He had been a resident of Santa Monica for nearly all his life and was very familiar with all the streets. Most of his life he had worked as a salesman, and in his retirement, he volunteered to assist his church and the local library.

After the Santa Monica Police Department assessed the situation, it brought in the California Highway Patrol accident-reconstruction experts to render an opinion as to the cause of the accident. The CHP took six months to write a 900-page report finding the incident was a matter of 'Pedal Error.' They explained it as follows: *"When the brain is too busy, it simply assumes muscles are performing as ordered and ignores signals, even when the opposite may be the case. The brain remembers the neuromuscular command it gave, rather than the responses to that command."*

The report didn't recommend any criminal action against Mr. Weller except maybe a speeding violation. The Police Chief wanted some type of criminal charges brought against Mr. Weller. During these six months, everyone had been waiting to see what the public opinion would be. By the first of 2004, there was a groundswell feeling that someone would have to be held responsible for such pain and suffering that so many had been living through.

The news media had produced story after story of the suffering that so many were enduring. The pressure from the police and the public became so intense that someone had to pay for this tragedy. The idea that it was a mere accident to be settled in the civil courts was not the solution the masses wanted. The community wanted someone to be criminally prosecuted.

The case was submitted to the DA's Office in West Los Angeles, where the public pressure continued to intensify. The DA's Office was faced with the dilemma of rejecting the case and being painted with the broad brush of being soft on crime. The DA's branch office seemed to feel the pressure for filing of criminal charges, and it was recommending such. A meeting with the top DA administrators was scheduled Downtown to make the ultimate decision.

Prosecutor Ann Ambrose was given the task of reviewing the CHP report and all the other documents and expert opinions that had been generated about the incident. The DA's Office knew that a decision needed to be made as to whether to file charges or not. At this meeting Downtown, Ann Ambrose and her head deputy were asked to explain their opinions on what should be done with the case. Present at this meeting were the DA and his top administrators.

Ann was a relatively new prosecutor but was well respected for her accomplishments. She had impressed the DA administration when she tried the Winona Ryder shoplifting case against the well-known Defense attorney Mark Geragos. It was a case of 'David against Goliath' proportions. The media and practically everyone believed that Geragos would get the actress off. However, he didn't realize the tenacity and creativity of this redheaded prosecutor. In the end, the glib Geragos had to have been more than shocked when the Beverly Hills jury convicted his actress client.

The Farmers' Market case would be decided in the so-called 'Granite Conference Room.' (The name comes from the fact that the conference table is made from granite, with the DA Seal inserted in the center of the table.) Ann had a high-tech PowerPoint presentation which spelled out all the mayhem caused by Mr. Weller. She emphasized that the driver appeared to be continuing to drive down the center of the street where most of the people were located. At no time did the driver try to stop the vehicle by turning into parked cars or stalls. She showed how the CHP report was incorrect and stressed the body count and seriousness of the injuries suffered by the surviving victims.

Some of the DA's administrators felt strongly against filing any criminal charges against an 86-year-old driver. These prosecutors were concerned with what to do with Mr. Weller if he were convicted. There was no place to incarcerate such an elderly man with severe mental and physical problems. Those opposed to filing charges emphasized that the CHP report strongly recommended against filing any Vehicular Manslaughter charges.

However, those administrators who were in favor of filing charges stressed the strong public opinion that someone must be held accountable for such a devastating tragedy. These prosecutors kept repeating the statistic of the ten dead and 63 seriously injured. The discussion was intense and passionate, splitting the supervising prosecutors almost down the middle. For more than an hour, the discussion seemed to intensify, with both sides' adamant as to the merits of their position.

Finally, the District Attorney, Steve Colley, himself weighed in on the discussion. Everyone in this conference room knew that whatever was decided would forever affect the District Attorney. Since the office of District Attorney is an elected one, public opinion can't be ignored. That was when the District Attorney turned to Ann Ambrose and asked, "Do you think there is sufficient evidence to prove the Gross Negligence element for Vehicular Manslaughter?"

Her response was in the form of reshowing all the unadulterated photos of the carnage, which stretched for three football fields. Then she said that was the evidence of the Gross Negligence. The DA fixated his attention on each and every slide showing the mangled bodies of the victims. Then he said, "If you think you can prove the Gross Negligence, then file it."

For several moments, there was an eerie silence in the DA's Conference Room. The lengthy debate was over. Ann Ambrose had done a masterful job of deflecting the attention from how to sentence an 86-year-old man facing 18 years in state prison to the issue of whether there was sufficient evidence of Gross Negligence to support the charges. The decision had been made to give a green light to filing ten counts of Vehicular Manslaughter with Gross Negligence against Mr. George Russell Weller.

CHAPTER 25. COURT PROCEEDINGS

Once the decision was made to file charges, it was time to get prepared. Factually the case was complex, but most of all the jurors had to thoroughly understand the law on Vehicular Manslaughter with Gross Negligence. Ann had had to explain the case to so many people over the past six months that she had honed her communication skills to the point that she knew what people needed to know to persuade them the charges were warranted.

The case was set in the West LA Courthouse for the arraignment. Mr. Weller appeared and he was advised of the charges. The DA asked for a modest bail of $50,000. The Defense's response was that he should remain on his Own Recognizance. Even though the judge recognized the gravity of ten Manslaughter charges in the Complaint, she didn't believe that the now 88-year-old was a 'flight risk,' so the judge permitted the defendant to remain on his Own Recognizance. Because of the seriousness of the offenses, the judge ordered Mr. Weller not to drive while awaiting trial. This wasn't necessary, since the DMV had already suspended his license.

The DA's Office decided not to proceed by way of a Grand Jury, but used the Preliminary Hearing process. This would give the prosecution a chance to see which witnesses would make for the strongest case. The hearing was held in Judge Katherine Mader's court in the West LA Courthouse. Most Preliminary Hearings take less than a day to put on. However, in this case there were ten deaths and 63 serious injuries, so the hearing lasted for seven days.

At the end of the proceedings, the judge said, "*This case is unprecedented. Whether or not Mr. Weller went into a hypervigilant state after pressing the wrong pedal and his error caused him to negligently drive the car through the busy marketplace, Mr. Weller continued to drive, with bodies flying over his car. Mr. Weller did not react to the bedlam, the screams, the crashing of the stalls. Therefore, I find sufficient evidence to bind the defendant over for trial.*"

After the Preliminary Hearing, the case seemed to go into slow motion mode with continuances one after another. Because of Mr. Weller's deteriorating health, it seemed that the case would never go to trial. It was agreed that Mr. Weller didn't have to be present for all of the proceedings. Eventually, the case was transferred from the West Los Angeles Courthouse to the Downtown Criminal Courts Building. The case was assigned to a Long Cause courtroom on the ninth floor. Because of the very nature of the case and the delicate health of the defendant, few judges wanted to be saddled with such a 'no-win' case. Judge Michael Johnson somehow ended up with the Weller case.

There were innumerable motions that had to be litigated and decisions as to the appointment of psychiatrists to interview and render opinions as to the defendant's mental condition. After many months, to everyone's surprise, the case actually commenced with the jury selection process. Then the case was set for the Opening Statements. Both sides were given an opportunity to explain what evidence they would be presenting to the jurors.

When the judge asked the prosecutor, Ann Ambrose, if she wished to make an Opening Statement, she responded that she did. She started out by looking all the jurors in the eye and said, "*This is a case about accepting responsibility and public accountability. Mr. Weller needs to take responsibility for his actions, and the victims and their families need to come to court and be heard. The defendant could have stopped his vehicle at any time if he had merely stepped on the brake. Mr. Weller should be held criminally responsible for the deaths because he failed to do anything to stop the carnage. Mr. Weller steered for the length of three football fields and avoided hitting any parked cars, at the cost of innocent lives. He stopped only when a body trapped beneath his car became a human brake.*

"*You will hear from witnesses who reported Weller appeared intent and drove his car through the crowded Farmers' Market along Arizona Avenue at speeds in excess of 60 mph.*

The case is much more than an accident, noting that witnesses said Weller was surly after the incident and told bystanders that the victims should have moved out of harm's way when they saw him approaching. Is the killing of ten people just an 'oops'? Oops? I stepped on the wrong pedal. Oops? 'You saw me coming, you should have gotten out of the way.'"

The Defense attorney was next to give an Opening Statement, which stressed the fact that the entire incident was a tragic accident. He said the incident was exacerbated when the car was about halfway through the market and its airbag inflated, knocking Weller's foot off the accelerator and his hands off the steering wheel.

After both attorneys were finished with their Opening Statements, it was time for the testimony to begin. The prosecutor called as her first witness Rachelle Delong, who stated, *"I was walking along Arizona Avenue when I saw Weller drive through a wooden barricade and speed into the crowded market. I saw him clearly through his open window, looking straight ahead, determined, grasping the wheel with both hands. People were laying on the ground, bleeding, injured. Some people went to help the victims. I saw a woman lying on the left-hand side of Fourth Street, she was laying by herself. She had just been hit. I held her hand and started talking to her, I told her help was on the way. I stayed by her side for ten minutes, maybe longer, leaving only when she passed away."*

Richard Wong had headed the CHP investigation, and his opinion was that Mr. Weller had caused the ten deaths, because he failed to stop after he bumped another car before he sped into the market. Pedal Error explained the acceleration. The Defense presented to the jurors a graphic recreation of the 20-second drive through the open-air market. It was the view that the 86-year-old Weller had had through the windshield of his 1992 Buick.

Throughout, witnesses testified to hearing him stomping on and off the accelerator. He had his hands on the wheel turning the car, awake and alert. Some witnesses thought Mr. Weller was trying to flee. The earlier incident near the post office had involved scratches—cosmetic damage, according to police, to a Mercedes that Weller had struck from behind at a slow speed.

The prosecutor argued that the Pedal Error may have caused the crash, but an ordinary driver does not mistake one pedal for the other while driving nearly 1,000 feet. Pedal Error in and of itself is negligent behavior. And then there were Weller's remarks to victims when he got out of the car, saying, "If you saw me coming, you should have gotten out of my way."

Mr. Weller didn't take the witness stand, and he wasn't present during the latter part of the proceedings. There wasn't much that the defendant could add to his statements he made to the detectives on the day of the incident.

CHAPTER 26. HOW DID IT ALL END?

After all the testimony was over, the attorneys argued the case. The jurors listened to the Argument and carefully weighed the evidence, and after eight days of deliberation, they came back with a guilty verdict of ten counts of Vehicular Manslaughter with Gross Negligence. Many were surprised by the guilty verdict, but now they had to face the $64,000 question which was what the sentence should be. The possible sentences ranged from straight probation all the way up to 18 years in state prison.

Judge Johnson must have wondered how the heck he ended up with this 'hot potato.' The Probation Department did a Sentencing Report recommending some type of time in state prison. On the other hand, Ann the prosecutor made no recommendation as to what sentence should be imposed. Then came the endless Victim Impact statements from the many victims who had suffered so much, including loss of limbs, loss of mobility, loss of the ability to work, loss of mental faculties, not to mention those who suffered chronic pain and would do so for the rest of their lives. When the members of the deceased families explained the impact of the loss of their loved ones, there wasn't a dry eye in the courtroom.

After the parade of horrors that so many had gone through, Judge Johnson realized the ball was in his court. How could he not throw the book at this now 89-year-old, senile Mr. Weller for such pain and heartache he had caused? Judge Johnson knew that everyone in the courtroom expected him to perform a gigantic miracle. For the next 25 minutes, the judge tried to put into words his view of what the sentence should be, by saying, "*At trial, there was a great deal of attention to whether Mr. Weller could have put on the brakes of his car or whether his feet were frozen because of Pedal Error and hypervigilance. Like the jury, I have a lot of trouble accepting those concepts. The fact Mr. Weller's advanced age and weak condition contributed to his reckless driving is not a mitigating circumstance. That is because all drivers have the same responsibility to control their vehicles and avoid injury to others, regardless of age or physical condition.*

"There were places along the Farmers' Market where Mr. Weller literally threaded the needle through very narrow gaps between structures and vehicles, and in wider areas he steered his car from one side of the street to the other... Given the choice between stopping his car by steering into an empty truck or continuing to move down the street by steering into people, Mr. Weller chose to steer into the people.

"Among his first words after leaving his car, Mr. Weller told the police, 'Just think how I felt.' A few minutes later, he challenged some bystanders by asking, 'Why didn't you get out of my way?' These are unbelievably callous statements.

"Yet he has never once expressed in court any remorse for his actions. I have received letters and statements on his behalf from others, but not one word from Mr. Weller himself's indifference to the victims in this case, and I will never understand his stubborn and bullheaded refusal to accept responsibility and help put this matter to rest for everyone—including himself."

The judge was emphatic that the defendant deserved prison for his crimes. However, when the judge reviewed the defendant's age of 89 and rapidly declining health, he came to the conclusion that the defendant wouldn't be able to mentally and physical survive in a prison setting. Prison would most likely kill Mr. Weller. None of that was right and made no sense. The judge backed himself into a corner where he said he couldn't place Mr. Weller in prison or jail and he had no option but to place him on five years' probation. Further, he required him to pay $57,500 in restitution and $44,200 in fines, penalties and fees.

After the sentencing was over, the victims and relatives left the courtroom. There, the news media began interviewing them about what was a 'Just and Fair' sentence in this case. Everyone was dissatisfied with the Probation Sentence. One woman who had had her father killed and mother seriously injured said, "I'm not satisfied at all. Weller was grossly negligent. This trial accomplished nothing."

The daughter of one of the women killed said that she would never be able to see her mother again, while the defendant would get to see and be with his family. Another family was torn apart by the killing of the grandfather. One family member stated, "I think the Weller family members have to deal with their own actions or inactions in not taking away the keys from this man. He was already in previous accidents, and they should have admonished him not to drive anymore." Another victim's brother was in court and heard the sentence of probation, and he agreed with the judge, but he said his feelings would be different if his brother had been a younger man.

CHAPTER 27. WHAT HAVE WE LEARNED?

What happened after the criminal case?

On November 20, 2006 (Incident occurred July 16, 2003), the criminal matter concluded. The civil court case followed the resolution of the criminal case. However, before the criminal trial, a civil judge had ruled that the City of Santa Monica wasn't liable for any of the injuries and deaths. This shocked many of the victims and their families. Mr. Weller could be sued, but he didn't have any net worth aside from his house. His auto insurance was limited to only $500,000.

Just the medical bills for the seriously injured were in the multiple millions. The losses for pain and suffering and death benefits involved millions. Since this was the largest pedestrian injury in the country's history, it became obvious some deep pocket had to be found. A group of attorneys appealed the civil judge's ruling that the city wasn't liable. The court of appeals ruled that the City of Santa Monica was liable, since they didn't have a safety plan for the Farmers' Market. The appeals court ruled that the city should have had sturdier barricades to prevent automobiles from entering the shopping area of the Farmers' Market. The very liberal and compassionate City of Santa Monica became the deep pocket that every victim could reach into to make themselves whole. The city paid out $21 million to settle dozens of civil lawsuits.

Who should pay for such a tragedy?

The City Attorney for Santa Monica said that the $21 million settlement was a good resolution for all involved. The bulk of the civil suits were filed against the City of Santa Monica and the Bayside District Corp, which operated the Farmers' Market. At all times, the City and the District maintained that they weren't liable. But the City Attorney said, "In a case this big, trial results are difficult to predict. The settlement eliminates the risks and difficulties of trial and allows the victims, their families and the city to put this tragedy behind them and move forward." This extremely upscale community wanted to do the right thing for their residents and visitors. (As to those killed, only one had been a resident of Santa Monica.)

Should the City and the District be liable because they had used wooden barriers to keep vehicles off the streets used for the Farmers' Market? How foreseeable is it that a person would intentionally or accidentally drive through such a wooden barrier? Of course, removable poles could be used to keep vehicles out. However, such barriers could be compromised if someone such as a terrorist was intent on driving through the street market.

The questions about municipal efforts to protect pedestrians at farmers' markets nationwide may not be the real question. In this Weller case, the victims and families were merely reaching out for a deep pocket. The civil courts seem to like to make injured parties whole, especially when they did nothing to provoke their injuries.

Should criminal charges be brought in such a matter?

Prosecutors are given wide discretion whether to file criminal charges against a defendant. There are two questions in the Weller case that involve whether criminal charges should have been filed against Mr. Weller. First, did Mr. Weller's conduct show that he had committed a crime? Vehicular Manslaughter requires the defendant to purposely act. The facts of the Weller case can be interpreted in several ways. If one believes that Mr. Weller did hit a Mercedes and immediately tried to speed away (committing the offense of hit and run) and in the process he lost control of his car, causing the deaths and injuries, those facts could support Vehicular Manslaughter charges.

The issue of Pedal Error could be considered a complete defense to the Vehicular Manslaughter charges. However, it would be a defense that the Defense attorney would have to prove during the trial. In the Weller case, the evidence showed that no one saw the brake lights go on, meaning that Mr. Weller was in fact pushing on the accelerator, not the brake.

Once the Defense established Pedal Error by Mr. Weller's statements to the detectives, then the prosecution attacked that theory on the basis that one can't reasonably claim Pedal Error for over 20 seconds and traveling nearly 1000 feet. Either way, the prosecution could show that they had a basis for filing charges against Mr. Weller.

But the bigger question was, assuming that charges could be filed, SHOULD THE DA FILE SUCH CHARGES, even when the defendant could not be punished for his actions. When the DA started the trial, Mr. Weller was 89 years old and in such poor health that he couldn't attend the trial.

Often, the objective of a prosecution is to deter law breakers from committing crimes. But in this case, Mr. Weller wasn't likely to commit this offense again of driving through a farmer's market killing people. The main tools to deter criminal behavior are incarceration, payment of a fine or requirement to perform community service. In this case, Mr. Weller was 89 and in poor health, totally unsuited for incarceration.

The question is what is gained by prosecuting Mr. Weller. Thousands of tax dollars were spent trying Mr. Weller during a seven-week trial. Most large DA's Offices and Court systems can handle such expenses; however, smaller jurisdictions would have to reflect if this is a useful expenditure of public funds.

The District Attorney in Los Angeles County looked at the mayhem created by Mr. Weller's actions or inaction. The prosecutor works closely with the police and the victims of crime. When a prosecutor looked at this case and evaluated it as a civil matter, there was a storm of criticism that the DA was soft on crime. In order to be a well-respected prosecutor, it is easier to file cases like the Weller case in the courts to let them handle the problem. Here, in this case, Judge Johnson had to do the task of saying that the defendant deserved prison but it was impracticable to place a 89-year-old man in prison.

It was interesting that the DA's Office had persistent determination to prosecute the case but the DA's Office didn't make any recommendation what Mr. Weller's sentence should be. It is always easier at the end of a case to gain a better perspective as to what really should have happened at the start. When the criminal trial was over, there was a sense of "why did we do all of this for nothing?" Did the convictions give the victims' families closure? There was a feeling that if Mr. Weller was criminally convicted, then the matter of the civil liability would have been already proven.

How can we get dangerous elderly drivers off the roads?

Putting aside the merits of the criminal prosecution, the big issue was what should be done to get dangerous elderly drivers off the road. A corollary issue was whether the family and/or the children have a responsibility to prevent unsafe elders from driving. The Weller case brought the issue of safety of elderly drivers to the forefront. A knee-jerk reaction is that the elderly are more dangerous drivers. However, the facts don't support such a conclusion. Although older adults do lose motor skills and cognitive abilities as they age, statistics show that seniors often adapt to their limitations. Many of the elderly learn to take less trips, shorter drives, time the travel when there is less traffic as well as use familiar routes. As a group, the elderly do less risky driving such as speeding, texting or using alcohol than is done by younger drivers.

Those who have studied elderly driving find that drivers after age 75 have a higher crash rate including fatalities. The other rule of thumb is that most seniors stop driving ten years before their death. The studies show that mandatory age limits to driving don't seem to work out, since all seniors are different as to when they become dangerous drivers.

As a result of the Weller case, Katherine Freund, founder of the Independent Transportation Network, renewed her efforts to find volunteers who would be willing to drive seniors around in order to have them give up their keys to their automobiles. This concept can be effective if there are enough volunteers to do the driving.

Most studies show that for seniors to survive they need to get to the market as well as doctor's appointments. In the urban setting, the senior has access to public transportation and even taxi cabs to navigate through the daily needs for transportation. Many communities have senior citizen vans that help supply reliable transportation. However, in rural areas, many of these forms of transportation don't exist; therefore, the elderly are forced to fend for themselves.

Some states have enacted new laws that require the DMV to test seniors more often. These states have tried to create tests that give a better prediction of a senior's motor capability and mental ability to drive. So far, such tests are costly to preform and aren't that accurate at predicting a senior's ability to drive.

Many adult children have had to have the serious conversation with an aging parent about their ability to drive. Such conversations are often difficult, because the ability to drive is the opportunity to be independent. Most children want their parents to be independent so they don't have to personally supply the transportation. There are a few things the child can do to assess the capability for the parent to drive. One is to let the parent do the driving while the adult child is the passenger and can get an idea how well the parent can drive. Another is to constantly look at their car to see if there are new dings and dents, which may indicate difficulty in driving. Also, listen to the parent explain difficulty in parking or getting warnings or tickets for minor vehicle violations.

The Weller case created the perfect conversation for all children to talk to their aging parents, merely saying to the parent "we don't want you to be a new Mr. Weller, who became the number-one disliked person in the community." No senior citizen wants to end up like Mr. Weller. He was the most despised human being to ever live in his beloved City of Santa Monica, even up to his death on December 9, 2010, at the age of 94.

Thus ended the last chapter of one of the cases that impacted so many people, in which so many wonder whether JUSTICE WAS REALLY SERVED.

WHAT WAS ROUTE 66?

Why so Famous?

CHAPTER 28. NEED FOR A NATIONAL HIGHWAY

Up to this point, we have discussed three major cases, all occurring in the City of Santa Monica within blocks of the terminus of old Route 66. Before we continue reviewing more killings along this famous highway, let's spend a moment reviewing the history of old Route 66. What made it so unique and memorable to so many?

Today, everyone takes for granted the American Interstate Highway System. However, what most people don't remember is that America's highways didn't just magically happen. In the colonial days, streets and roads were pathways in villages and towns. Over time, trails and lanes were used to connect the various cities. At first, they were no more than horse paths that were narrow and hard to maneuver through. As wagons and carriages became more common, the rural roads became wider, with primitive bridges to cross streams. When America became a country, the new government began to grapple with the concept of major roadways between communities. At first it was a patchwork of country lanes used to transport commerce between communities, especially farming products.

Shortly after the founding of the nation, there was a impetus by President Washington to find more efficient ways to open up the new western frontier of Virginia (now West Virginia) to the Ohio Territory. The new government recognized that the public couldn't rely on the individual states to plan and construct such highways connecting territories outside their borders. This was where the federal government was vital to figure out how to carry out such a task. It was recognized that a highway was needed, starting in Maryland and continuing through the Cumberland Valley. It was in 1806 when President Thomas Jefferson authorized construction of the National Road, in which the first segment was called the Cumberland Road. It would extend from Cumberland, Maryland, to the Ohio River, replacing the footpaths and wagon roads of the old Braddock Road used during the Revolutionary War.

The early federal officials decided to carry the plan for the so-called **National Road** by allocating funds in 1810 for its construction. However, these great plans didn't lead to much building of the highway, since the British interrupted the plans when they attacked Washington D.C. during the War of 1812. We all remember during our childhood hearing the story how Dolly Madison grabbed and saved the paintings in the White House before the Red Coats burned the place down.

It wasn't until 1820 that the government was able to redirect its efforts to construct the next segment of the National Road. At that time, Congress authorized an extension of the road to the Mississippi River. Much of that road followed the old Ebenezer Zane Trace. The construction continued westward, reaching Vandalia, Illinois, which was the territorial capital of the Illinois Territory. Because of the Financial Panic of 1837 resulting in a national depression, the federal government ran out of funds and the National Road never reached the city of St. Louis as planned.

The federal government concluded that trying to maintain the National Road was too costly for them and transferred maintenance to the various states the road passed through. At that time, toll booths were established to raise money to maintain and repair the road. Back in the 1800s, the main vehicles traveling were commercial wagons, mail coaches, stage coaches as well as long processions of Conestoga wagons migrating westward. What was interesting was much of the road was constructed of crushed rocks, and in several places wood planks were used where the foundations were made up of soft sand or mud. However, later, in the 1830s, the road surface was covered by the macadam process (included a foundation of larger crushed rocks covered by smaller aggregated), which was pioneered by Scotsman John Loudon McAdam.

Through the remainder of the 1800s, the National Road went through periods of deterioration when other forms of transportation became more popular. Part of the time, there was a brief period that the American canal system was a more reliable means of travel, especially with commercial goods. Later, it was believed that the railroad would be a more efficient and faster method of travel from the East Coast to the Mississippi River.

America continued to move west with the expansion of the states and territories. It became imperative to find a way to connect all these new settlers. The first connection was done by the expansion of the First Transcontinental Railroad in 1869, which stretched 1,907 miles from Omaha, Nebraska, to San Francisco Bay. When the automobile came on the scene in the early 1900s, it became obvious that roads had to be constructed to accommodate motor vehicle traffic. **Route 40** came about in 1926 as a patchwork of roads allowing a person to travel from New York (Atlantic City, New Jersey) to San Francisco. It consisted of the basic path of the National Road combined with the Victory Highway, which was built in memory of the World War I veterans and ran from Kansas City, Missouri, to San Francisco. It was a gravel road in places and occasionally consisted of only a single lane.

Around the same time in 1926, U.S. **Route 66** was unveiled. It originally ran from Chicago through Missouri, a mere slice of Kansas, Oklahoma, a small section of northern Texas, completely crossing New Mexico and Arizona before ending in Santa Monica, California. It stretched a total of 2,448 miles and was given various names from the 'Mother Road,' 'Main Street of Americana' to even the 'Will Rogers Highway.' The road consisted of gravel and graded dirt, and it wasn't until 1938 that Route 66 became the first highway to be completely paved.

Because Route 66 avoided crossing the Rocky Mountains and other mountain ranges, it was relatively flat, which made it ideal for truckers who were transporting supplies across the country. Route 66 became famous in American folk history during the 1930s Dust Bowl years, when thousands of Midwesterners left their homes and farms decimated by the endless droughts. Author John Steinbeck in his book *Grapes of Wrath* vividly described the life of Dust Bowl immigrants traveling westward on Route 66 in hopes of finding a new life in California.

Not long after that, World War II broke out, and Route 66 took on a new purpose. Since the country was fighting two wars, one in the Atlantic and another in the Pacific, there was a need to move military equipment and troops across the country. Often, military families needed to be relocated, and Route 66 was utilized for that purpose. Also, Route 66 played a vital link in the development of the Atomic Bomb, since it passed through New Mexico, where White Sands was located.

After the war, the country experienced an economic boom that resulted in the expansion of auto sales. Many citizens in the USA were restless and wanted to explore the country. Massive numbers of people were anxious to take vacations by traveling in their new cars. They wanted to explore the West, and Route 66 provided the perfect highway, with all of its interesting attractions along the way. The new concept of 'motels' were built along the route, which allowed tourists to have convenient accommodations to make the trip pleasurable. Also sprung up along the highway were many 'mom and pop' diners with various specialties such as gigantic steaks to delicious BBQ ribs to satisfy the hungry travelers.

CHAPTER 29. MEMORIES OF ROUTE 66

Traveling along Route 66 became an American legend that resulted in a television series titled *Route 66* starring Martin Milner and George Maharis. It was a series that ran from 1960 to 1964 which was about two young men traversing the country in a Corvette convertible and all their adventures. Few highways have been the inspiration for a song such as ***Get Your Kicks on Route 66,*** composed by Bobby Troup in 1946. It was first performed by Nat King Cole by his trio and later sung by Bing Crosby, Chuck Berry and even the Rolling Stones. The lyrics are as follows:

Well, if you ever plan to motor west,
Just take my way, it's the highway that's the best
Get your kicks on Route 66
Well, it winds from Chicago to L.A.
More than 2000 miles all the way
Get your kicks on Route 66...
It goes from St. Louis down to Missouri,
Oklahoma City looks oh so pretty,
You'll see Amarillo and Gallup, New Mexico,
Flagstaff, Arizona, don't forget Winona,
Kingsman, Barstow, San Bernardino
Would you get hip to this kindly trip
Take that California trip
Get your kicks on Route 66

Get your kicks on Route 66
And I'll meet you on Route 66
Get your kicks on Route 66.

Later, in 1977, the musical group the Eagles alluded to Route 66 in the first several lines of their famous song "Hotel California," as the lyrics described what it was like to drive into Los Angeles on Route 66:

On a dark desert highway, cool wind in my hair;
Warm smell of colitis rising up through the air;
Up ahead in the distance, I saw a shimmering light,
My head grew heavy and my sight grew dim, I had to stop for the night.

Route 66 stayed a main thoroughfare for years, even after the **Interstate Highway System** was enacted in 1956. Since it took 35 years to complete the original version of the Interstate Highway, there was a need to continue to use Route 66 until 1985, when it was completely decommissioned. At that time, the roadside signs of Route 66 were torn down and tossed in the trash bin of bygone eras. Some history buffs had the good sense to confiscate some of the signs as collectors' items.

The idea of the Interstate Highway System for the USA was mainly due to President Dwight Eisenhower's urging. As a military man, he remembered back in 1918 the difficulty he had had transporting military troops and equipment during World War I, since the country didn't have a highway grid to all parts of the country. After his experience during World War II, he learned about the advantages Germany had with their Autobahn System. He recognized that America needed a federal transportation system which was direct and fast.

Eventually, the national government recognized the need for another plan to connect the various states to one another by the use of the Interstate highways. At first, the idea was to take existing roads and select them to be widened to provide better transportation. Others recognized the best way to speed up traffic was by redesigning the highways to follow a straight line instead of using existing connecting roads. Making these straight roads required large expenditure of resources in purchasing new properties and excavating for faster and safer roadways. The word 'infrastructure' was created to illustrate what was needed. The federal government officials recognized that they would have to draw up the plan for the intercontinental highways and not rely on cities and states to dictate the best route of travel. It was agreed that only the federal government had the resources to carry out such grandiose plans.

What this new highway plan was based on was the concept that the highway would have **'limited access.'** This method allowed for speeding up transportation by having the routes go around civic centers or in some cases totally bypass cities. This was a foreign idea from the old Routes, which were established to connect various communities. In other words, in the past, the traffic was directed to the center of a community. Thereby business districts prospered by the increase in traffic, although the traveler experienced substantial delays by having to drive through congested civic centers. For years, local communities fought the federal government's Interstate Highway plans.

Because of lawsuits that have been brought by some cities, there are portions of the original Interstate Plan that have not been completed. In several communities, major interchanges have never been built because of objections by local groups. Route 66 is a perfect example of how many communities along the old route have become ghost towns since traffic started speeding by on the nearby Interstate Highway. All those local motels, service stations and greasy spoons have faded away from lack of business, causing individual lives to be adversely affected. Several historic Route 66 Associations have been set up to preserve whatever is left of this important era of 'America's Mother Road.'

Route 66 without a doubt had a lasting impact on the areas it crossed through. Because of all the books which have been written about Route 66, people throughout the world come to visit the path of the old Route 66. Some are looking for nostalgic memories of when life was simpler. Others are hoping to experience how the West was won. For all those who crave to relive the past, Route 66 is still alive, even though this book points out it may be littered with more dead bodies as we retrace its old route.

IS IT DEATH BY NATURAL CAUSES OR MURDER?

People vs. Kenneth Hunt

CHAPTER 30. DEATH OF JEAN ORLOFF

Putting the City of Santa Monica in our rearview mirror, we continue eastbound on old Route 66 using today's Santa Monica Boulevard. As we pass under the 405 Freeway, we come to an intersection with Sepulveda followed by a small side street named Bentley Avenue. That will be the site of our next crime scene, involving a most unusual death. What makes this case so haunting is the chilling facts of how many murders go unnoticed or undetected.

We like to believe that when a dead body is found, we automatically know whether it is a homicide or not. In most situations, it is obvious when there is a gunshot wound or stabbing injury. Often dead bodies are found in homes where there is no evidence of trauma or deadly instrument. The most common situation is when elderly individuals live alone and a friend or relative goes to check on them and finds them dead.

Graphics Page

Old Route 66
Santa Monica Blvd.

Kenneth Hunt
Handyman Killer

A similar situation occurred on March 28, 1998, when a woman by the name of Jean Orloff did not answer her phone calls and hadn't shown up for work. This was strange for Jean in that she was a spunky 60-year-old and was always in communication with her family. Her elderly mother called one of her neighbors and asked her to check on her daughter to see if she were sick or if the phone was out of order. The neighbor went over to Miss Orloff's apartment and noticed newspapers at the base of her apartment door. She became suspicious and tried the doorknob. To her surprise, the door opened, which was unusual since Jean always kept it locked. Not knowing what she would find next, she walked into the kitchen and noticed a chicken floating in the tap water.

She called out Jean's name and there was no answer. Slowly and quietly, she went down the hallway that led to her bedroom. She felt like she was invading her neighbor's privacy by poking her head in the various empty rooms. As she reached the master bedroom's door, she stopped and wondered whether she was going too far. What if she had met some guy and had invited him over to her bedroom? Was she invading the privacy of a good friend? By now she wanted to leave, but she had promised Jean's mother that she would check out her apartment. With a slight tap, she pushed the bedroom door open.

Her eyes froze on what they saw. There on the bed was her neighbor, Jean Orloff, totally nude, lying face down on the bed. She didn't know whether to feel embarrassed because she was naked or shocked by the fact she wasn't moving or seemingly breathing. All she could do was try to utter her name, but her voice was too frightened to make a sound. "Oh my God" was all she could say to herself.

Now she wished she had brought someone else with her. She stood there questioning what to do next. Should she try to render aid or run out of the apartment? She realized she was an adult and she should try to act like an adult. Okay, when an adult finds a dead body, should she call Jean's mother and tell her the bad news? Or are you supposed to call the police? She didn't see any criminal activity, like a gun or blood. Or do you call the Coroner to come out and pick up the body?

She had all these questions and no one there to help her. As she headed for the front door, she had a flash in her mind that she could walk out of the apartment door and close it and pretend that she had never entered. In that way she could leave it to someone else to find Jean's dead body. But she got up the nerve to make the appropriate contacts.

Shortly the police arrived and checked things out. The one in charge was a long-time sergeant who had worked the field for years. Also, Jean's sister was reached and came over to the apartment and met with the neighbor. They noticed that the smoke detector had been removed from the wall and the fringe around the bed seemed to be singed in some way. They didn't know what to make of it. They mentioned this to the LAPD sergeant.

He asked a few questions that Jean's sister was able to answer. He asked about her sister's habits, in particular whether she smoked or had any medical problems. With ashtrays full of cigarettes, there was no secret that Jean was a long-time smoker. Her sister mentioned that she had always had an irregular heartbeat for which she took certain medicine. On the bedroom light stand was a full bottle of heart medicine.

After a half hour, the sergeant went over to Jean's sister and told her that from all he could see it was his opinion that Jean had died of Natural Causes after having a heart attack, possibly because she hadn't taken her heart medicine. He said he based this on the fact that she was 60 years old, a smoker and a person with heart problems.

Jean's sister said that she was skeptical that she died by way of Natural Causes. She couldn't figure out why the smoke detector had been removed. The sergeant responded back regarding her doubts by saying, "I have been to hundreds of homicides, and this isn't one of them." To support his opinion, there wasn't any gunshot or stab wound. There didn't appear to be any noticeable trauma or bruises.

The Fire Department paramedics responded to the scene. The captain from the Fire Department examined the victim's body. He discussed his findings with the LAPD sergeant. He believed that the victim had been murdered. The basis for his opinion was the fact that the nude body was face down on the mattress. He said that if the victim was having a heart attack, she would have had her face turned to the side in order to breathe. When told about the chicken in the sink, the captain said that he didn't think a woman would try to cook a chicken in the nude. Also, he noticed a suspicious mark on the back of the victim's neck.

The sergeant took note of the captain's thoughts but indicated that he believed that it was the usual heart attack of an older person who lived alone. He indicated that the Coroner's investigator would render the final opinion, and he was on his way. Shortly, the Coroner's investigator arrived and immediately examined the deceased and walked around the apartment.

The neighbor and Jean's sister went over to the investigator and said, "There is something really wrong here." They pointed out that the dust ruffle was burned as well as the phone wasn't where it normally should have been and that Jean would never have left the door unlocked. After listening to the women, the Coroner investigator consulted with the LAPD sergeant and ruled it was death by Natural Causes.

CHAPTER 31. BODY SENT TO MORTUARY

Jean's sister was told that she could request an autopsy but by now the Coroner's investigator and the LAPD sergeant had ruled that her sister's death was due to Natural Causes. She had never been in a similar situation, so she went with the opinions of the so-called experts. She said, "What's next?" They told her to select a mortuary to come over to pick up her sister's body. Also, they told her to obtain Jean Orloff's doctor's signature on the Death Certificate.

The police officer and sergeant who originally responded said they were leaving. They instructed Jean's sister that after the body was picked up by the mortuary home, they could clean up the apartment. Jean's sister got rid of the chicken in the sink and other things in the refrigerator that could spoil. Then she contacted another member of the family to help her remove the bed cover on which her sister's body had been lying.

The next thing the family had to decide on was the funeral arrangements. Because of their family religion, the service had to occur as soon as possible. Within a day they had a memorial service, which was well attended by friends and family. After the service, the body had to be immediately cremated according to tradition. However, the mortuary wouldn't do the cremation without a signed-off Death Certificate from Jean Orloff's doctor. When the doctor was contacted, he refused to sign it, since he hadn't seen Jean for over a year and he knew of no reason for her Natural Death.

Again, the mortuary called the Coroner's Office for them to issue the Death Certificate. The Coroner checked their files and found no investigation report and no photos. They possibly could sign off the documents, but a staff member said that he wouldn't issue the Certificate until he had a filled out an investigation report. The Orloff family kept contacting the Coroner's Office just to sign off so Jean could be properly cremated.

The Coroner's Office was feeling the pressure from the family as well as the mortician. Someone at the Coroner's Office assigned another Coroner's investigator to go by the mortuary and look at the body and sign off the paperwork. This second Coroner's investigator had to wonder why he was wasting his time checking out a dead body that another investigator had ruled as a Natural Death. This was bureaucracy at its worst. All he had to do was to check out the body and check off the right boxes on the Coroner's form, and within minutes he would return to Downtown with the completed form.

At the mortuary home, he found the assistant, who took him back to the Body Storage room. In the summertime, it was always a delight to visit the refrigerated body locker. But this March day was cool, so there was no thrill visiting this cold storage room.

A woman's body was pulled out, and he checked the name and number with the body tag. He assured himself this was the body he needed to sign off on. He looked at the initial report that contained the large words 'DEATH BY NATURAL CAUSES.' He took a second look at the body, and his eyes fixated on the victim's neck. Clearly there were crimson-red marks that extended around her neck. Glancing over the initial report, he saw written words stating 'slight red mark' on her neck.

Over the years, this Coroner's investigator had seen numerous strangulation cases, and the reddish marks on her neck area looked very similar to ligature strangulation. He stopped and took a deep breath. The assistant mortician had told him that the family was waiting for him to okay the body for cremation. For religious reasons, the family wanted to quickly complete the cremation so the deceased could join the afterlife.

The Coroner's investigator felt he was in a pressure cooker. He didn't know with any certainty that the deceased had been strangled, but he had a serious concern that the theory of a 'Natural Cause Death' may have been incorrect. The mortician and the family just wanted him to sign his name on the paperwork so a Death Certificate could be issued. The investigator phoned Downtown headquarters and told his supervisor that he had discovered reddish marks around her neck.

The supervisor wasn't feeling the pressure from the family. His reaction was to bring the body Downtown and do an autopsy to find out if his suspicion was right. The investigator at the mortuary had to be the one who gave the family the bad news. Immediately, the body of the deceased was shipped to the Coroner's main office on Mission Road, where an autopsy was performed. Upon conducting the autopsy, the Coroner/Medical Examiner found extensive bruises around the neck. Also, there was hemorrhaging in the eyes and mouth, indicating strangulation. Further, the Coroner found two ribs were broken. But most significant was the fact that the victim had been raped. The Coroner took vaginal swabs for testing for DNA.

So what had been ruled three days before as death by Natural Causes was now a full-scale homicide investigation. The Coroner's Office immediately notified LAPD. Within minutes, police cars were racing to the apartment house so the detectives could see if there was any evidence still left in the apartment. The crucial bedsheets that the sister had thrown in the dumpster had long been picked up and were buried under tons of dirt and trash in some dump site.

One would say that these things don't and can't happen. However, it is the prosecutor who has to stand up in front of a jury and explain how all these mistakes can occur while still wanting the jurors to believe the testimony of the authorities who had misdiagnosed this homicide. At least by now the police knew it was a homicide, but who was the likely suspect? There didn't seem to be any forcible entry into the victim's apartment, meaning probably the victim had let the person into her apartment. So the belief was that the victim must have known her killer. The apartment didn't seem ransacked, so burglary and robbery seemed to be ruled out. But what was the motive? Was it a sexual predator who had a fetish for older women?

The case went unsolved until the police received a phone call from a parole agent who said he had received word that the detectives should be checking out a parolee by the name of Kenneth Hunt. The parole agent said that Kenneth Hunt's brother-in-law called him up and stated that the police should be checking Hunt out for the death of Jean Orloff and possibly for the death of another woman, Myra Davis, some ten years earlier.

Since the homicide detectives didn't have any workable leads, they embrassed this new information with open arms and dusted off the old Myra Davis to take a look. They soon realized there were similarities.

CHAPTER 32. DEATH OF MYRA DAVIS

Some of the old-time detectives remembered the unsolved Myra Davis case and noticed that there were some similarities between her case and the more recent case involving Jean Orloff. However, there were some minor differences in their ages in that Myra Davis was in her 70s while Ms. Orloff was only 60 years old.

But some personal similarities were that they both had been married and had a grown family that included grandchildren. Also, both lived alone. Their residences were almost three miles apart from each other. The feeling was that in the Myra Davis matter the suspect could have been a burglar or rapist who worked in this general area. But again, the Jean Orloff crime scene didn't indicate anything had been taken. In fact, no drawers had been opened, and on the other hand in the Myra Davis case the house had been ransacked. But the homicide detectives were certain that there must be a connection. There were more similarities than dissimilarities.

In order to determine if there were resemblances to follow up on, the detectives reviewed the files from the Myra Davis case. That case occurred in June of 1988, when everyone was preparing for a hot summer in Los Angeles. The weather in June is often overcast with little in the way of sunshine. That is why this hazy condition is called the 'June Gloom.' The day was June 7th, and it was a typical dreary day. Myra Davis was a 71-year-old Hollywood actress who was often cast as the quintessential grandmother in TV commercials. She lived alone in a basic stucco house that she tried to keep up on her own. However, as time went on it became more difficult for her to maintain her house and yard. There were repair projects that she needed help with. Myra's concern was who could she find and trust to help her out.

Fortunately for Myra, she had a reliable manicurist who lived next door who she confided in. Often woman rely on their manicurists or hairdressers for advice, much like today's people rely on 'Angie's List' to find a good repairman. Myra mentioned that she needed someone to fix some things around her house. She said that she wanted a good 'handyman' who was dependable and reasonable. Her manicurist listened attentively, just like a therapist. Then her manicurist indicated that she had a solution to her problem in that she knew a good 'handyman.' She said he was great and could fix anything. Further he could be completely trusted because this 'handyman' was her **son-in-law**.

This was great news to Myra, since she didn't feel comfortable using the Yellow Pages to find a handyman. She would rather use someone who was recommended to her. So she got the handyman's name and phone number and called him to come by her house to see if he could do the jobs that needed fixing. The handyman's name was **Kenneth Hunt**, and he was excellent at doing woodwork. He was able to patch up everything Myra needed repairing. On several other occasions, Myra called Ken, and he always did the job and was very reasonable as to what he charged for his work.

Everyone was happy. Myra was pleased that she had found someone she could rely on and felt comfortable calling Ken at any time to help her around the house. He was happy because he needed the jobs, and of course his mother-in-law was ecstatic he was making money to support her daughter.

Myra had been married and had children. As the years went by, her husband passed away and her children moved out, leaving her to live alone. For years she had worked as a 'stand-in' in various movies. She had received noticeable attention when she was the 'stand-in' for Janet Leigh in Alfred Hitchcock's movie *Psycho*. She did the shower scene in which Janet Leigh's character was stabbed to death as she was taking a shower.

Later on in her career, she did numerous commercials playing the grandmother role. Because of her gray hair, she looked the part of the caring and loving grandmother. She certainly wasn't considered a star or even an outstanding actress, but she was always able to find work as a 'stand-in.' She seemed to blend into the crowd well, and that was what the directors were looking for. She was considered quite versatile and had a face that could project many expressions and emotions.

Everything was going well in Myra's life. She was in relatively good health for a person of her age. She still was regularly receiving work in Hollywood, not anything that made an enormous amount of money but she had enough work to keep her busy.

Then, on the day after June 7th, several people mentioned that they hadn't seen Myra and wondered if anything was wrong. Eventually, her family and friends were so concerned that one of her friends agreed to come by her small house to see if she was okay. The friend knocked on the door and waited but she didn't receive any response. Maybe she had gone on a short trip and forgotten to mention it to anyone. But as the friend was speculating on where she might be, she noticed that Myra's car was in the back. So she discarded that possibility. After waiting for several minutes, the friend didn't know what to do next. She had promised the family that she would check everything out.

Then she turned away from the front door and walked down the driveway that went to the backyard. As she did, she went up to the closed windows and tried to look inside. Nothing seemed to be suspicious. Finally, she was able to squeeze between several shrubs to look into the bedroom window. She cupped her hands in such a way to prevent the glare so she could look inside.

She was tittering between shrubs and tried to get a clear view of the bedroom. As she managed to focus her eyes on the interior of the room she gasped. There she saw Myra's body stretched out on the bed, not moving or breathing. First was disbelief and the thought that her eyes were playing tricks on her. After gazing at her friend's motionless body, she thought what she should do now. In an automatic response, she rushed to a door and with considerable force was able to push it open. As she ran to the back bedroom, she was in hopes of saving Myra's life. At Myra's advanced age, it was possible that she could easily have passed out after having a heart attack.

When she swung the bedroom door open, the sight halted her in her tracks. If the shock of seeing a dead body wasn't enough, there was something so appalling she couldn't comprehend what she was seeing. Myra's pants were pulled off and she had no underwear on. Her friend's mind was trying to process the entire eerie scene when the realization hit her that Myra had been viciously sexually assaulted.

The homicide detectives were called in, since this didn't appear to be death by Natural Causes. When the detectives arrived, they examined the victim's body and noticed red marks around her neck which were indicative of a person who had been strangled. There was something coiled around her neck. It was like a belt had been placed around her neck and pulled tight.

The detectives concluded that the victim had been raped and strangled. The next question was who would have done this. Because of her age, it made it especially hard to comprehend what type of person would commit such a heinous crime on an elderly woman.

The detectives continued to look around. Was there something that the killer had left that could be useful in tracking down the suspect? Since the killer hadn't used a gun, the forensic tool of ballistics would be helpful. Also there was no knife used, so that eliminated linking up a knife to the murder. This was 1988, and DNA hadn't been fully developed as a forensic tool. Since the victim had been strangled, there was no blood trail that would lead to the killer. The detectives were having difficulties knowing how to classify this murder.

The detectives searched all over her house looking for some type of clue that would shed some light on who the killer was and what his purpose was for the killing. Her dresser drawers had been gone through. This would be suggestive of a burglar. It was as though someone such as a burglar was looking for valuables such as money or jewelry. One scenario was that the victim came home and found the burglar inside and she confronted him.

The bed where the victim's body was found also had her purse lying on it with all the contents spread out. It appeared someone had gone through her purse, possibly looking for money, credit cards and blank checks. However, the burglary theory didn't seem to add up. The detectives looked at the doors and found no 'Forced Entry.' All the doors and windows were in good shape and hadn't been broken into. So the detectives deducted that the victim must have let the person into her house, possibly because she knew who he was.

CHAPTER 33. POSSIBLE SUSPECTS

The detectives knew there were certain group of sexual predators who delighted in attacking elderly women. But those individuals weren't burglars. In this case, the taking of personal property may have been an afterthought of the attacker. There wasn't anything that clearly indicated whether the killer was a sexual predator or just a common burglar.

The detectives asked the family members personal questions about Myra and who might have committed this heinous crime. Myra's granddaughter didn't want to cause family friction but had a thought. She said that one of Myra's grandsons had a drug problem. He wasn't working and often needed money for drugs. If he came over and knocked on her door, she would have readily let him in. He may have demanded money and she may have told him that she wouldn't give him any money unless he received help. This might have infuriated him and he may have struck her and attacked her. Since the detectives didn't have any good leads, they looked into the possibility that the victim's grandson was a possible suspect.

It wasn't likely, though, that a grandson would rape his 71-year-old grandmother. The detectives contacted the grandson and questioned him about where he was at the time of Myra's murder. After thoroughly talking to the grandson, the detectives came to the conclusion that the grandson had a credible alibi, and they eventually eliminated him as a possible suspect.

The detectives were running out of likely suspects, and they drove over to Myra's house. The victim's granddaughter was there cleaning up the house. The detectives related that unfortunately they weren't coming up with any suspects for the murder. The granddaughter, in a flippant manner, said, "Maybe you should check out the guy next door." She was referring to a young man who lived next door with the manicurist who seemed a little strange. She was referring to the **manicurist's son** who was always staring at the granddaughter every time she visited her grandmother. She was **not** referring to the **son-in-law handyman** Kenneth Hunter, who also lived there.

The detectives didn't know how to take this tip. However, they made a note in their files stating the words, "You should check out the guy next door?" For whatever reason, the detectives never checked out any of the guys living next door in the house of the manicurist. Possibly if she had given a reason why she had this suspicion, maybe they would have followed up on the suggestion. The irony was that the killer Kenneth Hunt was one of the guys who lived next door—although he wasn't the one the granddaughter was referring to.

Otherwise, the detectives listened to everyone who was willing to talk or give some workable leads. The detectives continued to talk to burglars who were caught burglarizing the area. They thought maybe a burglar might have talked the victim into letting him into her house under some type of pretext. But nothing seemed to materialize. Now the case was over a year old and there was nothing new to help solve the case. The detectives were swamped with other murder cases. They had to prioritize their time to work the cases that had leads to follow up on.

Myra's case was put on the back burner and the crime-scene evidence was tucked away in the evidence locker. About the only thing going for the case was the fact that it was so heinous as a crime that all the homicide detectives often talked about it in frustration that it had never been solved. The Myra Davis case made the transition from being an **ACTIVE** file to a **COLD CASE** file placed in the dusty file cabinet.

CHAPTER 34. HOW COULD DNA WORK ITS MAGIC?

The detectives in the Jean Orloff case were thrilled when they received the phone call from Kenneth Hunt's parole agent. When the agent revealed that he had been contacted by a person who suggested that the authorities should be checking out Kenneth Hunt for the Orloff murder the detective were excited to have a workable lead. What was more surprising to the detectives was the fact that this person suggested that Hunt was also involved in the murder of MyraDavis.

This was welcome news for both sets of detectives, so immediately they ran the name Kenneth Hunt through their criminal history computer. To their surprise this Kenneth Hunt had a lengthy record for assaults on women. With a little more investigation, they learned that Hunt had worked as a handyman for both victims. As a result, he knew both women and was familiar with their habits of coming and going to their residences. If he had come to either woman's door, they would have willingly let him in. Based on information that the detectives had gathered, they prepared a search warrant to obtain Hunt's blood to be used for DNA testing. Next they found a judge to sign the search warrant for Hunt's blood sample. Shortly thereafter they obtained a blood sample from Hunt.

Next the detectives had to obtain the samples of body fluid from both victims. The police luckily had been able to take several vaginal swabs from Ms. Orloff's body. These samples could be test and the results compared up to the suspect Hunt' DNA.

But the question was whether there were any swabs still in existence from Ms. Davis case. The police went through the police evidence locker looking for such samples. The records showed that there were two vaginal swabs taken of Ms. Davis.

Myra Davis's samples had been taken over ten years before. One of her swabs had been lost either in transit to the private Cellmark Lab or lost in the Cellmark Lab. The other swab sample that still existed had to be analyzed using a different DNA procedure. As to Ms. Davis, only the DQ Alpha & Polymarker & CTT method was used.

The samples from Ms. Orloff were tested by using three slightly different methods on three different dates. The results of those tests showed that the vaginal swabs of Ms. Orloff were a match to Kenneth Hunt's DNA. As to the Myra Davis vaginal swab, it showed a match to Hunt's DNA. Therefore, these results proved that Hunt had had sexual intercourse with both victims and he was likely the killer of the two victims.

When the prosecution went to trial, they were relying heavily on the DNA evidence. Hunt's Defense attorney knew that the DNA evidence if believed by the jury was going to convict his client, Hunt. So the Defense wanted to cast some doubt on this crucial DNA evidence. They attacked the procedure used to analyze the samples. The Defense next tried to attack the manner in which the samples had been collected, stored and shipped to the DNA lab.

Further, the Defense tried to attack the 'Frequency' rate. This involved the Cellmark expert rendering an opinion as to how likely it was the DNA could match another person. This is what is called 'statistical probability.' The DNA experts break it down according to the defendant's racial background. Statistically, the Frequency will vary depending on the race of the defendant. So the expert will list the Frequency for Caucasians, African Americans and Hispanics.

The prosecutor wanted the jurors to understand and appreciate the high unlikelihood that the piece of evidence came from any other human being. Since Kenneth Hunt appeared to be Caucasian, the Defense could point out that the Frequency rate was 1 in 1.7 quintillion. To put the number of 1.7 quintillion in perspective, it is more than all the people who have ever lived on the Earth. In other words, one could say with a high degree of certainty that the DNA was that of defendant Kenneth Hunt. Once the jury understood the statistical probability, the

Defense had a much more difficult task of creating a reasonable doubt regarding the DNA evidence.

The DNA evidence was quite compelling, but every prosecutor knows that some jurors will have difficulty in convicting a defendant solely on the DNA evidence. Some jurors would require some type of corroborating evidence. This is why the prosecutors decided to put on additional evidence regarding the manicurist referring her son-in-law, Kenneth Hunt, to work as a handyman for both Jean Orloff and Myra Davis. The manicurist had encouraged customers to use her son-in-law, Kenneth Hunt, as a handyman. She talked Ms. Orloff into hiring him to do several projects around her apartment, just like Myra Davis who had hired him to do various jobs around her house.

CHAPTER 35. TRIAL

GUILT PHASE

The prosecution believed that they had a strong case against defendant Hunt by relying on the DNA evidence coupled with the fact that Hunt had worked as a handyman for both victims. The DA's Office recognized that this case would have to rely on new methods of analyzing DNA. As a result, the administration assigned two knowledgdable DNA prosecutors. Deputies John Gilligan and Laura Jane Kessner were willing to take on this challenging case. One of the real concerns of the prosecutors was whether the jurors would be able to navigate through the numerous legal steps. First, the jury had to decide if there was sufficient evidence to prove beyond a reasonable doubt that defendant Hunt was guilty of **Murders.**

The next task for the jurors was to decide if the killings were **First Degree Murders**. What becomes confusing is that First Degree Murder can be proven several different ways. One way would be by proving the killing was done with **Premeditation and Deliberation**. Another way would be by relying on the **Felony Murder Rule**. That would apply if the killings were committed during the commission of a Felony such as Rape, Burglary or a Robbery. Either way, the jury could reach the conclusion that the murders were of the First Degree.

Once the jury arrives at that step, they need to next decide if one of the **Special Circumstance** allegations has been proven to be true. In this case, since it was a multiple murder case and the killings were done during felonies, the jury could easily find the Special Circumstance allegation true.

The jury was able to navigate through all the various legal hurdles to return guilty verdicts of two First Degree Murders and both with Special Circumstance to be true. This concluded the Guilt Phase of the trial, and it was time to move on to the Death Penalty Phase.

DEATH PENALTY PHASE

The prosecutors needed to show that the Aggravating evidence substantially outweighed the Mitigating evidence. The prosecution put on numerous witnesses that the jurors hadn't heard before. The prosecutors wanted to show a pattern of violent behavior by defendant Hunt starting in 1991 that continued all the way through 1998. Between these two murders of Myra Davis and Jean Orloff, there were seven assaults on other women and a Manslaughter conviction. The prosecution called witnesses regarding the assaults committed by the defendant in domestic violence situations.

One of the most telling pieces of evidence during the Death Penalty phase was when the prosecution called witnesses in regard to the defendant's Manslaughter conviction in 1992. The facts were that the defendant lived next door to Mr. Bernard Davis (not related to Myra Davis) and his wife. This was another neighbor of Hunt in addition to Myra Davis who had been a neighbor back in 1988.

In March of 1992, Mr. Davis and his wife were walking out of their home when they saw the defendant Hunt next door kicking his dog. This continued to the point that Mr. Davis couldn't ignore this beating any longer. Mr. Davis asked defendant Hunt to stop mistreating the dog. At that point, Hunt stopped the beating of the dog and walked over to Mr. Davis. Hunt pulled back his right arm and coiled his fingers into a fist. Without a word he used his right hand like a slughammer and propelled it with all his strength at the head of the elderly Mr. Davis. His clenched fist made a bullseye hit on Mr. Davis' head which snapped backwards. The force of the blow knocked him off his feet causing him to fall to the ground and hit his head on the pavement. The consequence of this violent attack resulted in Mr. Davis being taken to the hospital where he went into a coma. After a short time in the hospital, the victim died of the injuries he had suffered.

The prosecution argued that there was more than enough Aggravating evidence from the manner in which he killed the two murder victims. Adding to that was his Manslaughter conviction of the elderly Mr. Davis combined with all the women he had attacked. Clearly the Aggravating evidence substantially outweighed the Mitigating evidence, therefore the Death Penalty should apply.

Hunt's Defense attorney concentrated his Argument on the fact that while growing up Hunt had had an alcoholic father and an unstable home environment. His Argument was that it was the bad childhood that was at fault. All the violent behavior by the defendant only supported the fact of how bad his childhood really had been.

After hearing all the additional evidence and listening to the Arguments, the same jury that had just convicted defendant Hunt of murder was sent out to deliberate his fate as to Life or Death. They deliberated for several days without a verdict. Eventually they told the judge they were at an impasse. The judge told them to continue to try to reach a conclusion. After more deliberations, the jury returned and this time said they were hopelessly deadlocked. At this point, the judged declared a mistrial and a hung jury. Afterwards, it was determined that 11 jurors were in favor of imposing the Death Penalty and just one juror held out for Life.

The prosecutors and the victims' families were extremely disappointed. With such a lengthy pattern of violence, it seemed a reasonable juror would vote for the Death Penalty. The prosecutors discussed the options with the family members, and it was all agreed to retry the Penalty Phase. So the case was set for another trial on the issue of the Death Penalty. The prosecutors analyzed every step of the previous Penalty trial. They were looking for ways they might be able to better persuade all 12 jurors this time.

Several months later, another 12 jurors were selected for the second Death Penalty trial. The presentation of the evidence seemed to go even better than the first trial. The jury heard all the evidence from both sides and started to deliberate. After several days the jury came back with bad news that they were hopelessly deadlocked. The judge encouraged them to continue to work to see if they could reach a verdict. Finally they came back like the other jury, hopelessly deadlocked. However, this time the numbers weren't as good for the prosecution in that there were only ten in favor of Death and the other two were for Life.

This was devastating news for the prosecution. The DA's Death Penalty (Special Circumstances) Committee met and decided that there wasn't any new or different evidence to present. It was felt that an additional jury wasn't likely to unanimously agree on Death any more than the other two juries. The prosecution agreed not to put on another Penalty trial. Then the judge gave the defendant Hunt a sentence of Life in Prison Without the Possibility of Parole.

This case illustrates how important DNA evidence can be in murder trials. If law enforcement had had the forensic tool of DNA back in 1988 when Myra Davis was killed, very likely Jean Orloff would be alive today. This is especially important in rape cases, when a rapist is detected early on and removed from society before, he can create more victims. The other lesson we learned from the Jean Orloff case is how often murder situations can be misdiagnosed as 'Death by Natural Causes.' It is essential that First Responders are better trained to know what to look for in deciding whether a death was due to Natural Causes or a possible Homicide.

HOW A DOMESTIC VIOLENCE CASE CHANGED TRUE CRIME REPORTING

People vs. John Sweeney

CHAPTER 36. LIFE OF ACTRESS DOMINIQUE DUNNE

As one continues to travel eastbound on Santa Monica Boulevard, one approaches Rangely Avenue. If one drives down the street, one comes to Dominique Dunne's West Hollywood house. From the outside, the house gives the appearance of an owner who is someone starting out in the entertainment industry. Nothing fancy, but well located to be able to attend auditions at the nearby studios and production companies.

Graphics Page

Old Route 66 In West Hollywood (October 30, 1982) **Strangling of Dominique Dunne**

Dominique Dunne came from a distinguished Hollywood family, growing up in Beverly Hills. It wasn't a perfect family in that her parents divorced when she was eleven. Unfortunately, her mother had been diagnosed with multiple sclerosis, which confined her mom to a wheelchair. This meant that Dominique had to learn at a young age to care for her mother. Eventually, she was able to attend college in Colorado, which allowed her to escape from Tinseltown. She had an opportunity to travel to Italy, where she stayed to soak up the history and culture. When she returned to the States, she attended Colorado State University, where she majored in acting.

With her family and upbringing, she was a natural for acting. When there were openings, she came back to Hollywood. She received small parts in popular TV series such as ***All in the Family, Chips,* and *Fame.*** Although these weren't leading roles, these jobs looked good on her resume. When Steven Spielberg was filming ***Poltergeist,*** he auditioned Dominique and selected her to play the role of the older sister. Since the film was a hit, she gained recognition, allowing her to be noticed in the entertainment industry.

Dominique's career was kicking into high gear. As her professional life was on an ascent, her personal life had hit a low point. A year earlier, she had met a handsome lad by the name of John T. Sweeney (this surname is thought to be of Irish origin, but in reality, is a Scottish name from the Gaelic word *suibne,* meaning a 'pleasant' or 'well-disposed' person. Later that was a misnomer in describing him). She enjoyed his company, especially since he demonstrated an intense interest in her as a person and was impressed by her achievements as a rising movie star.

It was as if he couldn't get enough of her. He was always trying to assist her. Eventually, she rented a house on Rangely Avenue, which was perfect since it had a large backyard for all of her pets. He knew how much she loved animals, so on various occasions he presented her another pet, one time an endearing puppy. With this cozy little abode, it almost seemed natural for him to move in with her so they could play the role of an aspiring upstart Hollywood couple. For almost a year, it seemed like endless bliss or a real version of the 1970 movie ***Love Story,*** with Dominique playing the part of Ali MacGraw and John Sweeney a stand-in for Ryan O'Neal.

However, as time went on the practical world appeared, as it does for most couples. That is when true love takes on the role of compromise and routine. Years earlier, another couple had lived several blocks away by the names of Marilyn Monroe and Joe DiMaggio. They had two careers totally dissimilar from each other. Marilyn was a Hollywood actress, and he was a New York Yankee baseball player. Their careers demanded that they both live on various sides of the country. Neither was going to give up their professions for their marriage, which may explain why this world-famous couple's nuptial lasted a mere nine months.

The same could be said for Dominique and her boyfriend John Sweeney. She was an actress. What the public doesn't realize about actresses is that there is an unglamorous side of working in the movie business. When an actress is filming, she has to wake up very early in order to be on the set for the makeup and hair styling. So Dominique's routine was going to bed early and arising around 3:30 a.m. in order to be at the studio by 5:00 a.m.

On the other hand, Sweeney was a chef at Ma Maison restaurant, and his work hours were from 3:00 p.m. to midnight. That meant he returned home after midnight, when Dominique was deep in sleep. When he arrived home, Sweeney was highly charged and would wake up Dominique to explain how his day had gone. That was followed by sexual activity, which he loved but which curtailed Dominique's quest for a good night's sleep.

Dominique tried to be a good sport to please Sweeney; however, her daytime acting was suffering, since she would be exhausted on the movie sets. Eventually, she realized this relationship wasn't working out for her. Although she had feelings for Sweeney, the hours of their two varied careers were tearing them apart. That was when she told him that it would be better if he moved out. Her hope was that if they weren't living together, they could have a more normal relationship.

Sweeney didn't like the idea of the separation and felt she was being disloyal to him. Since he wasn't the one who was experiencing the lack of sleep, he couldn't comprehend the justification for the breakup. His view of the termination of the relationship was that Dominique was rejecting him because of his lack of sophistication. Simply put, he felt she didn't think that he was good enough for her. Sweeney came from modest means, and his family would best be described as 'commonplace.' As the couple parted, he begged for a chance to reconcile, and her answer was "let's wait and see." In other words, she was ready to move on with her life. She was young, attractive and from a prominent, prosperous family. There was no shortage of respectable men for her to meet and socialize with.

From Sweeney's vantage point, he had caught one of the most promising young actresses on her path to stardom. No way would he let her slip away so some other guy could move in on his true love. From that point on, he became **obsessed** with Dominique. And when he wasn't at her side, he wanted to know what she was doing and who she was with. His jealousy drove him to stalk her. On several occasions, he showed up at her rehearsals. Sweeney became distrustful of her friends when they related, they didn't know where she was.

Obsession at first seems so delightful. That may be why the Calvin Klein perfume 'Obsession' is so dearly desired by women. What woman doesn't relish all the attention being showered on her? A woman who is obsessed over by another has to be elated that she possesses a quality which drives another to feel that they can't live their lives without totally being with that woman. However, at some point that 'obsession' becomes like an albatross around the woman's neck, choking off her individuality. The woman wakes up to realize her separate life has been taken away from her by the one craving her.

At first, Dominique believed that she could control the situation, since he would do anything to persuade her to reconcile with him. He would do anything to win her back by baking special dishes or pastries for her. Dominique was an optimist and believed things would work out just like they had through her entire life. The old saying that 'Time can solve all problems' gave Dominique some peace of mind.

What Dominique didn't recognize was that Sweeney had entered the Domestic Violence spiral of no return. The mental abuse took the form of threatening her if she didn't reconcile with him. At this point, he wanted her to understand that he was in control and she needed to recognize it. The mental abuse soon was transformed into physical abuse. At first it was only minor pushing and shoving. It seemed harmless, since it was like a couple playing the roles in the 1966 movie ***Who's Afraid of Virginia Woolf*** starring Elizabeth Taylor and Richard Burton.

On August 27, 1982, the mental abuse escalated to physical abuse when he pulled her hair and knocked her to the floor. At that point, Dominique questioned if she really could control the situation. On September 26, 1982, Sweeney came over to

Dominique's place. Dominique had several old friends come into town to visit her. Both couples decided to go out together for dinner and have a few drinks. By the end of the evening, everyone was mellow and both couples went to their separate bedrooms. At first everything was congenial, and the visiting couple decided to go to bed. However, sometime after midnight they were woken by loud shouting and a heated argument, like a volcano ready to erupt. The other couple in the guest bedroom didn't know what to do. Should a guest in someone else's house step in to play referee on their host?

The visiting couple lay in bed, paralyzed, not knowing what to do. The shouting worsened to yelling, and on several occasions, they could hear Dominique's voice scream out for help. As the emotional exchange reached a high pitch, Brian, the male visitor, couldn't ignore it any longer. To gain enough nerve to step in, he raced to the master bedroom and found himself banging on the door. He shocked himself for having the nerve to intervene. What surprised him was his knocking had silenced the argument. He didn't know what to say, since he didn't want to appear as a person trying to meddle in someone else's personal situation. All he could think of saying was, "Could you cool it? We can't sleep with all the noise."

Although Brian sheepishly returned to the guest bedroom, not knowing if he had done the right thing or forever lost the good friendship he and his girlfriend had with Dominique, what Brian didn't realize was that the stage had been set for the beginning of a major DOMESTIC VIOLENCE incident.

CHAPTER 37. FINAL CURTAIN

Almost a month later, on October 30, 1982, the next phase of this case was about to unfold. Dominique was home rehearsing for a new TV series. She had invited her fellow actor, David, over to rehearse their lines for this science-fiction-type TV series which was being called "V" until a real name could be decided on.

Around 4:00 p.m., Dominique's phone rang, and she was hesitant to answer. After several more rings she gave in, just in case it was her mother calling. When she noticed it was Sweeney, her tone changed, and she began thanking him for the Halloween card and gifts he had sent her. He had reconciliation on his mind, but she wasn't ready to agree to anything. As the conversation continued, he suggested that they get together for lunch on the next day. Dominique realized that would be a good way to end the conversation, so she agreed to lunch.

Sweeney was at work reflecting on their conversation and realized that Dominique didn't sound like she was ready for him to move back in with her. At 8:30 p.m., he made a second call, only to receive a busy signal on her phone line. Sweeney sensed the urgency of this situation, so he called the operator to break into her line. Dominique was surprised by the interruption by Sweeney on her line, so she promised that she would call him back as soon as she finished her call.

After that conversation, Dominique wondered what she should do. She was a mature female who was from a celebrated Hollywood family and receiving accolades for her acting. At this moment in her life, the most important thing was crafting her resume with more acting roles. At the age of 22, she had accomplished much, but she wanted more. She wasn't ready to have anything interfere with her career.

As much as she had feelings for Sweeney, she recognized that their relationship would impact her acting career. His working hours as a chef would never change, and early-morning calls at the studios were part of the price of being an actress. After mulling over the impossible situation, she decided to make the phone call to Sweeney.

She told him, "I've been thinking about our relationship and I don't want you moving back in with me." Further, she said that their relationship was starting to affect her career. This wasn't the message that Sweeney wanted to hear. All he wanted was another chance. He needed a ray of hope that reconciliation could be possible sometime in the future. Dominique was running out of various ways to say "no" to him moving back in with her. She tried to say that they could continue to talk about it at lunch the next day.

The dreaded phone call finally ended. Sweeney was at work at Ma Maison, and he was rethinking every word that Dominique had just related to him. He could see that his Halloween card and gifts had not won her back. It was like having tunnel vision in that he was so obsessed with winning her back. All he thought about was not giving up but being more forceful, conveying to Dominique how much she meant to him.

Sweeney saw a break in the dinner orders and told his buddy, the co-chef, to cover for him for ten minutes so he could walk over to Dominique's place and try to work things out. Sweeney didn't have a car or a driver's license, so he had to walk for several blocks to Rangely Avenue. Arriving at the front door, he rang the doorbell. Within seconds, Dominique was at the door and she pulled it open.

Sweeney could see that Dominique was dressed as though she was going out. She had on a blue sweater with purple Sassoon women's cords, finished off with purple ankle boots. Behind her, Sweeney could see a young man, David, the actor she had been rehearsing with for the "V" TV pilot. David could see that a tense situation was unfolding before his eyes. David was a runner from danger and had no desire to be a hero in saving a damsel in distress. His response was that he was willing to leave so the couple could talk privately by themselves.

Dominique thought that she didn't want to be left alone with her ex-boyfriend. Her quick response was, "No, stay, we will both talk on the front porch." As Sweeney closed the front door, David could hear the two discussing their relationship. First was Sweeney asking for a reconciliation, and Dominique responded that at this time in her life she wanted to live alone. They went back and forth, and David could sense that Sweeney was becoming exceedingly infuriated.

At that point, David was observing a Dr. Jekyll and Mr. Hyde moment. It appeared that Sweeney was being transformed into a hideous person, who raised both of his hands and placed them around Dominique's neck. Instinctively she backed away to get away from his grasp. But his large chef's hands that had been useful in squeezing tomatoes and other vegetables were like a vise clamping off her breathing.

At this instance, Sweeney realized that he was in total control. She tried to dislodge the grip by turning away from the front door. He pushed her off the front porch onto the driveway. All she could do was move her feet backward, trying to get away. Sweeney's grasp was so intense that he pushed her into the neighbor's driveway.

The two of them moved slowly into the neighbor's backyard, where she tripped and fell backward and he landed on top of her. The net effect was that now he was straddling her with his hands squeezing her neck with all his strength, thrusting his thumbs down on her windpipe. Eventually, he took off his chef's rolled-up scarf and removed two of his chef's jackets. What happened next is vague. What is known is he strangled her long enough that she stopped breathing.

Sweeney became aware of what he had done and he switched into the save-my-girlfriend role. First, he administered mouth-to-mouth resuscitation. When Dominique didn't respond, he reached in and pulled her tongue out so she wouldn't choke on it. At that moment, he noticed David leaning over the fence which divided the two houses. Sweeney yelled at him to call the police.

After considerable time, Sheriff's deputies arrived on Rangely Avenue. Sweeney got up from lying over Dominique. He walked over to the deputies and stated, "I killed my girlfriend and I want to kill myself." The deputies were more than surprised, since they had never been greeted that way. One of them got his handcuffs out and walked behind Sweeney and cuffed him. They had to wonder how often in their careers they would arrest a murder suspect within 15 seconds of responding to a crime scene.

CHAPTER 38. WAITING FOR THE DUST TO SETTLE

One of the deputies went to the back of the neighbor's yard, and he saw Dominique lying on her back. There wasn't any movement such as breathing, so he called for paramedics to assist. When the emergency personnel arrived, there was an attempt to resuscitate, but it didn't have any positive results. The advantage for Dominique was that Cedars Sinai Hospital was only blocks away.

She was whisked away and the ER personnel started doing their magic. They were able to attach her to a resuscitation apparatus, and the EEG indicated slight brain activity. The detectives needed to know whether this was going to be a full-scale homicide investigation or a mere Domestic Violence situation in which the victim would be begging law enforcement to later drop charges.

The detectives did the preliminary investigation such as searching Dominique's house. The only thing of interest was finding a check written by 'John Sweeney' for the amount of $2,000, which was apparently for rent. A more thorough search by detectives uncovered the name of Dominique's mother, Ellen Griffin Dunne, living on Crescent Drive in Beverly Hills. They contacted her at 3:00 a.m. and advised her that her daughter had been injured and was being treated at Cedars.

Dominique's mother didn't sound surprised about the attack and told the detectives that a similar incident had occurred back in August which resulted in Dominique moving back in with her mother. She had described how her boyfriend had grabbed her hair and she bumped her head on the floor. She related that the couple was having difficulty with their relationship. He would come home late and wanted to talk to her after she had already gone to bed. This was becoming so disruptive that Dominique had decided between her career and her relationship with him. She was trying to be as gentle as possible in conveying to him that their two careers didn't mesh.

After listening to Dominique's mother, the detectives drove over to Cedars Hospital, arriving around 4:00 a.m. The head nurse showed them to Dominique's room, where they found her lying lifeless. They walked closer and had to step around various medical devices. They looked directly at her neck and saw large abrasions around her throat area. These abrasions wrapped around the front of her neck. The nurse escorted the detectives to the corner of the room and in a low voice she announced that the patient was critically ill and she wasn't likely to live much longer without the ventilator.

These were the words the detectives were hoping not to hear. That meant that this simple DV case was going to be a homicide case involving people in the entertainment industry. The detectives knew it was time to start their 'A' game where all the 'i's are dotted and the 't's crossed.

The detectives knew that it would be important to know more about the prior incidents when Sweeney had been violent. Back at the station, they were busily doing their paperwork at their desks when the phone rang. The one detective nearest the phone picked it up, and a Brian, 24, from Chicago was on the line. He indicated that he was a good friend of Dominique and he had some information which might be of interest to the detectives. He explained that a month earlier, on September 28, 1982, he and his girlfriend had flown out to spend a weekend at Dominique's place.

He related that he and his girlfriend had gone out to dinner and had some drinks with Dominique and Sweeney. Afterwards, they came back to her place and both couples went to their respective bedrooms. After a short time, he heard a thud and could hear the sounds of an argument. When it didn't subside, he went to Dominique's bedroom and asked them to "cool off and go to sleep."

Things quieted down, and he went back to his bedroom. Within a minute, he heard Dominique screaming, so he got up and went to the hallway, where he saw Dominique run out of her bedroom. He could see that she had abrasion marks around her neck. She told her friend to call the police, since Sweeney had choked her. She went into the bathroom and closed the door. The next thing he heard was Dominique's VW starting up. He surmised that Dominique had climbed out of the bathroom window in order to escape in her car.

As he heard the VW engine start up, he saw Sweeney run out of the bedroom and continued out the front door. Brian wondered if there was going to be a confrontation outside, so he followed Sweeney out of the house. Then he noticed that Dominique had successfully backed her VW out of the driveway onto the street. As Dominique turned her head to see if it was clear to back onto the street, Sweeney jumped onto the front of the VW to prevent Dominique from driving any farther.

Brian couldn't believe what he was seeing as he saw Sweeney grabbing the windshield wipers in order not to fall off. At the same time, Brian could see the fear and determination in Dominique's eyes as she maneuvered the VW onto the street. She put the car in drive and took off. Sweeney yelled at her to stop since he was about to fall off. She put on the brakes and Sweeney went flying off. As he fell to the side, she steered around him and gunned the engine to get out of there.

The detectives knew Dominique moved out of the house and wouldn't return until Sweeney had moved his belongings out. Eventually, she had her locks changed and returned to her house, hoping things would return to normal without Sweeney around.

Who was the Dunne family? Most people recognize the family name as part of the entertainment industry, as well as the book world. First, her father was the famous True Crime author Dominick Dunne, who wrote about how high-society folks interact with the judicial system. That was all due to this case, which gave him an introduction to the courts in the worst possible way. Prior to being a True Crime author, he had been a TV and movie producer in his earlier days in Hollywood. He married Ellen Griffin, an heiress with ranching money. They had three children—two boys, and Dominique was the youngest. They were a prominent Hollywood couple living in Beverly Hills.

The family relationship deteriorated, and they divorced in 1967. He continued to produce movies, one with Elizabeth Taylor called ***Ash Wednesday*** (1973), which turned out to be a major flop. However, like so many who were in the entertainment industry, he became addicted to drugs, and by 1979 he knew he had to move out of town to save himself. He moved to Oregon and lived a boring life and dabbled in writing, and as a result he wrote the book ***Winners,*** which was a success. That encouraged him to continue with his writing.

Dominick's brother was John Gregory Dunne, a famous American novelist, screenwriter and literary critic. He married Joan Didion, and the two collaborated on a series of screenplays including ***The Panic in Needle Park*** (1971), ***A Star Is Born*** (1976) and ***True Confessions*** (1981). John Gregory Dunne wrote numerous best sellers such as ***The Studio, Vegas***, and ***Playland,*** as well as ***Monster: Living off the Big Screen***.

There was no question that Dominique came from a recognized Hollywood family which moved in the elite circles of society. On the other hand, John Sweeney came from humble means from Pennsylvania. His only claim to fame was that he had studied in France to be a chef. His ability to work his way up at Ma Maison restaurant was a major accomplishment. He was being groomed to take over after the celebrity chef Wolfgang Puck moved on.

CHAPTER 39. DIFFICULT TIMES

For any family it is hard to pull the plug on a loved one. Even when one knows that a person is brain-dead, there is the hope that a miracle will intervene and bring that dear soul back to life. However, what made Dominique's situation so difficult was the fact that she was a vibrant young woman who had so much to live for. It was going to be a struggle for her parents to decide to take her off life support. By November 4, 1982, all the Dunne family members had said their final goodbyes, and the family wishes were carried out and the plug pulled.

When that occurred, this DV case was elevated to a homicide. The Detectives presented the case to the DA's Office, and a murder complaint was filed against John Sweeney. Thus started one of the most convoluted and contentious criminal cases of all time. Dominique's parents wanted Sweeney, the killer of their beloved daughter, to go away to prison for the rest of his life. At the outset of this case, her father and mother knew little about the Criminal Justice System in California. However, what they saw and endured over the next year would forever change them.

To begin with, there was a preliminary hearing held several months later at the Beverly Hills Courthouse. Several basic witnesses were called to prove that there was sufficient evidence to bind the defendant over for trial. At this hearing, the prosecution called Lillian, who was a former girlfriend of Sweeney. She testified that Sweeney had beaten her at least a dozen times in which her nose was broken and she had a ruptured eardrum. The purpose of this witness was to show that this defendant had a propensity to beat up women.

After the preliminary hearing, the case was transferred to the Santa Monica Superior Courthouse, where the case was assigned to Judge Burton Katz's courtroom. The case was set for trial in six months. When July arrived, it was time to select a jury who could sit on a trial that would take possibly four weeks. Both sides exercised their pre-emptive challenges, and eventually a jury was selected. It consisted of nine men and three women. Then the pretrial motions were held to decide how the case would be tried. The major pretrial motion was whether the DA could call as a witness, Lillian, to testify to the beatings that the defendant committed on her during their prior relationship.

Late in the day, around 4:30 p.m., prosecutor Stephen Barshop was questioning witness Lillian, who had lived with Sweeney from 1977 to December 1980. Barshop asked her whether her family was wealthy, and she was about to say "no." Then suddenly Sweeney rose up from his seat at the counsel table and began walking toward the rear door of the courtroom, which led to the holding cell area. The bailiff quickly threw both arms around the taller defendant and wrestled him down, in the process slamming Sweeney into some filing cabinets. The judge and the clerk activated the security alarm that brought Sheriff's deputies sprinting into the courtroom. Sweeney didn't resist, but he was handcuffed to the chair.

After the ruckus quieted down, the Defense attorney said that Sweeney wished to address the court. The judge said okay, and they waited for a minute for him to speak. And haltingly, between convulsive sobs, he said, "I'd like to apologize to the court, to Mr. Barshop, and to the bailiff. I wasn't trying to escape. I was just becoming very tense and needed to move around." Then the judge said that he accepted the defendant's apology. The judge explained that he needed to keep decorum in the courtroom and if the defendant found that he had too much stress on him, he could choose to remain outside the courtroom.

The witness, Lillian, resumed her testimony in this pretrial hearing. The judge ruled that her testimony could be brought in for rebuttal, but the prosecution couldn't use her testimony during their 'Case in Chief.' Next, the judge said that due to the excessive publicity in this case, he ruled that he was imposing a gag order on both the attorneys not to talk to the news media about this case.

The jury was selected, and it was time for the actual trial to begin. The defendant was seated at the counsel table with his public defender. Sweeney was dressed in a suit and tie, and in his right hand he was clutching a tattered Bible. Whenever he was brought into the courtroom by the bailiff, he had his Bible at his side.

Then the judge announced that it was time for the Opening Statements by the attorneys. He turned to the prosecutor and asked if he wished to make an Opening Statement. Mr. Barshop responded that he would as he stood up and looked directly at the jurors. He said, "Mr. Sweeney was arrested at the scene and confessed. There is no question in this case as far as who killed Dominique Dunne, not at all." Then he went on to explain about the similar incident that occurred a month before. He said that the jurors would hear from two witnesses who would testify how Mr. Sweeney attacked Dominique. They would relate to them that they heard a thump, then gasping for air and crying from the victim, in which she called out for them to help her. When the bedroom door was opened, she ran out, hysterical, and claimed the defendant had attempted to kill her. Then the victim ran out of the house through a bathroom window and drove away. She wouldn't move back into her house until he moved out.

Then on October 30, while she was working on a mini-series titled "V," she and actor, David, a friend and her co-star, were present when the defendant knocked on the door. She opened the door but didn't remove the chain link. The prosecutor said Sweeney said, "We have to settle this matter now..." David said, "Do you want me to leave?" Sweeney said, "Please leave," but Dunne said, "You don't have to leave, I will talk to him out on the porch."

Then Barshop told the jurors that David would testify to hearing an argument in which he heard screaming so he called authorities. When he tried to leave by the back, he saw Sweeney in the neighbor's backyard, and Sweeny told him to call the police.

Then Barshop explained to the jury that by the time help arrived the victim was brain-dead, and four days later, she was taken off of life support.

The prosecutor went on to explain that the jury would hear from an expert who would testify that the cause of death was manual strangulation of the air supply, which takes four to six minutes to kill the victim. In order to impress the jury as to how long this was, Barshop remained silent for four minutes, so the jurors would realize that it is a long time.

After the prosecutor finished, the judge asked if the Defense attorney if he wanted to make an Opening Statement, to which he indicated he would reserve his Opening Statement for a later time in the trial.

CHAPTER 40. CALLING WITNESSES

Now it was time for the prosecution to prove their case by calling the witnesses to testify. The first prosecution witness was Deputy Frank DeMilio, who was one of the deputies who responded to the scene. He described what he saw when arrived, which was Sweeney walking toward the street from the rear of the house next door. He and another deputy went to the backyard and noticed Dominique's lifeless body, and he assisted in giving her cardiopulmonary resuscitation until the paramedics arrived.

After Sweeney was arrested, DeMilio was assigned to transport Sweeney to the West Hollywood Sheriff's station for booking. During this drive to the station, Sweeney kept saying "Man, I blew it, I killed her." "I didn't think I choked her that hard. I just lost my temper. I blew it." When the deputy was asked to describe the defendant's expression, he said that the defendant appeared "dumbfounded."

One of the most crucial witnesses to testify was Dr. Eva Heuser, the Deputy County Coroner. She testified that the victim, Dominique, had been strangled by hand, and it took in excess of two or three minutes and perhaps as long as five or six minutes. However, on cross-examination by the Public Defender, she agreed that there could be irreversible brain damage due to lack of oxygen caused by strangling for as little as two minutes. Further, the Coroner agreed with Sweeney's attorney that a 'brush mark' on the victim's neck could be due to the victim's violently turning her head as she was being strangled.

Lastly, the Defense questioned the coroner if the discoloration on the back of the victim's neck could be from natural pressure during the five days she had lain in a coma at the hospital. The prosecutor tried to show the coroner the photos of the victim's neck; however, the Defense objected, claiming the photos were inflammatory. The judge had a conference outside the presence of the jurors. The judge ruled that two of the **autopsy photos of her neck** could be used. Further, the judge ordered an incise mark be cut out of the photo, so, using scissors, the prosecutor cropped the photo as ordered by the judge.

Dr. Miles Saunders was a neurosurgeon from Cedars Sinai Medical Center and the next witness. He testified that when he examined the victim at the hospital, she was not totally brain-dead. She showed some reflexes when she was brought in. The victim had a weak heartbeat, could blink when her eye was touched and could cough. He testified that five days after the attack, all of the victim's life functions stopped while she was still on a respirator to help her breathe. At that point, Dr. Saunders declared Dominique to be totally dead.

The prosecution called Norman as the next witness. He was the friend that Dominique drove over to on September 26th and visited with after being attacked by the defendant. The next morning, he took **personal photos of her neck** which showed the bruises. In court, he identified the three photos of her neck. Barshop asked why in the last photo Dominique had a smile on her face. He responded, "I was trying to make light of the situation. She had an audition the next day for a role as a battered child. I told her she wouldn't need makeup, and she smiled as seen in the photo."

On cross-examination, the Public Defender asked if Dominique was intoxicated, since Brian indicated they all had been out drinking earlier in the evening. This witness, Norman, indicated that Dominique didn't seem intoxicated but she was horrendously distraught about the attack on her.

Eventually, the DA called the homicide detective Harold Johnston to testify to what Sweeney had told him at the station. Det. Johnston indicated that Sweeney said he had left Ma Maison at 8:30 p.m. and walked to Dominique's house several blocks away. When he got to her house, he and Dominique had a conversation on the front porch. She was adamant she didn't want any reconciliation with him. He became angry and grabbed her by the throat. Dominique, who was only 5'2 and weighed 112 pounds, was easily pushed off the porch. From there she crossed the driveway and through some bushes separating her property from the vacant house next door. Eventually she tripped and fell, and he landed on top of her. He kept choking her until he noticed she wasn't breathing. At some point, he started to apply CPR to revive her.

The Public Defender asked the detective if Sweeney explained what the reason for their breakup was. The detective related that Sweeney claimed that the biggest obstacle was the hours he worked at Ma Maison, from 3:00 p.m. to midnight. When he got home he would want companionship, but Dominique would be asleep because she had to get up early to be at the studio for makeup and hair styling. Earlier, the judge had ruled and instructed the detective that he couldn't testify what Sweeney had told him about the other incidents where he had pushed, shoved and choked Dominique. He could only tell the jurors what he had said about this incident that killed her.

There were a number of other witnesses who testified for the prosecution, which included other chefs that Sweeney worked with. They testified that Sweeney had one of them take gifts over to Dominique's place to try to get her to reconcile with him.

CHAPTER 41. DEFENSE TAKES SHAPE

The Defense called very few witnesses but mainly relied on defendant Sweeney's testimony. The Defense attorney announced to the court that the defendant John T. Sweeney wanted to testify before the jury. As the defendant slowly rose from his chair next to his attorney, he strolled over to the witness stand, looking downward at the carpet. The courtroom clerk asked him to raise his right hand and recite the oath to tell the truth. His answer was an almost inaudible, meek "I do." Everyone in the courtroom was waiting for this moment. Dominique's parents were on the edge of their seats waiting to hear what their daughter's last minutes of life had been like. The Defense attorney had to be sweating as to what type of appearance Sweeney would make in front of the jury. The attorney was confident that he could hold his own when he was questioning him, but he was concerned how well he would withstand the cross-examination by the prosecutor.

The Defense attorney started out by asking Sweeney to tell the jury what he had with him when he went over to Dominique's place. Sweeney stated that he was carrying a letter Dominique had written to him. After their breakup, she placed all his belongings in a box and took it over to Ma Maison restaurant, where she had left it with a letter for Sweeney. The Defense attorney asked the judge to read the short note. It stated, ***"I need more time. I do think good thought of you but I need to go slowly. Please try to give me that time. Given enough time, I'll probably beg you to come back."***

Then he related that four days before her killing, he had gone over to her place and the two of them had sat down and had a heart-to-heart conversation. At that time, he mentioned to her that he had been seeing a therapist who told him "not to be pushy..." He said Dominique was touched and they hugged and kissed. They talked of marriage. They talked of having children together. They talked of when to announce the wedding. After that chat, his mindset was that everything had been patched up and they had both agreed that they had a future together.

Further, he testified that on Oct. 30th, he had sent her the gifts of a chocolate face and pumpkins for each of her animals. He told the jurors that he was certain that she was going to reconcile with him. When he talked to her on the phone and she said she didn't want to get back together, this stunned him. He believed what she had said in the letter and related to him during their heart-to-heart discussion.

So when he arrived at her house and she told him again that she didn't want to reconcile, he was shocked. "She explained that my love for her was too obsessive. I lost my temper. All I remember was being on top of her with my hands around her neck. I don't remember choking her. All I remember is picking her up to walk and I was shaking her and talking to her. I don't remember what I said. She wasn't responding."

The Defense's approach was that it was Dominique's fault in that she had led her lovesick boyfriend along. Then the Defense attorney asked him if Dominique had lied to him. His response was that he had believed her and thought she was being truthful. The Defense had been successful in creating a situation in which **Sweeney was the victim of deceit perpetrated by Dominque**.

After he had his opportunity to tell his story to the jury, it was time for the DA to cross-examine him. Prosecutor Stephen Barshop asked him how long the attack took, to which he claimed he couldn't remember. The DA asked, "Do you remember reaching out for Dominique?" He claimed he had no recollection. The DA continued, "Don't you remember reaching for her throat?" Again, the response was "Don't remember."

The prosecutor wanted to show the jurors how long Sweeney had to reflect on what he was doing. More questions were, "Did you hear her scream? Did you hear her gasp? Did she thrash about? Did she cry for help?" All were answered in a quavering voice from a crying defendant pleading that he didn't remember. When asked what he remembered next, he replied, "I remember looking into Dominique's face beneath me on the ground at the rear of the neighboring house on Rangely Avenue."

The prosecutor turned to the prior choking incident on September 26, 1982 and asked questions about it. Sweeney conceded that at that time he grabbed Dominique by the neck when she tried to walk out on him. Sweeney wouldn't admit that he was trying to choke her. Then the prosecutor asked Sweeney to step down in front of the jury and show them how he had his hands on Dominique's neck. Barshop then asked the Public Defender to stand in for the victim.

Sweeney demonstrated how he grabbed Dominique by the back of the neck, and pulled her back towards him when she got up from the bed and tried to leave the room. At that point, Sweeney said, Dominque spun around until his hands were on her throat. After that, he said, they rolled off the bed and onto the floor. Throughout the entire demonstration, Sweeney maintained that he didn't attempt to CHOKE her.

Prosecutor Barshop reminded the defendant that when Brian testified earlier, he said that when Sweeney came out of the bedroom, he had claimed that he never touched Dominique. Sweeney claimed Cook was wrong. "I'm not denying I grabbed her. I didn't say I never touched her." He also denied telling the victim "Stop acting. You're not on camera now."

The most that Sweeney was willing to concede to the DA was that he didn't want her to leave the house during the September 26th incident and the August 27th incident in which he tackled her to prevent her from leaving. After the defendant testified, the Defense called a few additional witnesses and then the Defense rested its case.

CHAPTER 42. INTRODUCTION OF PRIOR ATTACKS

When it was up to the prosecution to call any rebuttal witnesses to challenge what the defendant had testified to. The prosecution wanted to call Sweeney's longtime girlfriend Lillian, whom he lived with from 1977 to 1980. She would testify that Sweeney had beaten her on numerous occasions. She was hospitalized at least twice, once with a broken nose and once with a perforated eardrum and collapsed lung. The Defense objected, claiming this wasn't permissible evidence since there was no evidence presented by the prosecution that this attack was deliberate or premeditated.

The judge ruled that this wasn't a First-Degree Murder case but at most was a Second-Degree Murder or a possible Voluntary Manslaughter. The judge said that the defendant's actions were impulsive. The prosecutor tried to argue that the defendant had sufficient time to premeditate and deliberate up to five minutes, according to the Coroner's report.

The judge stated that if the Defense presented a Mental Defense, the prosecution had the right to ask the psychiatrist about Sweeney's attack on his prior girlfriend. However, if his mental condition was not going to be an issue and no psychiatrist would be called, then the testimony of his ex-girlfriend wouldn't be relevant (not permitted).

During an earlier evidentiary hearing, the Public Defender got the judge to rule that if Sweeney testified in place of the psychiatrists, then the prosecution would not be allowed to call his ex-girlfriend. The Defense had locked the judge into agreeing to exclude Lillian from testifying. Even after the defendant's testimony, the Defense claimed nothing had been changed to allow her testimony.

The judge's strange ruling prevented the jury from hearing about the defendant's pattern of behavior in attacking women. This judicial ruling would not go unnoticed by Dominique's father Dominick Dunne.

CHAPTER 43. ARGUMENT

After a lengthy, contentious trial, it was time for the parties to argue their cases. The prosecutor started out by telling the jury, "If you do not find the strangling of actress Dominique Dunne to be murder, then you will have sanctioned this conduct, excusing this conduct. This is not a crime of passion but it is a crime of domestic violence." He alluded that half of domestic violence cases involve unmarried couples, like in this case. The prosecutor argued, "Any one of us who finds themselves in a crumbling relationship doesn't go out to kill the other person."

Then the prosecutor wanted to remind the jurors how this violence had continually escalated from pushing and grabbing during the August 27th attack. That was when Dominique told friends that Sweeney had pulled on her hair so hard that tufts of her hair came out, which terrified her. Then, on September 26th, Barshop recounted what Brian testified about how he was awakened in the middle of the night when he heard sounds of an argument coming from the master bedroom. Then Brian said he heard a thud and there was a gasping for air. That witness asked, "What is going on?" Then Dominique emerged from the bedroom and she ran into his arms hysterically. She said, "He tried to kill me. Can't you see the bruises on my neck?"

Barshop reminded the jury how scared Dominique was of Sweeney. He said that she moved out, petrified of Sweeney. But he wouldn't move out until she had the locks changed. Not until October 26th did she feel safe to move back in. That was four days before the attack that killed her.

Then, on October 30th, he continued the cycle of violence when he went over to Dominique's house and ultimately choked her to death. The prosecutor turned his Argument to defendant Sweeney. He referred to his testimony last week in which he said he didn't remember strangling Dunne, only lunging at her during an argument over her decision not to resume their romance. Looking right at Sweeney in the courtroom, Barshop said, "Why don't you recall what you did? Was it so horrible to kill a person by strangling?" Then Barshop walked up to the courtroom board of the two autopsy photos of the victim. "Is it so horrible to look at these photos of what you did to Dominique Dunne? Look at what you did to this girl—for absolutely nothing." This was one of those high drama courtroom moments. Sweeney timidly turned his head slightly, looking at the prosecutor. His expression was that of a scared creature wishing it could find a place to hide.

The prosecutor had earlier introduced a letter Dominique wrote about how afraid she was of Sweeney's mood swings. The prosecutor reminded the jury of that letter by saying, "On October 30th there was a mood swing in front of the house on Rangely Avenue. As a result, this defendant killed Dominque Dunne, and the crime is **Murder in the Second- Degree**." The prosecutor went on to tell the jury, "There is no justification or rationalization for a verdict of Voluntary Manslaughter. You should conclude this is a **Second-Degree Murder**, nothing else. To do otherwise would amount to sanctioning this conduct, excusing this conduct, which is unacceptable to every person here."

Barshop finished by anticipating what the Defense was about to say to the jurors. He reminded them to remember what Sweeney had told the detectives, "I tried to stop. I really did. I need help. I can't believe I did something that will put me behind bars forever. I've been rejected all my life. I couldn't handle it. I strangled her."

That ended the DA's Argument and it was now time for the Defense to state their case. The Defense attorney rose up from his seat, starting his Argument. He slowly weaved the web of the Big Spin of the facts. He wanted to convince the jury that Dominque had been leading on **his poor client, who was the real victim in this case**—misleading Sweeney into believing that she loved him when she was only going to dump him.

The Defense attorney said, "It was almost an adolescent love. On October 30th, he sent her a chocolate face; he sent her four pumpkins with the names of her animals on them." The Defense attorney read the letter she had sent him earlier which gave him hope that he might reconcile with the actress. The letter said, "If given enough time alone. Absence makes the heart grow fonder. If we spend enough time apart, I'll probably beg you to come back."

She played his client for a fool by telling him four days before the attack that they had a future together, then they talked about marriage and having children. They even discussed when to announce the wedding. Then, on Oct 30th, he called her after he had sent her the various gifts and she told him that she felt their relationship was over and would talk to him about it the next day at the Mandarin Restaurant. This came as a shock to him, and his attorney said, "Sweeny felt desperate and went over to see her."

As they talked on the front porch, she started to scream at him, and his attorney recounted Sweeney's version of what was said. "**You have lied to me** about loving me. **You have lied to me** about wanting to marry me. **You have lied to me** about wanting to have children with me."

The Defense attorney paused and then went on to quote the defendant. "You have been all this time lying to me, and all you are saying that all we've had together has been a sham? After all we've had together, after what I'm going through and need to talk to you now, you'd decided to spend this evening with David because you want to go to a movie?"

Sweeney's Defense attorney then paused for a moment, looking up and down the row of the jurors' faces. His voice intensified as he asked the jurors a question: "Would an ordinarily reasonable man become enraged in learning this was all untrue? The answer to the question is obviously **yes**." The Defense attorney inserted a 'pregnant pause' so the jurors contemplated the disappointment he felt. Then he told the jurors that this wasn't a case of Murder but merely a sad case of **Voluntary Manslaughter** in which the defendant killed in the **Heat of Passion**.

The Defense attorney had finished his Argument by dramatically using the Big Spin doctrine. Since the prosecution has the Burden of Proof, the prosecutor, Barshop, had an opportunity to Rebut the Defense Argument. He stood up from the counsel table and walked to the lectern and with a strong voice explained that this wasn't a case of Voluntary Manslaughter because Sweeney felt betrayed by Dominique. "It's murder. It's not a case where you can compromise. You can't justify this kind of conduct. You shouldn't mitigate the death. Do not sanctify this killing by calling it other than what it is. **It is a murder.**"

CHAPTER 44. IT'S OVER, BUT IS IT REALLY OVER?

After a lengthy trial, the beginning of the end was near when the prosecutor finished his Rebuttal Argument and the judge had read the last jury instruction. The jurors deliberated for a number of days. Then, on the eighth day, the jury signaled that they had a verdict. All the parties congregated in Judge Katz's courtroom. All the attorneys were present with the respective families, and the jurors filed back in to announce their verdict. The clerk read the verdict, stating that the defendant was found guilty of **Voluntary Manslaughter**, and as to the prior attack on September 26, 1982, that occurred a month earlier, it was declared **a misdemeanor**.

Dominique's father and mother shrieked with anguish as the court clerk read the verdict. Judge Katz thanked the jury on behalf of both the Dunne and Sweeney families. The tension in the courtroom was released when Dominick Dunne shouted out, "Not from our family." Later, the judge said that Dominique's father would have a right to speak when Sweeney was sentenced. Dominick, her father, responded, "Too late then. You withheld important information from this jury about this man's history of violent behavior."

Later, when the attorneys talked to the foreman, he reported the jurors accepted the Defense attorney's contention that his client had acted in the **Heat of Passion** when he realized Dominique did not want to resume their romance.

On October 31, 1983, the defendant was sentenced to six years in state prison, of which he served less than three and was released on parole. Her father Dominick Dunne never forgave Judge Katz for his rulings in not permitting the defendant's ex-girlfriend's testimony and restricting the prosecutor from arguing First Degree Murder. Dominick stated to the judge that the prosecution can't appeal the court's bad ruling.

From that day forward, Dominick became an advocate for victims' rights and began writing about the judicial system. He wrote the book ***Justice***, in which Dominick complained that Sweeney received a sentence of six and a half years but served only two and a half after his conviction. Later, in 1984, he wrote the article ***Justice: a Father's Account of the Trial of his Daughter's Killer,*** published by *Vanity Fair*. As a result, he became a steady contributor for *Vanity Fair*. His True Crime books became popular and were all best sellers: ***People Like Us*** (1988), ***An Inconvenient Woman*** (1990), ***A Season in Purgatory*** (1993), ***Another City, Not My Own*** (1997) and big hit ***Justice: Crimes, Trials and Punishments*** (2001). And the one he was working on at the time of his death, ***Too Much Money*** (2009). He eventually hosted the TV series ***Dominick Dunne's Power, Privilege, and Justice*** on Court TV.

What was interesting about Dominick was he continued to cover famous murder trials, even though he was a well-recognized figure from his TV program. He covered famous trials including those of O. J. Simpson, Claus von Bulow, Michael Skakel, William Kennedy Smith, the Menendez Brothers, Phil Spector and his last one, which was O. J. Simpson's Las Vegas case.

In 2008, the documentary ***Dominick Dunne: After the Party*** permitted Dominick to reflect on his success and tribulations as a big name in the entertainment industry. In the film, he remembers his past as a World War II veteran, falling in love and raising a family, his climb and fall as a Hollywood producer, and his epic comeback as a writer.

(I, the author, feel compelled to share a few personal memories I have about Dominick. I often saw him in court, with his old-fashioned way of taking notes with a pen and spiral notebook. He had a talent for catching unique moments during a trial. He might notice a reaction of the witness or a candid response by one of the attorneys. He was a master at seeing through his distinctive glasses what all the other writers in the courtroom didn't see. He could weave those facts into a subplot in one of his articles.

I remember having a private conversation with 'Nick,' as he was called. Since I knew the judge who handled his daughter's case, I asked Nick if his feelings about the judge had mellowed over time. He slowly turned his head upward to look me in the eye and in a peeved voice said, "I will never forgive that judge as long as I am alive.")

In 2007 he was diagnosed with bladder cancer, but it didn't diminish his zeal for his celebrity life. But he had a scare at the Vegas trial when he passed out. His traveling was curtailed, although he wanted to finish the O. J. Simpson case, since he had a desire to see justice finally done although it took so many years. Then on August 26, 2009, at 83 years, he checked out of the mundane life and somehow continues to live on in his books and TV reruns.

As to John Sweeney, you won't find much on him, since he changed his name and basically went underground. He has stayed in the culinary field. So be careful if you ever complain to the chef that your meal wasn't any good. You never know, your wayward chef may be John Sweeney.

As to Dominique, she was buried in the Westwood Cemetery, where Marilyn Monroe is buried. Her grave is a few rows over from Natalie Wood's grave. Although she is in good thespian company, we will never know how great an actress DOMINIQUE DUNNE could have become.

WHAT'S THE ANSWER—MENTAL HOSPITAL OR PRISON?

People vs. Keven Graff

CHAPTER 45. GUESS WHO JUST WALKED IN?

Now we steer our way back to Santa Monica Boulevard to rejoin the old Route 66 through West Hollywood. We pass by Fairfax Boulevard, which in earlier times was the heartland of the Jewish community in Los Angeles. Shortly we come to Stanley Avenue, which is the street where many agree was spot of the most horrific, grotesque murders of all times. We turn left on Spaulding Aveune and proceed north for several blocks. We come to a quaint residential area sandwiched between Hollywood Boulevard and Sunset Boulevard. This area gives the appearance of a peaceful oasis from the usual hectic pace of the Motion Picture Capital.Graphic Page

Old Route 66 Hollywood (June 13, 2004) **Graff Beheads & Mutilates Elderly**

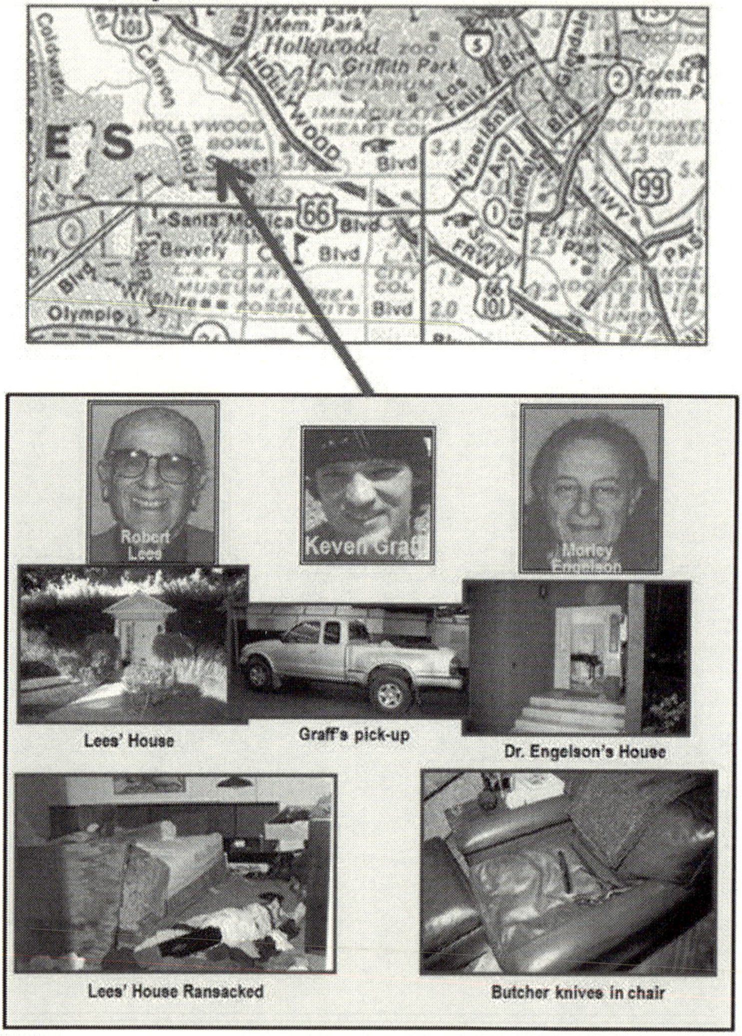

The street changes name to Courtney Ave., which is lined with Spanish tile houses interspersed with small bungalows dating back to the 1920s and 1930s. On this Sunday morning, June 13, 2004, many of the residents were attending their local churches. However, Robert Lees, who was a 91-year-old writer, was proud that he was an atheist and didn't feel any obligation to go to church.

He lived in a cozy, diminutive cottage house on a street with a canopy of trees covering the street. His house was valued at around $850,000, like most of the other houses, and everyone felt safe and locking doors during the day was unnecessary. On this pleasant, serene day, Keven Graff (27) had parked his Toyota pickup truck on Hollywood Boulevard a block to the north. After walking away from his truck, he roamed aimlessly around this Hollywood neighborhood. He strolled up the driveway to Robert Lees's house and stopped at the side door. He twisted the doorknob and found that it was unlocked. As he pushed open the door, he entered the house. Graff continued to the kitchen and for whatever reason he picked up a meat cleaver he saw next to the stove. With cleaver in hand and several kitchen knives he quietly proceeded to scout through the house, looking for any resident.

Not finding anyone, he headed to the back of the house, toward the rear bedroom. Possibly Graff heard the movement of the elderly Mr. Lees. Without any words being spoken, he used one of long kitchen knives to stab Mr. Lees, who was so surprised offered no resistance. After stabbing the victim several times the victim fell to the floor. Then Graff took the meat cleaver and hacked at Mr. Lees's head until it fell off. Graff had never met Mr. Lees nor ever been in this house before.

Needless to say, the act of beheading a person created a bloody scene. For several moments, the victim's heart was still spewing blood from the stub of his neck. The attacker leaned over the body of the victim and started cutting open his chest making a long incision from his neck to his waist line with one of the butcher knives. It was as if he was butchering a side of beef. For whatever reason, Graff reached into the open chest cavity and tried to remove the old man's heart. But he needed to use the knife to sever the remaining tissue holding the heart in place. Graff continued to mutilate the victim's body by slicing off his penis.

Then the butcher turned his attention to the victim's head lying on the floor a short distance away. It was unclear what the fascination of a severed head was, but he grabbed a smaller knife and gouged out one of the eyes. For whatever gratification, he decided that he wanted to carry around the victim's head as some type of trophy. He took a leather belt with a large buckle and wrapped it through the victim's mouth and pulled it out through the severed neck. This permitted him to easily carry the victim's head, as to show others that he had a new toy to play with. There are no words in the English language to accurately describe the bloody scene. The words *ghastly, despicable, abominable, monstrous, atrocious, repugnant, revolting, vile, repulsive, appalling, grotesque, surrealistic, horrific, awful, deviant, vicious, wicked, brutal, venomous, noxious, gory, gruesome, grisly* don't express the depth of the depravity.

With the dead resident unable to protect his property, Graff began his rifling through the closets looking for cash or anything of value that he could convert to money. Grabbing the dresser drawers covered with a fine mist of blood spatter, he dumped the contents unceremoniously on the floor. As clothing and keepsakes tumbled to the blood-soaked shag carpet, he turned the bedroom upside down. He violently shook the drawers, and possibly in disappointment at not finding valuables, he tossed the empty drawers on top of the victim's lifeless body.

In his fit of rage, he dropped his keychain, which was attached on a 'Jägermeister' strap which contained the keys to his pickup truck. Further, his actions somehow loosened his homemade necklace he always wore. It was unique in that he had made it of links of a chain which were wrapped together by thin wire. This primitive metal necklace held a special meaning to him, possibly representing how his bizarre thoughts were chained to his brain. As meaningful as this necklace was to him, he didn't notice it falling off his neck and landing on the floor near the meat cleaver he had used to behead the victim.

Years earlier, Mr. Lees had created a bulletin board in his bedroom which was made of a large sheet of plywood which was covered with a thin layer of cork. This was attached to the wall, and it was covered with dozens of snapshots of family members and scenic views he had captured on film. Most of these photos had a yellowish patina tint and ragged edges, indicating they were from times long ago. Why Graff ripped this bulletin board off the wall is a mystery, but it ended up tossed on the floor, with some of the aging photos falling off onto the carpet. One photo showed family members posing in the back of a hatchback, possibly from some family outing. All the photos were from happier times.

After his dissection of the corpse, it was unclear why and at what point Graff became ravenous for sustenance. It most likely was around breakfast time when Graff left the bedroom to check out the kitchen. With his bloody hand, he reached for the handle of the refrigerator and flung it open. Leaning down slightly to peer inside the fridge, he looked for ingredients to make a sandwich. He madly grabbed some lunch meat and poked around for mayonnaise and butter. He stacked his sandwich high with whatever he could find in the refrigerator. He loaded up the kitchen table with peanut butter, salad dressing, syrup and a half-used bottle of ketchup.

While hunting for food, he found a carton of Tropicana orange juice in the back of refrigerator and plopped it onto the small kitchen table. After gathering all his food, he sat down and devoured it all in short order. Graff had seen on the bottom of the fridge several bottles of beer, which he used to wash down his meal. Graff may have been disappointed with the high he was hoping for from the three beers he had consumed. He was not familiar with Clausthaler beer, which was a nonalcoholic beer. Apparently the 91-year-old victim preferred this specialty beer.

It may have been an afterthought, but Graff had meticulously peeled a banana. After gobbling down the banana, he dropped the peel on the floor where someone could slip and fall on it. Since the banana was partly peeled, a fine mist of blood was on the remaining part of the banana, which indicated that he may have been eating the banana during the savage attack.

Graff had an occasion to use the bathroom and he may have wanted to wash some of the victim's blood off his hands and clothing. He walked into the bathroom and leaned on the tall bathtub. Possibly to steady himself, his bloody hand reached out for the top of the bathtub. As a result, he left a large bloody smear of his finger and palm prints.

Since the victim was a screenwriter, he had one of his rooms set up as a mini-office with a computer on his work desk. With Graff's bloody hands, he attempted to use the computer keyboard and even touched the monitor, making a bloody streak across it. Without a password, he was frustrated and possibly agitated that he couldn't access the internet. There was a wadded-up paper soaked with blood lying on the desk.

For all of Mr. Lees's neighbors, it was just another lovely, peaceful Sunday morning. Most residents were contentedly sitting reading the Sunday newspaper while enjoying a hot cup of coffee. By 10:00 in the morning, Graff was ready to continue his reign of terror of the Hollywood area. By this time, it was late morning when Graff walked out into Mr. Lees's backyard. The rays of sun were peeking through the swaying trees to cover his grassy backyard. This tranquil sight was erased by the ghastly sight of Graff gripping a leather belt holding upright the mutilated head of Mr. Lees. What purpose was served by carrying a severed head through a backyard surely could be known only by Keven Graff.

CHAPTER 46. CLIMBING OVER THE FENCE

After eating and cleaning up, Graff was ready to leave Mr. Lees's house to continue his mayhem in the neighborhood. His next target was Dr. Morley Engelson (69), whose home on Stanley Avenue was directly behind Robert Lees's house. In other words, their houses were back-to-back with each other and separated by a Dog Eared Cedar fence. Around 10:00 a.m., after Graff had left the back of Lees's little cottage, he proceeded to the back fence. He had to look for some way he could gain a foothold to climb over the fence. This was tricky for Graff because he had only one hand to pull himself up and over the fence, since his other hand was busily carrying the dead victim's head. As he grabbed the top of the fence with his bloody hands, he left blood stains on the fence. Then he jumped down into Dr. Engelson's backyard, which looked like an urban forest with tall trees providing a covering blocking the midday sun.

At that time, Dr. Engelson was in his house making a phone call to Southwest Airlines in order to make reservations for a business trip to San Jose, California. He was concentrating on what the reservation clerk was saying, since he didn't want any misunderstanding about the times of the flights. Dr. Engelson, being a retired doctor, was patiently working with the reservation clerk. Then, to the surprise of the airline clerk, she heard an unusual noise with some shouting and the sounds of some type of commotion. Since their conversation was businesslike without any background noises, she couldn't understand why the caller wasn't responding to the inquiries she was making. The airline clerk heard the voice of some person on the other end of the line say, "Help me! Help me! Somebody help me!" Then the line went silent.

The airline clerk didn't know what to do, let alone what to say. She tried to call back on the line and only received the sound of a busy signal. Fortunately, she had her wits about her and remembered that she had received another phone number from Dr. Engelson. She immediately dialed that secondary number and waited to see if there was any response. Within seconds, a different voice (Graff's) came on the line, saying "Hello." This unnerved the clerk and she asked if everything was okay, to which the person on the line said in a detached voice, "Everything is fine now."

The proverbial question is when an outsider should become involved in someone else's problem, especially if the outsider is a clerk from Southwest Airlines in Phoenix, Arizona. Certain companies don't want to interject themselves into customers' personal problems. The clerk was so bothered by the desperate cry for help from the petrified voice on the phone that she went to her supervisor and explained what had just transpired. He good-naturedly listened to the clerk's description of the phone call. Since the call center for Southwest Airlines was in Phoenix, there wasn't much the supervisor could do. This was one of those uncomfortable moments that occur in one's life when the GOLDEN RULE grabs your conscience. What would I want someone else to do if I were the one yelling for HELP? What was amazing was how the supervisor had the good sense to know what to do.

First they needed to figure out where the customer's call was coming from. It could be anywhere in the country, but the area code of the caller's phone indicated that the call came from the Los Angeles area. The supervisor needed the help of someone in law enforcement to trace the phone number to a location. Fortunately, the supervisor thought the best place to start was the Los Angeles Police Department. However, he was dealing with the second most populated city in the country, of over three million people.

Luckily, the LAPD dispatcher he reached was well rested or just a caring, accommodating person. The airline supervisor explained the situation and that they were in Phoenix and had heard some type of person asking for help on a phone call that came from the LA area. The easiest response from the dispatcher would be for them to call back when they had more information and could verify that a crime had been committed. With the 9-1-1 emergency system, the police can use the phone number to show them the address where that phone device is registered. The dispatcher ran the phone number, and she received back an address on Stanley Avenue in the Hollywood district.

Apparently, the moon, planets and stars on this Sunday June 13th were all lined up in a row. It may have been the fact this was a slow Sunday around noon, when the radio calls were at a minimum. For whatever laudatory reason, the dispatcher said that she would send a police unit to that address to check things out. The dispatcher recorded the names and phone numbers of the airline employees and indicated that detectives would be in contact with them if anything had happened. No one knew if anything would come of all this, and the employees went back to work making airline reservations.

One of the Hollywood patrol units received the radio call to check out the household on Stanley Avenue. Two officers from the LAPD pulled up their black-and-white in the front of Dr. Engelson's house. They both exited the vehicle and walked over to the driveway that led to the front door. Right at the entrance of the driveway was a prominent security company's yard sign. The officers wondered why they hadn't received a call from the security company if something really was wrong. The birds were chirping from the top of the cypress trees. As the officers approached the front porch, the best words to describe the atmosphere were peaceful and serene.

The house was recently painted light beige, and the front yard was postcard perfect. The lawn had been mowed and edged precisely and not a leaf had fallen to disturb the manicured look. One of the officers rang the doorbell. They quietly waited, knowing this 'courtesy call to check things out' would be resolved in minutes. As they stood on the porch, one whispered to the other something about where they should go for lunch. After three rings of the bell and not hearing anyone respond, the other officer looked through the beveled glass of the windows on the side of the large front door. His view was distorted by the beveled glass, but his eyes seemed to see a person's legs lying on the floor.

This couldn't be, and the officer squinted his eyes to get a better view. Realizing that he couldn't see clearly from that position, he went to the other side of the door to look into the interior of the house. From that position, he could see more of the person's bare legs, with socks on the feet, lying on the floor.

At that moment, the officers recognized that they possibly had a medical emergency where someone may have had a stroke or passed out and couldn't get up. The front door was made of hardwood and had the appearance of being solid and definitely expensive. The officers looked at each other, wondering whether they should kick in the door to render aid. But if they were wrong, they didn't want to have to explain to their sergeant why the city had to pay $1500 for a new front door for the upset resident.

The officer quickly moved to the side yard, looking for another door which might be open. While walking around the house, they saw a rear window wide open with the screen off. As they approached to look into the window, they looked down for a place to safely step. There was a four-inch butcher knife on the ground. This caused the officers to realize they may have more than a medical emergency on their hands.

Instantly, they entered the house to check out the person on the living room floor. As they rushed in, they weren't prepared for what their eyes viewed. They understood they were working in Hollywood, where many horror movies were produced for the Halloween market. But what they saw was more horrific than any movie writer could ever envision.

There on the living room floor was an older man, stretched out on the floor without any clothes except for a sweatshirt pulled above his chest. What grabbed the officers' attention was the fact that a fireplace poker was stuck into his neck, protruding upward in the air. His chest was cut wide open, revealing his heart and organs. This jagged-edged cut had penetrated through layers of body fat that was oozing out of the chest cavity, spilling blood onto the floor. The officers quickly assessed the situation and realized there was no need to test the victim's body for a pulse. The fact that the victim's body was lying on his back with his legs apart made the scene even more bizarre. Why were the victim's pants completely removed, revealing his private parts? Was the killer trying to send some type of message?

The officers were shocked at the sight before their eyes. Their police training kicked in and they knew they had a murder and needed to notify the station. However, their training required them to search the remainder of the rooms of the house to look for other victims and possible suspects. As sickening as the crime scene appeared, they looked around and saw a hefty stuffed leather chair filled with large and small kitchen knives on the seat cushion. One of the knives they saw was covered in blood.

Next they checked out the kitchen and didn't find anything unusual, so they moved down the hallway to the back bedroom. They swung open the door and stepped in. There appeared to be a red soccer ball in the middle of the bed. This seemed strange for a soccer or volley ball be on a bed. The officers walk further into the bedroom and to their shock and surprise disovered it to be a decapitated head (that of Mr. Lees) oozing blood onto the pristine white bedspread. If that wasn't ghastly enough, there appeared to be a leather belt tied through the mouth. The LAPD officers were well trained to handle unusual emergency situations. However, nothing had prepared them to face this gruesome sight, which was more than nauseating, and any thoughts about going to lunch after this call had disappeared from their minds.

CHAPTER 47. TIME TO INVESTIGATE

The officers were pleased they didn't find anyone else in the house. They immediately radioed the station that they needed the homicide detectives to respond immediately. The patrol officers were anxious to get out of the house, which they must have thought to be the 'House of Horrors.' They remained to secure the scene, but couldn't wait to get away from the house. When the detectives arrived, they asked for a short briefing and couldn't believe their ears and quickly wanted a walk through the crime scene after receiving the summation from the patrol officers.

The detectives knew that this type of bizarre crime scene would become a popular attraction for law enforcement personnel. They contacted the CSI services in order to make sure the right technicians arrived at the crime scene before the evidence became contaminated by all the lookie-loos. They could see that the floor surface was that of highly polished hardwood flooring. Certain areas of the hardwood were covered with expensive throw carpets.

The living room was well furnished, with a baby grand piano in the corner. It consumed a substantial portion of the space, across from the large stuffed leather chair filled with kitchen knives. One detective examined the knives for blood and instructed one of the CSI technicians to bag one of the bloody knives. Then they noticed a phone receiver on the floor. They looked at the phone and noticed that it had printed out on the phone's screen the words 'Southwest Airlines' with its 800 number listed, stating the 'Call time:' 9:59:59. Now the phone corroborated what the original caller had said regarding talking to Dr. Engelson about reservations for airline tickets.

The detectives examined what appeared to be an office with a desktop computer mounted under the desk. The computer monitor and keyboard were located on top of the desk. Nothing seemed out of place or contained any evidence pertaining to the homicide. The detectives turned to the back room of the house and saw a window screen lying on the floor. By looking at the various windows in the room, it was apparent that one of the windows was missing a screen. As they proceeded to that window, they could see bloody handprints on the inside and outside sill of that window. At that point, the detectives believed that was the point of entry of the killer.

As the detectives moved from one room to another, they couldn't help but notice the extremely highly polished hardwood floors in most of the rooms. While looking at the floors, they noticed shoeprints of some type of athletic shoe, which they marked for the CSI team to take close-up photos of the shoeprint. As they continued, they entered the master bedroom. They had been warned by the patrol officers that there was a head of a person lying on the bed. However, the detectives weren't prepared for the sight of Mr. Lees's bloody head plopped in the middle of the white comforter on top of the bed. In all their homicides they had investigated, they had never encountered a severed head such as this.

As surreal as it seemed, the one detective leaned over to better look at the facial side of head. He noticed a deep cut across the forehead of a head of what appeared to be an elderly gentleman. The right eye seemed to be gouged out, making it look more like a gory Halloween mask. The detective's reaction was, where was the rest of the body? The idea was to continue from room to room hoping the remainder of the body would pop up. As the detectives turned around, they returned to the kitchen area, where they saw a number of knives lying on the counter. However, everything else seemed to be in order. A turquoise tea kettle stood boldly on the stove, looking as though it had been used in happier times.

As the detectives proceeded to make a full circle of the house, they returned to the living room with the stretched-out corpse that wasn't missing a head. The other detective went over to the body to get a closer look at the body. Starting from the top, he could see that this body had a head attached to it, so he confirmed that the head in the bedroom belonged to someone else. He noticed the dead man, who was lying flat on his back, had his right hand stretched out above his head while his left hand was partially bent over his chest. The incision across his abdomen exposed his heart and some of his organs.

After leaning down checking out the body, the detective stood up slowly, shaking his head, wondering what human being would do such a horrific killing and why? This homicide didn't have the earmarks of a simple murder to solve. Even though this had been a beautiful leisurely Sunday afternoon, the detectives called the Hollywood station asking for more detectives to be called in to assist with the initial investigation. Aside from keeping the CSI team on track, someone needed to contact the neighbors to see if anyone had seen or heard anything. Initially the detectives wanted to find out the possible name of the victim, so wallets and identification were checked and the name Morley Engelson was determined to be the victim lying on the living room floor. The next of kin needed to be reached immediately, before the news media plastered photos of the house on their news broadcasts.

One of the detectives checked the driveway for any car, and none could be found, so the DMV computer system was used to learn what type of car this Morley Engelson owned and determine where it was located.

Just as the detectives were getting their hands around this horrendous homicide, a phone call was received at the station that would spin this case into one of the most diabolical murders in Hollywood's recent history. A woman, Helen (86), reported that she had gone to Mr. Lees's house around 4:00 p.m. to pick him up to go to a function at the Academy Awards in Beverly Hills. Since he didn't answer the door, she looked through a side window and called his name. Without hearing any response, Helen looked through the bedroom window and saw what appeared to be a body covered with stacks of clothing with an empty drawer stacked on top. She entered the house and was shocked to find Lees's beheaded body under a pile of clothes and blankets, with empty drawers cascading to the side.

When the police heard the word "beheaded" and realized that this was directly behind Dr. Engelson's house, they quickly recognized the connection between the two killings. Like a puzzle, the pieces were fitting together. The head on Dr. Engelson's bed belonged to Mr. Lees, who was lying dead in his bedroom, missing a head.

The police responded and verification was made that there was a body missing a head. The detectives working the Dr. Engelson homicide had their hands full and told the officers to merely stay outside of Mr. Lees's house. The detective bureau called in more detectives to respond to the crime scene location of Mr. Lees's house. By the time these backup detectives arrived, it was dark. One female detective was given the task of checking out Mr. Lees's house with her flashlight. They didn't want to compromise the crime scene by flipping on lights.

The female detective was aware of the dead bodies and that one had been beheaded and the other had a fire poker inserted in his neck. She started searching each room of Mr. Lees's house for possible suspects, possible victims and other possible body parts. With latex gloves she clutched her faithful flashlight and trusty service pistol in the other hand. She cleared the living room easily and continued on to the dark kitchen. She couldn't help but notice the kitchen table was stacked high with different food products.

As she headed to the back bedroom, she could smell the scent of death. Mr. Lees's body had been lying there in the heat of the day for at least eight hours. She had been informed that there was a deceased on the floor missing a head. But she was not prepared for the scene of an elderly man's body slit open with body parts missing. In order not to disturb the crime scene, she tried to tiptoe past the body so she could open the closet to see if there were any surprises hidden inside.

As she tried to open the closet, the door made a deep creaking sound that reminded her of the radio program ***Inner Sanctum***. Hurriedly she shined the light from side to side, not knowing what she was looking for. She could see there was no person or parts of a person in the closet. From the master bedroom, she walked to the other bedroom, which had been made into an office. She flung open the door and directed the flashlight to the left-hand corner of the room and slowly moved the light beam in an arch to cover the entire room. She felt a relief that she hadn't found anything.

As she returned to the front door, she took a deep breath and hoped that would stop her heart from racing. She had done her job of clearing the crime scene, but she couldn't remember when she had been so scared. She knew that she would never be able to completely clear her mind of the horrific sight of viewing the beheaded corpse with his innards cut out. This would be a night she would long remember, although she would try to block this horrendous ghastly crime scene out of her memory.

CHAPTER 48. WHO WERE THE VICTIMS?

Robert Lees (91) lived an extraordinary and full life. He was born in San Francisco and graduated from Lowell High School in 1929. He started in show business as a dancer before moving up the ranks to become a writer for MGM Studios during the boom years. His first screenplay was for the 1936 film ***The Perfect Set-Up,*** which was the first of a series titled ***Crime Does Not Pay***. He had carved out a niche for himself and was well respected for his writing talent during and after WWII.

As the 1950s evolved, he was caught up in the hunt for Communists and their sympathizers in Hollywood. The pressure was applied to everyone in the entertainment business including actors, directors and screenwriters to reveal the names of fellow sympathizers to the 'Red Plague upon America.' To retaliate and object to the attack on the film industry, most of the entertainment employees closed ranks and refused to cooperate in providing names of their professional friends to the government authorities.

Without realizing the impact, it would have on his career, Mr. Lees, and most Hollywood folks, refused to cooperate, and he took cover behind the Fifth Amendment when he was called to testify before the House Un-American Activities Committee being chaired by Senator Joseph McCarthy. Many actors and directors were shunned by the studios and lost the opportunity to work.

However, the writers found themselves without jobs, since their names were placed on the Blacklist. Initially, it was extremely difficult to find jobs, and Mr. Lees at the age of 60 went back to school to earn a credential as a nursery school teacher. However, he found limited jobs for teachers and wanted to restart his writing career. Writers are naturally creative people, so after much struggling for work, he learned by changing his 'pen name' to J. E. Selby he was able to find work writing for the studios.

Just one of his achievements in writing was when he co-wrote the 1948 comedy classic ***Abbott and Costello Meet Frankenstein***. Other films he wrote were ***The Black Cat*** and ***Holiday in Havana*** starring Desi Arnaz. Then he worked with a new comic team consisting of Dean Martin and Jerry Lewis and wrote the movie ***Jumping Jacks***. Later, he wrote for several popular TV shows such as ***Alfred Hitchcock Presents*** and ***Rawhide***.

With all the writing success, his greatest loss was when his beloved wife died of cancer. That loss was devastating to him, and he continued living alone in his little cottage of a house. He was loved by all his neighbors and they looked after him. Helen, who lived across the street from him, eventually became a close companion, and they enjoyed each other's company.

Dr. Morley Engelson (69) was a native of the area and had been an athlete when he attended Fairfax High School, where he was captain of the football team. He went on to college and eventually medical school, becoming a medical doctor. For years he had his practice in the Bel Air area, where he treated and cared for the very rich of Los Angeles.

He had recently remarried, and he and his new wife wanted to live in the Hollywood area but wanted to downscale. They had found this smaller house on Stanley Avenue which was perfect for their new life together. The house had been remodeled, with new windows that were bright and cheery and with the hardwood floors polished to perfection. What made the house so exclusive was the fact that it had a complete wall of trees and shrubs all the way around it. Even the front of the house was walled in with eight-foot cypress shrubs that blocked the view of the house to give it a secluded look. As one retreated down the driveway, there was a feeling of entering a private estate where one felt safe from the madding crowd.

CHAPTER 49. WANDERING ARRESTEE

The next day after these ghastly murders, life returned to normal according to Hollywood standards. Movies were still being produced at the Paramount Studios, over a mile away from the two crime scenes. A strange young man was standing at the guard gate to the studios. He continually asked to see a friend by a name not printed on the studio personnel list. After being told that there wasn't any person by that name working at the Paramount Studios, this young man still wouldn't leave. The security guards were busy checking people in and asked him to leave, but he continued to stand around near the studios' main entrance, which contains the giant arch emblazoned with the words 'PARAMOUNT STUDIOS.'

Over the years, the studio guards had seen some strange people 'called actors' who pass under their gate. But this guy looked homeless, with his long-disheveled hair and unshaven face. His tattered clothes looked like he had slept in them without the benefit of a shower for some time. They noticed that he was acting erratic. At times he seemed to be talking to himself, and other times he would shout at the cars driving by on Melrose Boulevard. At times he seemed confrontational as he flipped off passing motorists, yelling obscenities at them.

As the studio guards watched in wonderment, they had no idea what should be done. This irrational young man wasn't committing any crime. He wasn't blocking the entrance to the studios, and he was on the public sidewalk when he was ranting and raving. The guards thought there wasn't any need to call the LAPD unless the situation escalated to some type of criminal activity. In the guard house, the security personnel had a TV set which was tuned to one of the news channels. All of a sudden, the TV announced that there would be a public service announcement by the Chief of Police for Los Angeles. One of the guards walked over to the TV and turned up the volume. Then the LAPD Chief William Bratton came on the TV as part of a news conference. The Chief requested the public's help in locating a person of interest who might be involved in a double homicide in the Hollywood area. Then a booking photo appeared on the screen of a Keven Graff, taken from a prior arrest. One of the studio guards watched the TV news conference and focused his attention on the photo of the suspect. The individual looked familiar, and then he realized that it looked like the strange young man who was yelling at the cars outside the studio entrance.

The studio guard couldn't believe his eyes. Immediately he discussed this situation with his fellow guards, and it was agreed to call LAPD indicating that they had under surveillance a person who looked like the person they were searching for. Within minutes, officers arrived and found the stranger sitting on a wall under a row of ficus trees near Melrose Boulevard. He was carrying a frayed Bible in one hand and a small can of Mace in the other. When questioned about the crimes, Graff claimed that a man on the streets of Hollywood gave him methamphetamine and Ecstasy the night before the murders. Graff continued to claim he had no memory of committing the murders.

This man admitted he was Keven Graff. His hair was almost shoulder length and his face looked sunburned from being outside for too time. His eyes had a blank stare, as though his mind and his body were disconnected. The officers noticed that his hands and fingernails were covered in blood and he had a cut on the top of his right hand. They handcuffed him, and as soon as they could, they placed his hands in paper bags to preserve any evidence that may have remained on his hands.

After his arrest, he made a statement to the Associated Press where he stated, "*I just wanted them to leave me alone. I was a lot of positive energy, but people would try to pull that positive energy from you. The happier you are as a person, the more people want to take that from you. This Earth is hell. I'm just an innocent lamb. It's up to God. He's the only one who can judge. But really, I wish I could take what happened all back because I don't understand this.*"

CHAPTER 50. WHO WAS KEVEN GRAFF?

Keven Graff was a good kid born and raised in the sleepy rural town of Irrigon, Oregon. He was raised basically by his father after his parents divorced. In high school, he played football and baseball. Shortly after high school he joined the Marines and was stationed at Camp Pendleton near Oceanside, California. For whatever reason, the experience in the Marine Corps changed him somehow. He eventually wanted to get out of the Corps, but he feared receiving a dishonorable discharge. Eventually there was a parting of the ways when he was released on a medical discharge for an injured ankle. As a result, he received his honorable discharge and exited the Marine Corp.

To support himself, he worked as a personal trainer and did a variety of odd jobs. Through his various jobs he mixed with various groups. Between 1997 and 2002, he was working for local gay clubs, mainly performing as a go-go dancer. Since he was good looking, pleasant and down to earth, he fit in well with his new lifestyle. Then, in April 2002, he appeared on the front cover of the *Gay and Lesbian Times*. The article discussed the various circuit party scenes. He gained popularity as a male dancer for gay parties and enjoyed all the new companions. While having several girlfriends, he also lived with various well-known members of the gay community. This combined lifestyle got him the moniker of 'Gay for Pay but Love for Women.'

In his mid twenties, he began exhibiting mental problems. On one occasion he was found wandering in streets of Merced, California. His family became concerned and wanted him to receive some help. Then, in May of 2003, he was living with his brother, and for some unknown reason he called the Fullerton Police Department to report that someone was threatening his girlfriend. When the police checked it out, they determined he was suffering from certain delusions. The police referred him for a psychiatric evaluation; however, after several days, he was released.

Later, in the fall, his family had him admitted to the Veterans Affairs Hospital in Long Beach for observation. But again, after a psychiatric evaluation, he was released. This was disappointing for Graff's family, since they realized how strange his behavior had become. His brother seemed to blame his strange behavior on his experiences in the Marine Corps. After enlisting, he was never same.

His illness continued to worsen, to the point where he was arrested in Las Vegas for lewd behavior when he exposed himself to a woman. Afterwards he was sorry for his conduct. When he was arrested, he was wearing the chain wire necklace which he later dropped in Mr. Lees's house. Then on May 5, 2004, he went into court and pleaded guilty to disorderly conduct.

It is unknown what motivated him to come back to the Hollywood area. He had no money, so he was using his new Toyota pickup truck as his home. Basically he was homeless, and his little truck represented his home. In the rear compartment, he had dumped a large suitcase and a backpack. In the truck bed, he dumped a clothing tub and another backpack. In the driver's compartment, he had an empty water bottle with Styrofoam cups.

It was impossible to tell if someone was really trying to live in the trashed truck or had merely abandoned it. Since Graff continued to leave the Toyota parked on Hollywood Boulevard, it continually received parking citations, which accumulated on the windshield. During much of 2004, Graff became heavily involved in using methamphetamine. His behavior was a result of his unstable mental condition mixed with these drugs.

CHAPTER 51. BUILDING A CASE

During the investigation, the detectives noticed that Dr. Engelson's 2001 Mercedes was missing. His wife wasn't driving it, and Dr. Engelson had had it in the driveway when his wife had left. The LAPD put out an all-points bulletin to stop the vehicle if seen. Not until the next day was the Mercedes found, at Third Street and La Brea Boulevard, less than a mile from the crime scenes. The car was parked behind a business. When the detectives examined the interior of the car, a smear of blood was found on the seat and a smudge on the steering wheel. Samples of the blood were taken and submitted to the crime lab for DNA testing. The results showed that the blood in the car belonged to both Graff and Mr. Lees.

The detectives were able to find an eyewitness to say he saw a person similar to defendant Graff driving Dr. Engelson's car out of the driveway and onto Stanley Avenue. There was another eyewitness who saw certain items of clothing being thrown away by a person looking like Graff. Neither eyewitness was absolutely certain as to their identifications. However, the latter witness was able to point out the trash dumpster where the athletic shoes were thrown. The soles of those shoes were compared to photos of the bloody shoeprints found in Dr. Engelson's house. A forensic expert was able to render an opinion that those recovered shoes were the ones that made the shoeprints in the house.

After the defendant was arrested and booked, the CSI team took swabs of his bloody hands. When the samples were tested, they came back with both victims' blood on them. Also, when some of the blood samples were tested from Dr.

Engelson's house, they proved to be from defendant Graff. So the DNA evidence connected Graff to both murders.

The other forensic evidence that linked Graff to the killings was the fact that his fingerprints were found in both houses. In Mr. Lees's house, the defendant's latent prints were on the top of the bathtub, while in Dr. Engelson's house, the latent prints were found on the knives on the kitchen counter.

The detectives were able to find a previous booking photo that showed Graff wearing the exact same necklace that had been dropped in Mr. Lees's bedroom. The booking photo was enlarged with a photo of the found necklace. Since the necklace was so distinctive with the various chain links wired together, no jury would have difficulty identifying it. Likewise, the belt buckle used to carry Mr. Lees's head was identified as being the same type of belt Graff had worn previously.

The Toyota car keys on the Jägermeister strip which was found on the floor in Mr. Lees's bedroom perfectly fit the defendant's truck.

When the detectives received the autopsy reports, they learned that both victims had been sexually assaulted with a foreign object, possibly the defendant's finger.

CHAPTER 52. WHAT'S THE ANSWER?

What should happen to Mr. Keven Graff? The Defense wanted to have Mr. Graff found not guilty by reason of insanity, and therefore he would be committed to a mental health facility until he recovered his sanity. The problem with this disposition of the case was that if this defendant were later found to be sane because he had responded well to therapy or possibly certain medicines had helped him, he could be released back into society. All it would take was for a psychiatrist in the future to declare that Graff had regained his sanity, and if the mental health committee agreed he had sufficiently recovered, he would have to be released from the state mental hospital. The thought of Mr. Graff walking the streets again scared prosecutors, who wanted to protect the public from dangerous individuals. This scenario was too scary to ignore. The community needed to be protected from the likes of Mr. Graff.

The mission of the DA's Office is to file charges and prosecute individuals when there is sufficient evidence to prove beyond a reasonable doubt that the person committed a crime. However, many DA's Offices and most prosecutors believe that they should do whatever is legal to protect the safety of the community. To achieve that objective, prosecutors may have to act and argue contrary to logic.

ISSUE OF NOT GUILTY BY REASON OF INSANITY

Two of the top prosecutors of the DA's Office, Ricardo Ocampo and Alan Jackson, were assigned the Graff case. The DA's Office recognized the dilemma it was in. Any person who was told the facts of the Graff case would invariably conclude that the person who committed those acts was absolutely 'CRAZY.' Everyone's logic told them that anyone who beheads someone, cuts out their heart and severs their penis and sexually molests that person has to be 'CRAZY.' And when they heard the additional facts about the vicious acts against Dr. Engelson, the average person would say that the killer had to be more than 'CRAZY.' To most people, 'CRAZY' is the equivalent to being 'INSANE.'

The prosecutors knew that they were going have a difficult task of convincing jurors not to find that the killer was 'INSANE' (at the time he did all those horrific acts.) However, the legal concept regarding insanity is murky at best. Basically, the question is whether the defendant knew the difference between right and wrong when he or she committed the crime or crimes.

In this Graff case, the DA's Office needed to find a psychiatrist that would render an opinion that Graff was 'SANE' at the time he committed the crimes. The DA's Office was able to obtain the services of Dr. K. Sharma, who was one of the most highly distinguished psychiatrists used by the courts to render opinions regarding 'INSANITY.'

Dr. K. Sharma filed a report with the court which stated that Graff, the defendant, had a significant and documented history of mental illness and treatments. He had been diagnosed as being bipolar. He indicated that Graff was being treated by the Veterans Administration and was receiving medication to treat his mental illness. *(However, he knew the difference between right and wrong at the time he killed both victims.)*

The Defense was able to find psychiatrists who were willing to testify that in their opinion they believed the defendant, Graff, was so severely mentally ill that he didn't know the difference between right and wrong. These types of cases are called the 'Battle of the Experts.' Jurors often tend to disregard the testimony of the experts from both sides. Regularly, jurors become so confused by the testimony of expert witnesses' opinions that they tend to cancel each other out. This is particularly true in cases where the psychiatrists are testifying to the defendant's 'Specific Intent' to commit the crime.

However, this type of case was different, since the jurors would have to decide the issue of 'SANITY.' Here, the jurors can't totally disregard the psychiatrists' opinions. The jurors have to make a finding whether the defendant knew the difference between right and wrong. It's the Defense's job to persuade all 12 jurors that the defendant lacked that capacity.

The Defense attorneys never know if they can convince all the jurors to prove up the claim of Not Guilty by Reason of Insanity. Since the defendant's acts in this case were so bizarre, the Defense had a real possibility of proving that he was Insane. However, if the Defense wasn't successful of convincing all 12 jurors then the prosecution was in a strong position of proving him guilty of both murders since the evidence was overwhelming. With his fingerprints and his DNA in the victims' houses as well as the DNA of the victims on his hands, the Defense would have great difficulty explaining all that evidence away in order to obtain a not guilty verdict.

DEATH PENALTY ISSUE

With both the Defense and prosecution having their own significant problems with the case, the next issue to be considered by both sides was the Death Penalty. Seldom does the prosecution have a case that calls out for the Death Penalty more than this case. Putting aside the defendant's SANITY issue, the acts committed by the killer were the most despicable deplorable anyone could image. If the Death Penalty is to be reserved for the worst of the worst, then this case would certainly qualify for the Death Penalty.

The DA's Office policy regarding when to seek the Death Penalty starts by reviewing all the facts of the present case and the defendant's criminal record. Then all the prosecutors in the chain of command make a recommendation for or against seeking the Death Penalty. Within the structure of the DA's Office, there is the Special Circumstances Committee that makes the final determination whether the prosecution will seek the Death Penalty. Once the decision is made to seek the Death Penalty, the DA's Office has a policy that they will not change that position, even if the Defense attorney indicates that the defendant is willing to plead guilty to all the charges in exchange for dropping the Death Penalty. The DA's Office doesn't want to appear to be using the Death Penalty as leverage to force a defendant to plead guilty in order to save his or her life.

One of the objectives of any Defense attorneys is to save their client's life. In this case if the Defense wasn't successful with the INSANITY Defense, it was highly likely the jury could convict Graff and, in all likelihood, return with a finding for the Death Penalty. The horrific nature of the crime made the Graff case a likely candidate for the Death Penalty. The Defense had to accurately assess the chances of them obtaining 12 jurors to agree to a Not Guilty by Reason of INSANITY.

This case was like a high-stakes 'poker game.' The Defense was holding one 'ace,' which was the likelihood that the defendant would be found Not Guilty by Reason of INSANITY. However, the DA's Office had two 'aces' in their hands. If they escaped the INSANITY issue, the prosecutors would easily be able to convict Graff, and secondly, they had strong possibility of convincing the jury to recommend the Death Penalty.

Both sides had to evaluate what they wanted most out of this case. What the prosecutors wanted most was to prevent Graff from ever being released. Their only guarantee of that was making sure he was not referred to a state mental health hospital. In other words, they wanted him in state prison for the rest of his life. The prosecutors felt that they had a strong case to obtain the Death Penalty. However, what was different about this case was the fact that both of the victims' families were opposed to the Death Penalty. Often, in other cases, the victims' families are adamant and put pressure on the DA's Office to seek the Death Penalty.

Here, in the Graff case, the victims' families were more interested in Life in Prison Without the Possibility of Parole.

GUILTY PLEA

The Defense was most interested in saving Graff's life. Both sides had to make tough decisions. Both sides assessed their situation, and Graff with his attorney, agreed to plead guilty to all the charges if the DA's Office didn't seek the Death Penalty. The prosecutors agreed, and Graff pleaded guilty to Murder in the First Degree, plus Sexual Penetration by a Foreign Object, Torture, Mayhem and First-Degree Residential Burglary. He also admitted to the Special Circumstances of Murder Involving the Infliction of Torture and Multiple Murders. He did this as to the killing of both victims Robert Lees and Morley Engelson.

Neither side received everything they wanted. However, the prosecutors knew that Keven Graff would never walk the streets to harm anyone else.

SENTENCING

On April 5, 2008, at the sentencing hearing, Dr. Engelson's widow addressed the court and the defendant and stated, "He died after fighting valiantly with this evil, satanic intruder who was a calculating, unremorseful, ruthless butcher who knew enough to lock the door behind him."

Robert Lees's companion of 23 years said, "I had the horrible, numbing experience of finding his beheaded corpse just a few weeks shy of his 92nd birthday. When I see a man on the street of Bob's (Lees's) size and shape, wearing the kind of outfit he loved... my heart pounds and my body starts shaking."

At the sentencing hearing, the defendant said, "I don't really remember. I don't understand. I don't say I have a mental illness... But apparently, I am, because who in their right mind could do something like this? This person gave me drugs that I didn't know what they were, and then this happened. It is senseless acts for no reason... absolutely makes no sense." The interesting part of his statement shows he didn't accept responsibility for being at fault for these appalling crimes. He placed blame on the person who gave him the drugs and not explaining the type and strength of the drugs. The defendant skipped over the fact that he willfully took the drugs on his free volition.

As he turned to address the victims' families, Graff continued on by saying, "I am not a violent person. I do yoga, study various religions and try to focus on positive things and be the best person I can be." The victims' family members had to wonder how yoga and religion and his belief that he is a good person created a monstrous person capable of doing all these horrific acts. The only part of his attempt to apologize to the victims' families that made any sense was when he said, "... I can say I'm sorry, but sorry doesn't cut it." He recognized that there were no words or phrases that he could say to comfort the saddened victims' family members.

The Criminal Justice System likes defendants to admit to their crimes at time of sentencing. The idea is that the defendant needs to be remorseful and apologize to the victims and their families. The court's rationale for this contriteness is that it is the first step to rehabilitation, so he or she can someday be reintegrated into society. However, when the judge sentenced Graff to two terms of Life in Prison Without the Possibility of Parole, there wasn't going to be any release and no need for rehabilitation.

As Graff continues to serve the rest of his life in prison, life goes on in the neighborhood where the crimes occurred. The victims' houses have been sold to new families. They are occupied by couples who have young children. No one seems to remember when this was the location of two of the most dreadful murders in the annals of LA history. When one asks one of the new neighbors walking down this serene, tree-covered street if anything exciting happened here, the answer by the new neighbor is, "I heard that Hugh Grant got arrested for having sex with a prostitute on this street." It is strange what some people remember about their community. The horrific fades from one's memory, but the licentious seems to be indelibly etched in people's memories.

WAS IT A KIDNAPPING OR JUST AN AFFAIR?

The Aimee Semple McPherson Story

CHAPTER 53. AIMEE SEMPLE MCPHERSON

In order to continue traveling old Route 66, one stays on Santa Monica Boulevard to its very end, where it merges into Sunset Boulevard. Most people have heard of Sunset Boulevard and are familiar with it traversing Hollywood. On the eastside, Sunset veers to the right and curves through a hilly area as it winds its way into the Echo Park area. Along the way, no one can miss the vision of the Angels Temple, with its huge rotunda building topped by a white dome.

Years ago, anyone traveling Route 66 would have been more than impressed with this gigantic church with massive radio antenna towers on top. The church was built by Aimee Semple McPherson in a circular design in order for the churchgoers to have an unobstructed view of the stage, where theater productions could be performed depicting stories from the Bible. Today most Angelinos don't have a clue what type of scandal occurred there which rocked the city and galvanized the nation.

Graphics Page

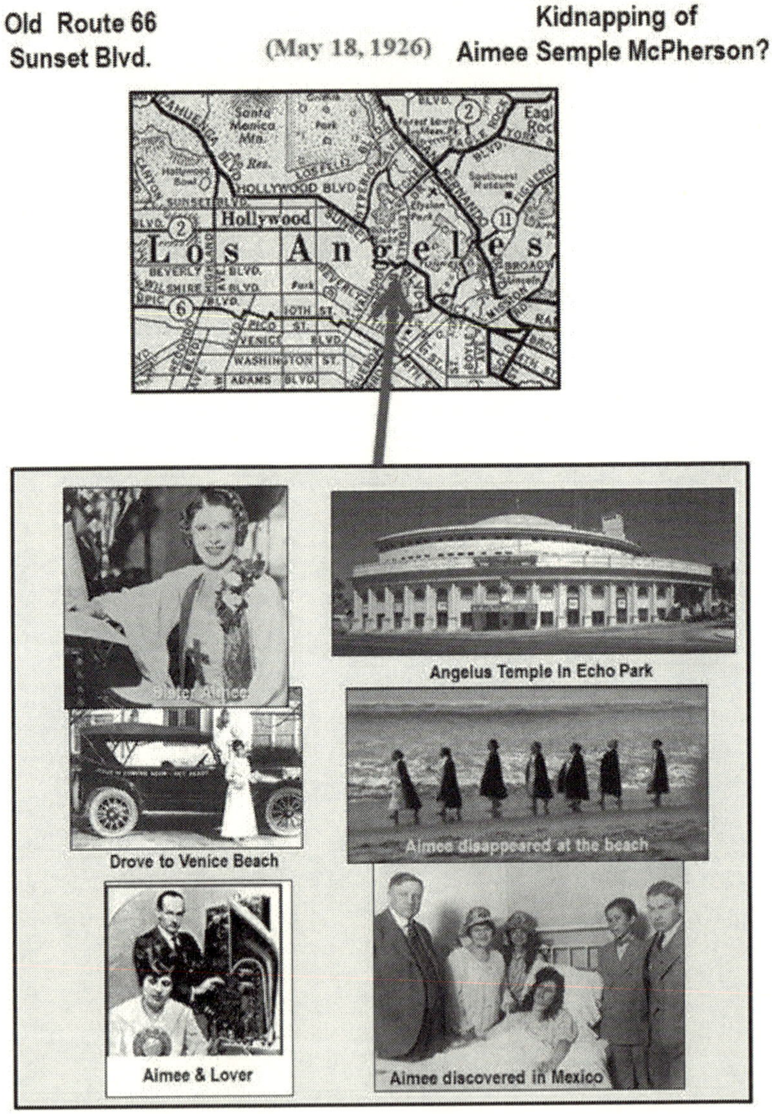

In 1926, America was fascinated by Pentecostal preachers who traveled all four corners of the country. They set up their circuslike tents on the outskirts of a lonely town and invited all 'God-fearing' people to come and join them for an emotion-packed evening. Since the meetings were free and most Midwesterners were starved for any form of entertainment, these events received wide attendance.

The preachers were born showmen and knew how to drive an audience into a frenzy. The end result was many people believed they somehow felt euphoric and even some believed that they had been cured of whatever ailment they may have had. Others were so emotionally overcome they passed out from feeling God's hand on them. These religious crusades expanded at the same time radio stations were able to expand their radio reception area. There was a merger between certain preachers and the use of the radio to reach a nationwide audience. Several preachers saw the advantage of the radio broadcasts to reach a larger audience. This was where Aimee Semple McPherson had an advantage, since she was located in Hollywood, where the pioneer radio engineers existed and radio equipment was being developed.

Aimee was on the cutting edge of religious broadcasting and quickly learned how to mesmerize large audiences to contribute funds to her worthy causes. She became incredibly successful as a radio evangelist. She was called **Sister Aimee** and was idealized by millions. She would dress in long, flowing white robes, which gave her the look of an angel. She was gifted in knowing how to blend religious teachings into theater productions, with all their spot lighting and rhythmic music to capture people's imagination.

As a reader, you may wonder why we are discussing Sister Aimee. What does she have to do with True Crime cases along old Route 66? The answer is that she was the center of the city's most publicized scandal investigated by the DA's Office. Although it didn't involve a typical murder case, it did involve the deaths of two men. The mysteries behind the scandals still linger on to this day. The unanswered question is whether Sister Aimee was really kidnapped from Venice Beach. One wonders whether, with new forensic tests, this mystery could ever be solved. So this book will attempt to answer some of these questions.

First you need to know the facts of the disappearance of Aimee Semple McPherson. It all began on a Wednesday, May 18, 1926. The weather was pleasantly warm and Sister Aimee knew it would be enjoyable to soak in some sun on the beach as well as taking a dip in the Pacific Ocean. She had done this on other occasions and appreciated this break from all her churchly duties. She felt obligated to work on next Sunday's sermon. She told her church assistant to put some material together and she would work on her sermon at the beach as she watched the waves roll in.

They packed up the church car and drove down to Venice Beach. There she headed to Ocean Park, which was an amusement park with a long pier which protruded out into the ocean. Since it was a weekday in the spring, they had no trouble finding parking and a sandy beach dotted with few bathers. Aimee loved to swim, so she took off for the water while her assistant set up the umbrella and laid the towels down on the sand, shaded by their oversize brightly colored umbrella. Sister Aimee dove into the waves and started floating on her back in the foamy salt water. How delightful the water was, not frigid but merely cool and refreshing. While floating on her back she could look directly up into the sky, seeing seagulls gracefully gliding overhead. She thought how free they were to fly wherever the gentle wind took them.

Sister Aimee's mind was always thinking of new ways to tell biblical stories in ways that the audience would connect with her religious topics. She made a note to herself how she could use the seagulls' flight in her next sermon. When she had had enough swimming, she floated in to the shore. She didn't want to be covered in sand, so she leaned down into the water and rinsed all the sand off. She walked out of the ocean as the tide seemed to be pulling her feet back into the water. She was met by her assistant with a large white towel, which she used to dry herself off. As the two of them walked back to the umbrella, she remembered that she needed to contact someone about the music for the next Sunday service. Since the choir had rehearsal that night, it was important to talk to someone in the choir.

Aimee continued to mention her concern about contacting the choir director about the music. Her assistant came to her aid and told her that she would find a pay phone and make the call. (Back in 1926 there were no cell phones, and pay phones were on just about every street corner.)

Aimee went over to her big towel on the sand and straightened it out while her assistant strolled off looking for a pay phone to make the call. As she plunked down on the sand, she couldn't have felt better. She could gaze out on the waves. One could be hypnotized by the repetitive motion of the surf. As she glanced up, she could see the outline of Catalina Island some 26 miles off shore. Later, in 1957, the Four Preps musical group made that island famous with the following lyrics:

Twenty-six miles across the sea
Santa Catalina is a-waiting for me
Santa Catalina, the island of romance
Romance, romance, romance
Water all around it everywhere
Tropical trees and the salty air
But for me the thing that's a-waitin' there, romance
It seems so distant, twenty-six miles away...

The only noise aside from the seagulls was the amusement rides, with a screech every so often from the riders on the roller coasters. Depending on the wind, one could detect the faint smell of cotton candy. With the umbrella blocking the sun, Aimee stretched her legs into the warm sand, which felt refreshing.

This is the exact point at which there are two versions of what happened to Sister Aimee. One account is that she was kidnapped and held against her will for a month in Mexico. The other version is that she madly ran away with a married man and spent some time with him near the seaside village of Carmel, California, and later covered this up with the kidnap story.

What we do know for certain is that her assistant came back and found her missing. Her assistant initially thought that she may have gone back into the water and drowned. We do know that Aimee's mother gave a sermon that night in which she told the audience that Aimee had gone to be with Jesus. That started a stampede of thousands of her followers flocking to Venice Beach to look for her.

In the frenzy, one man drowned when he swam too far out into the ocean. He apparently thought he saw a body, which turned out to be a group of seals. Another man died while trying to look for her on the beach. A shrine was set up and a vigil was established on the beach for someone to remain just in case Jesus or someone returned Sister Aimee.

CHAPTER 54. EXAMINING THE TWO THEORIES

After Aimee returned, she explained in detail what had happened to her. She claimed that as she was sitting on the sand while her assistant went off to make the phone call, a young couple approached her. Aimee said that this couple indicated that they recognized her. They said that they had a child who was in poor health, and they asked her if she would come to their car to meet the child and if she could bless the child. Aimee, hearing this, couldn't say no, so she followed the couple a short distance to their car. When she leaned into the car, someone placed chloroform over her nose and mouth. Then they pushed her into the car and tied her up.

They took her to various places to hide her as they figured out a way to set up a ransom demand. Eventually they took her to a rural place in Mexico where she was kept. On June 23, 1926, somehow Sister Aimee miraculously escaped her kidnappers. She wandered through the desert for 13 hours until she came to the sleepy region of Agua Prieta, in Sonora, Mexico. A Mexican couple heard a knock on their door and opened it to find the wretched body of a woman. At first, they were naturally frightened and didn't know what to do. As they gazed at this figure, they noticed a slight movement, so the woman got a blanket to cover her.

Aimee claimed she had been kidnapped, drugged, tortured and held for ransom in a shack by two men and a woman (named Steve, Mexicali Rosie, and another male). She convinced the Mexican couple to drive her to Douglas, Arizona, where she was taken to a convalescent hospital. The media flocked to the little township of Douglas, wanting answers to this unbelievable kidnap story. The Los Angeles County District Attorney traveled all the way there to talk to Sister Aimee, the victim of this unbelievable kidnapping.

This story received national attention, partly due to William Randolph Hearst. He had an eye for newsworthy stories. He realized that he could sell a lot of newspapers with this incredible story. So Hearst had his newspaper writers and editors find ways to keep this story alive. Reporters were everywhere, trying to find a new slant to poor Sister Aimee's disappearance. When Aimee was well enough to return to Los Angeles, she was greeted by over 50,000 people waiting to get a glimpse of her leaving the railroad station and being paraded to her church. The city fathers as well as many celebrities were anxious to be seen with Sister Aimee in her jubilant homecoming.

When she arrived at her Angelus Temple, she gave a heartfelt speech in which she thanked all her well-wishers. The public wanted to believe her and they gave her their full support. However, as time went by, some reporters noticed that some parts of her story didn't add up. Also, some other Fundamental preachers may have been jealous of her popularity or just fed up with her hypocrisy.

Sister Aimee had held herself out to her congregation as being a saintly person. She wore her white clothing representing purity and was a strong opponent of drinking alcohol and an ardent supporter of Prohibition. She preached against sex outside of marriage and had accepted the conservative principals of the church. Sister Aimee liked to preach about not throwing stones if you live in a glass house. This concept applied to Sister Aimee, since her social life was far from her teachings. Her close associates tried to shield her so the public wouldn't see the real Aimee. However, there were times when her reckless behavior didn't go unnoticed.

Now let us review the other version of what happened when Aimee was so-called missing. Instead of being kidnapped by this young couple, she was picked up by her lover, the radio engineer, Kenneth Ormiston. She had met him when they worked together on her radio program. They spent many hours and days rehearsing and broadcasting her popular radio programs. What made the situation dicey was the fact that he was married and had a young son. At that time, Sister Aimee was divorced, so she had no problem dating someone as long as they were single like her.

The Fundamental church beliefs prohibited sex outside a marriage. The ultimate sin was having an affair with a married person. The problem with Aimee was that she couldn't be discreet about her affairs. She seemed to have a recklessness that made her feel above it all. Whether it was her lover's idea or hers, they decided to run off to spend some quality time together. Spending one night together or even staying together until Sunday wouldn't have caused heads to turn. As long as she had taken the pulpit on Sunday to give one of her fire-and-brimstone sermons, no one would have been the wiser.

The two of them may not have been able to help themselves. They decided to drive all the way up to Carmel, California, and stayed at a secluded cottage. There aren't many more romantic spots for such a rendezvous than the beautiful Carmel Valley. Since Sister Aimee was best recognized for her voice, few people up in the northern part of the state would have recognized her. However, Aimee may not have realized how much publicity would be generated by her disappearance. The Hearst papers plastered her picture all over their pages, making her the most recognizable person on the face of the Earth.

Going out in public to eat was no longer an option for the happy couple. Her lover, Kenny, had to go to the market and purchase food for them to cook in their cozy cottage. Aimee had to write notes for him to know what to buy at the market.

At first, the couple must have been in euphoria reading how thousands of people were looking for the missing Sister Aimee. However, as the days went on and they read about how several men lost their lives looking for her, their happiness turned to "Oh my God, what have we created?" As much as they enjoyed each other's company, reality set in as to how much they had at stake.

Aimee, at the young age of 36, was the head of the most popular religious radio broadcast program, which reached millions and generated an endless supply of donations. What would be the reaction if the world learned that their beloved Sister Aimee was having an affair with a married man?

At some point, Aimee and Mr. Ormiston recognized that telling the TRUTH was not an option. The question was, how could the two of them reappear without raising suspicion? After trying to come up with a feasible story, they decided on one in which Aimee would claim she was kidnapped and held for ransom. As for Mr. Ormiston, he would claim that he traveled to Carmel to be with a friend.

The big question was how and where Aimee would reappear. For whatever reason, it was decided to use a remote place along the Mexican border as the place where Sister Aimee would claim she was able to escape from her kidnappers. To pull this off would require an incredible performance by Aimee. There was one thing Aimee didn't lack, and that was self-confidence.

She needed to be convincing to the Mexican couple when she knocked on their door asking for help. The next performance would be directed to the nice people of the little town of Douglas, Arizona, whom she needed to persuade everyone that she had been wandering the desert looking for help.

CHAPTER 55. TIME TO INVESTIGATE

It may not come as a surprise that the book ***Elmer Gantry*** by Sinclair Lewis was published at the same time, in 1926. It was a story of a Pentecostal preacher who was just like Sister Aimee. Elmer Gantry preached a fanatical fundamental religion while living a life of hypocrisy. Eventually, all his lying and debauchery brought him down. The book showed a different side of religion, which no one dared question at that time.

The Elmer Gantry phenomenon may have created a backlash for poor Sister Aimee. Her detractors were made up of the Chamber of Commerce, the head of the Church Federation and the press, which continually floated other reasons for her disappearance. Some of the reasons were that she went away to have plastic surgery, another that she had an abortion and the most common tale was that she ran off with a lover.

Aimee maintained that she was the victim of a kidnapping. When she was recovering in Douglas, Arizona, the Los Angeles County District Attorney Asa Keyes and his assistant Joseph Ryan met with Aimee. They noticed that her clothing and shoes didn't show any signs of a person wandering in the desert for several days. When the DA and his assistant returned to Los Angeles, they were met with many people who questioned the entire story of the kidnapping.

So on July 8, 1926, they convened a grand jury to take testimony about the events regarding the kidnapping. The grand jury adjourned after 12 days without any indictment, citing a lack of evidence to proceed with any charges against either Aimee or her mother regarding the kidnapping or the act of committing perjury.

That could have been the end of the court proceedings if Aimee would have dropped the idea, she was the victim of a kidnapping. What was happening was that the DA was being inundated with witnesses claiming to have seen Aimee and her lover Mr. Ormiston at the Benedict seaside cottage in Carmel-by-the-Sea. By August 3rd, the grand jury was reconvened and started taking testimony from all these witnesses. It was proven that Mr. Ormiston had rented the cottage in another person's name. Aimee's attorneys presented an affidavit from a woman who claimed to have been with Mr. Ormiston during that month. The DA called witnesses who claimed to have found grocery slips in the yard of the cottage, and an expert testified that it was Aimee's handwriting on those slips. Aimee's side denied it, but she refused to provide a handwriting exemplar for them to compare to the grocery lists.

The grand jury continued receiving evidence for over a month. The key witness for the DA was a woman who claimed that Aimee had told her to claim that Mr. Ormiston was with a woman who looked very much like Sister Aimee. On November 3, 1926, the grand jury decided that there was sufficient evidence to bring charges against Aimee and her mother for the charges of a Criminal Conspiracy To Commit Acts Injurious To Public Morals, To Prevent And Obstruct Justice By Manufacturing False Evidence—Falsely, Wickedly And Maliciously—As Well As To Prevent The Due Administration Of The Laws, and Of Engaging In A Criminal Conspiracy To Commit The Crime Of Subornation Of Perjury. If convicted, she could face a maximum of 42 years in prison.

However, by January of 1927, the DA Asa Keyes claimed that he was uncertain of the credibility of that key witness and dismissed the indictment. This gave Sister Aimee a new life of freedom; however, it wasn't the same for DA Asa Keyes, who was indicted for taking bribes (thought to be from Aimee's supporters), and the DA ended up serving time in a San Quentin cell.

That meant Sister Aimee and her mother would not go to prison for any false information they had given to the authorities regarding Aimee's disappearance. Although Aimee was free of prison, her status as a Pentecostal preacher had diminished and her following shrunk. However, for the rest of her life she had diehard supporters who believed every word she spoke. Others were more skeptical and listened to her sermons and may have believed every other word she spoke.

She continued to live the good life, with her followers making sure she lived in comfort. As a matter of fact, she married again—not to Mr. Ormiston but another man. Again this marriage didn't fare well and ended in divorce. Then, in 1944, at the age of 53, she was found dead in a hotel room in Oakland, California, from what was claimed an overdose of sleeping pills. It was ruled that she accidentally had taken too many pills when trying to fall to sleep.

Strange how old Route 66 provided the path for Sister Aimee's followers to come to her Angelus Temple to listen to her sermons. Although this infamous road has had a trail leading to so many homicides, it also has seen its share of some unbelievable **scandals**. Was Sister Aimee a mere TART or a poor victim? It is up to you to decide.

AMERICA'S FAVORITE PASTIME CAN BE DEADLY

People vs. Peter Marron

CHAPTER 56. TAKE ME OUT TO THE BALL GAME

After leaving Echo Park, we travel eastbound on Sunset Boulevard (old Route 66) for a mere short six blocks and see the sign pointing to Dodger Stadium. We veer left on the wide Elysian Park Avenue and we find ourselves entering the huge stadium parking lot. We transport ourselves back to Saturday, September 19, 2003, which was the perfect day to enjoy a baseball game in the stadium on top of the hill overlooking Downtown LA. It had been a warm day, but as evening approached, it was delightful weather for a couple of frosty ice-cold beers in the stadium.

The Dodgers were playing the San Francisco Giants, which was going to make for an exciting game. The two teams had what could be called a cross-town rivalry, even though the two cities are over 300 miles apart. Since it was a Saturday evening game, there would be a large crowd. Friends and families were looking forward to a pleasant sporting event.

Graphics Page

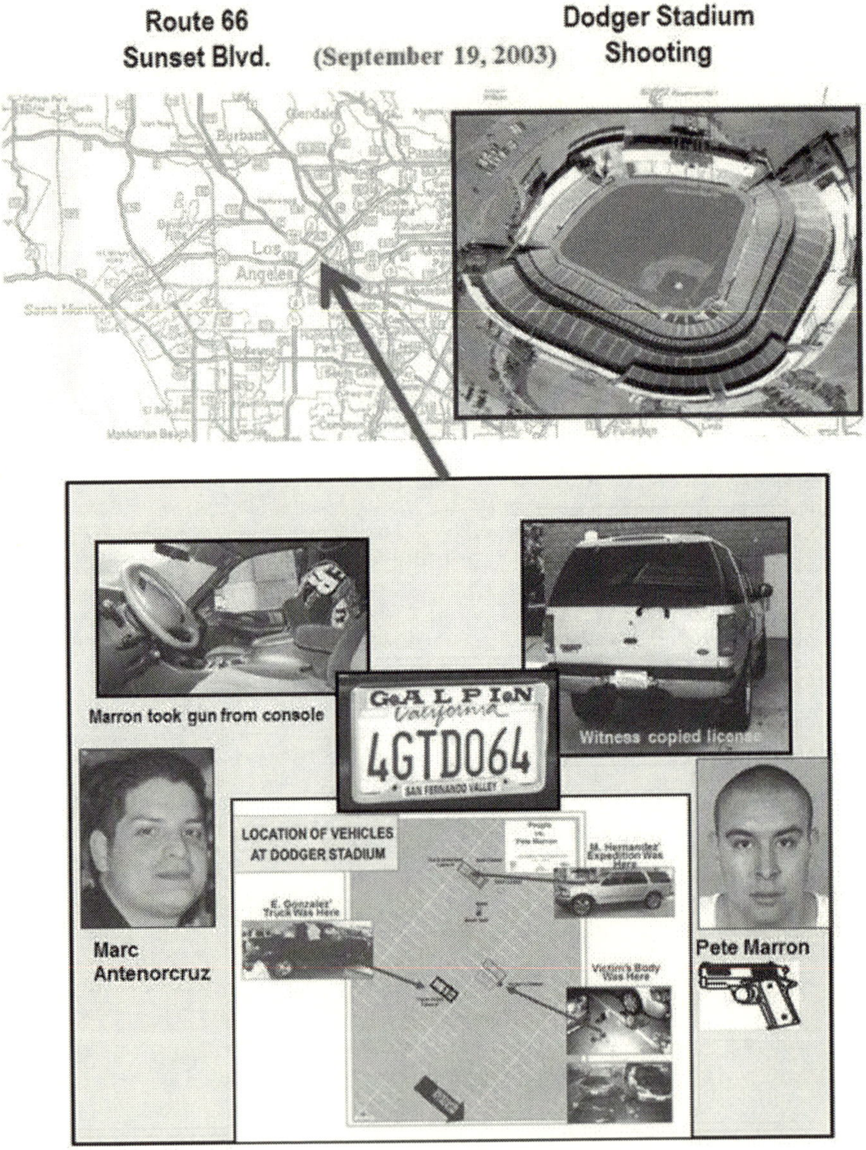

Parking at the Dodger Stadium can be challenging, since the parking lot is gigantic and rotates in circles around the stadium, which is in the center. When one drives into the huge circular parking lot, one wonders, "Where is this going to lead me and how far am I going to have to walk to get back to the stadium?" There is always a parking attendant who directs you to what seems to be the most distant section of the parking lot. When you finally get a parking spot all to yourself, everyone else comes swarming in around you. After getting parked, you exit your vehicle and you start loading yourselves up with jackets, hats and radio. Everyone around you seems to be in a hurry. There seems to be a race to the stadium. You realize you have designated seating and no one will take your seats, but there is this eagerness you feel and you don't want to miss anything.

While weaving yourself through the parking lot, you come across several groups having tailgate parties. They all seem to be in a jovial mood. You get a whiff of their barbeque, causing your stomach to beg for a mere taste of their ribs or tri-tips. You try to ignore those tailgaters and head for the stadium concession stands for your food and beverage.

As you walk briskly to the stadium, you feel the fresh air and notice a slight breeze which is fluttering the flags on the top of the stadium. Once you have passed through the turnstiles, you enter the gargantuan stadium. You head for a concrete tunnel that takes you to the vantage point where you can see the playing field. You assure yourself that the game hasn't started without you. You smile to yourself and make the decision to head over to the food concession stand. There you become well aware you aren't all alone as you stand in what seems like an endless line. It seems everyone has the same idea as you in getting the famous "Dodger Dogs" before the game starts. As you patiently stand in line, you can smell the hotdogs grilling and watch others in front of you burying their long Dodger Dogs in chopped onions while others entomb them in relish and mustard. You just can't wait until it is your turn to have your very own hotdog that you doctor up for your own culinary taste.

After loading yourself up with food amd drinks, then it is time to find your assigned seats. Your seats always seem to be in the middle of the row, requiring a juggling act to carry the Dodger Dogs and the drinks without spilling anything on the other fans. When you get situated, it is time to check out all the people around you. It is electrifying to see so many people. Part of the fun of going to a ball game is to 'people watch.' You try to see if you recognize any of the sea of people who surround you. It becomes apparent to you that it is a big world. As far as your eye can see, there are people who you don't know. Everyone seems to be smiling and laughing, appearing to have a delightful time. Subconsciously, you think how great it is that all these people with totally different backgrounds join together to support the same baseball team.

The stadium's organ is booming out happy tunes like "Take Me Out to the Ballgame" to create a congenial mood. Although the stadium is made up of Dodger supporters, since it is their stadium, the San Francisco Giants have a respectable number of fans to watch the great rivalry between the two teams.

Dodger Stadium is a great place to have such a big game, since this stadium is the largest Major League stadium, seating 56,000 fans. So it has the capacity, but some fans lament the fact that Dodger Stadium is the third-oldest field, only after Boston's Fenway Park, built in 1912, and Chicago's Wrigley Field, constructed in 1914.

Dodger Stadium was built in 1962 by Walter O'Malley, who was the owner of the Brooklyn Dodgers. When he couldn't get a new stadium built on the East Coast, he was attracted to the City of Los Angeles. There, the city fathers were willing to make available some public housing land that was never developed. The area was called Chavez Ravine, since many of the home owners were immigrants from Mexico.

O'Malley and the city excavated acres of hillsides, filling in the ravines to provide a leveled site for the stadium. The end result was an ultra-modern precast concrete stadium that sits on the hill overlooking Downtown LA. During the day games, the fans are treated to a gorgeous view of the majestic San Gabriel Mountains. At night, there isn't any finer view of the LA city lights than from the stadium's parking lot.

One of the remarkable advantages of Dodger Stadium is that it is called 'Pitcher's Park.' It has been the site of 11 'no hitter' games. What makes the park unique is that there are ocean breezes, especially in the evening, which play havoc with hard-hit flies. Balls that would be home runs in any other park are merely high flies that are slowed down by the sea breeze and come crashing down within the outfield, where they are caught. Many of hitters feel they were robbed of a home run if it hadn't been for the sea breeze.

Vin Scully was imbedded in his announcer's booth. Since 1950, starting back in the days in Brooklyn, his voice had announced the home games. Talk about tradition—for over 66 years, the Dodger games have started out with him saying, "It's time for Dodger baseball! Hi, everybody, and a very pleasant good day to you, wherever you may be." The baseball crowd has come to recognize his dulcet voice and lyrically descriptive style of announcing. The fans think of him as part of the baseball experience at Dodger Stadium.

Dodger Stadium is a mixed bag which many fans love to hate, but everyone has precious memories of the old ballpark. One of those nostalgic fans was Marc Antenorcruz (36), who went to school up in the Bay Area, so at an early age he became a dedicated San Francisco Giants fan. He loved and supported his Giants. This evening, he went to Dodger Stadium with a friend, his sister and a step-brother. They had driven there in his friend's four-door Ford F150 pickup truck. They were having a marvelous time. In order to get in the right frame of mind, they had a few beers on their way to the ballpark. Marc was a big fellow, almost six feet tall, and would be considered in good physical shape.

He may have had a Dodger Dog and some nachos, but he spent considerable time drinking several icy cold beers and discussing with his friends his new purchase of a Mustang. Since it was a warm nightfall, the idea of a frosty beer seemed refreshing. As the game progressed, the beers kept flowing. Marc knew he didn't have to drive, so he didn't feel constrained to say "no more."

Not too far away from Marc's group was another group, who were diehard Dodger fans. They all had come to the stadium with Manuel in his mammoth Ford Expedition. He was proud of his huge SUV and had had special rims added to it. It looked impressive and it was great for transporting everyone to a baseball game. Manuel was accompanied by his niece and nephew with a friend of his nephew. Manuel was 33 years old and had been involved with gangs most of his life but seemed to have outgrown it.

Manuel had brought along a much younger member of his old street gang. That young man's name was Pete Marron, who was 19 years old. Manuel had introduced this Pete to everyone else in the car as a friend with a moniker of 'Evil.' Everyone that went with Manuel knew Pete by the name 'Evil.' Manuel's group was thrilled to be attending the ballgame in his big Expedition. When they got into the stadium parking lot, they were just like Marc directed to go to a section of the parking lot near the old 'will call' ticket offices. The two groups didn't even notice each other, even though they had parked less than ten spaces away from each other.

Both Marc's group and Manuel's group thoroughly enjoyed the game. Marc's friends seemed happier, since they had been supporting the Giants, who eventually won by the score of six to four. However, Manuel's crew had been vocally shouting support for the Dodgers. Time went quickly by, and it was time for the 'seventh inning stretch.' Both groups were losing interest in the game, since it was certain that the Giants were going to be victorious.

Both groups decided to leave before the end of the game. Anyone who has parked at Dodger Stadium understands the predicament. You want to stay and watch the end of the game, but that requires paying a substantial price. If you leave early, you can actually get out of the parking lot and home in a fraction of the time it takes if you wait to the very end of the game. The saving of time is often more than an hour. If you are someone who doesn't like inhaling exhaust fumes and being blinded by brake lights while other cars try to cut in front of you, then the 'seventh inning stretch' is the time to pick up your belongings and start the trek to the parking lot.

So it is understandable why many fans opt to leave early. Both groups exited the stadium by walking down the exit tunnel that pours the fans into the parking lot. Marc had lost count of how many beers he had drunk, but the number had to be somewhere between six and eight. Marc was feeling no pain. He seemed to be walking okay, but he was moving slowly and taking his time. The clever fans were trying to make the 'mad dash' to beat the traffic nightmare. (He had a blood alcohol level between .10 and .15, which is higher than the .08 presumption of being under the influence of alcohol.)

CHAPTER 57. DISPUTE IN THE PARKING LOT

While walking through the parking lot, Marc and his sister Brandi started to discuss what they were planning to do after they left the stadium. There was a difference of opinion. Marc's sister wanted to invite her old boyfriend to meet them somewhere they could have some drinks and a bite to eat. Marc didn't want to have to deal with his sister's old boyfriend. Their discussion evolved into a shouting match between brother and sister. They had reached the parking row in which their group had parked the pickup truck. Manuel's group had arrived at the same point in the parking lot, and the young boy with Manuel stopped to look at Marc as he was yelling at his sister.

Marc turned to the young boy and said, "What the fuck are you looking at, kid?" At that moment, Manuel told Marc to cool it and not talk to the young boy that way. Marc turned to Manuel and 'Evil' and said, "Butt out; I'm not talking to you."

The word exchange continued to escalate. Marc said if they wanted to take him, on he would oblige them. Then it became the challenging of one's masculinity. They kept yelling at each other. Manuel, who was five six, and 'Evil' (Pete), who was five four, retreated to the Expedition. Pete reached into the console between the front seats. He removed a silver semiautomatic pistol.

Pete, who was short in stature, was now ten feet tall while he was holding the semiautomatic in his hand. Pete walked back to the rear passenger side of the

Expedition. While Pete was standing there with Manuel, Marc started to walk toward Pete, while Marc's friend David, who was a fair size himself, followed a short distance behind Marc.

One might describe it as 'High Noon,' where Gary Cooper takes on the bad guys in a gunfight. But in this case only one side was armed with a gun, and the other side only had bare fists to fight with, even though the two groups of men were kind of lopsided in size, since Marc and his friend were substantially heftier than bantam-sized Pete and Manuel. If this moment in time could have been stopped and frozen, it would have been highly beneficial to all involved.

The next several seconds changed their lives forever, especially Marc's, Pete's (Evil) and Manuel's. Instead of leaving in the Expedition, Pete (Evil) raised the gun and pointed it toward Marc. The question that doesn't have a valid answer was why point a loaded gun at someone some 50 to 100 feet away from you? Is it to scare the other guy? Or is it to show him that you are tougher than he is? At that moment, there was no imminent threat to Pete or his group to defend themselves from. Or could it be a macho thing, like proving your manhood?

Pete was standing behind the Explorer with both hands extended in a firing position. The $64,000 question was what would compel someone to pull the trigger in this type of situation? Was there a derogatory comment made that incensed Pete to pull the trigger? Maybe it was part of the 'gang mentality' to shoot first and ask questions later. We may never know the true reason for the shooting, but what we do know is that Pete shot Marc and hit the target as a good gang member is taught. Then, almost reflexively, he shot at Marc a second time.

The first bullet struck Marc in his chest cavity and perforated the lung and aorta. The second bullet entered his chest through the diaphragm and perforated the spleen. Both gunshot wounds were fatal. His hand reflexively reached out for the gunshot wound as he felt the cold steel go through him as his body lurched backward. As the slug went piercing through his chest, it came out on his back side, falling to the ground. Marc stumbled away from the shooter and darted between two rows of cars and collapsed.

As Marc fell and started his death spiral, Pete and Manuel ordered everyone from their group to jump into the Expedition, and they started to leave. By now it was the eighth inning of the game, and more fans were emptying into the parking lot.

Manuel ordered his sister to drive the SUV. She put it in reverse and backed into the lane to exit. In doing so, she almost struck a car that was coming down the lane. Then she made a hard turn to the left and started the slow exit out of the stadium. She got to the main exit and quickly pulled out onto Stadium Way. At that point, ironically, they were within 100 yards of the LAPD Academy. They weren't in any mood to talk to any police officers at that point. They went down the road and followed the long row of cars heading to the entrance to the Interstate 5 Freeway.

This is where there is a slight twist in the story. Seconds after Marc was shot, his friend David yelled at a couple who were driving down the lane and were almost hit by the Expedition that was backing out. David told the couple that someone had just shot his friend. He pointed to Manuel's gold-colored Expedition and said, "Those guys just shot my brother, follow them."

Everyone experiences these critical moments in one's life. The question is whether a complete stranger should become involved in something they don't know anything about. Most strangers can find reasons not to insert themselves, especially without knowing all the facts. Why was this couple, who was merely driving down the lane, willing to be 'Good Samaritans'?

This couple started to follow the SUV. By now the Expedition was quite a ways ahead of them. They couldn't get close enough to get the license plate number. He continued to follow the Expedition as it entered the Interstate 5 Freeway. After extensive maneuvering, he was able to position his car where he and his wife could see the license number, and she wrote the license number, 4GTD064, down on a piece of paper.

These 'Good Samaritans' didn't just get the license plate number, but they did more. They used good judgement by not taking the law into their own hands by trying to pull over the Expedition. They went out of their way to return to the stadium, which was a major task, since so many fans were still exiting the parking lot. Eventually, they maneuvered back to where the shooting had occurred and noticed a number of police officers standing next to the new F150 pickup that Marc had come in. The police were shocked and surprised that these 'Good Samaritans' had gotten a license number. Immediately, one of the officers went over to his police unit and entered the license plate number into the DMV computer system. Within minutes, they had an address of the registered owner of that license plate number. The address was located in Whittier, slightly over 21 miles from Dodger Stadium.

Two detectives were dispatched to the address listed to see if they could locate the shooters. When they arrived at the Whittier house, there were no visible signs of the Expedition vehicle. This was disappointing, but they thought that it might be in the enclosed garage. They contacted the residents and asked if they had an Expedition. The lady who lived at the house said that they didn't have an Expedition and the police were free to look in the garage. The police didn't know what to think. So they took the woman to the police station and took her photo and put it in a photo lineup and showed it to the people at the crime scene. Everyone looked at it separately, and everyone said that they couldn't identify anyone in the photo lineup.

The Whittier couple was asked if they had been anywhere that evening. They were able to establish by a sales receipt that they had been shopping at Costco that night and certainly they hadn't been to Dodger Stadium. The detective didn't give up, and he outright asked if they could explain why the DMV had an Expedition registered at their address. The lady said that they must be talking about her brother, who had her buy an Expedition under her name, since he had bad credit and couldn't buy one under his name. So she was reluctant to say much, since she didn't want to get him into trouble. The detectives explained that they weren't trying to get her in trouble with the auto-financing company. All they wanted to do was talk to the person who was using the Expedition license number 4GTP064 that night. Since she didn't know the details of why they wanted to know, she willingly told them that her brother, Manuel, had the Expedition and he lived in South Gate.

At the same time, the police had run the Expedition's license number through a Traffic Citation database. Surprisingly, Manuel's name came up as the driver of the SUV on several occasions. His address listed on the citations was in South Gate. So the police went over to that location and staked out the house. They looked in the driveway, and sure enough, there was a gold Expedition. The police continued their stakeout. Around 4:30 a.m., Manuel came out and got into the Expedition, at which time he was arrested. At this point, the police got a search warrant to search and seize the Expedition.

CHAPTER 58. WANT TO PROTECT EVIL

The detectives asked Manuel if he would waive his Miranda rights and talk to them. He agreed to and said that he wasn't involved in any shooting. He said that they had left Dodger Stadium before anything had happened. He was willing to identify everyone who was in the car, except he didn't mention his fellow gang member Pete Marron (Evil).

After Manuel had given the names of all the people in his car, the police detectives went out and obtained their taped statements from each one of them. When those occupants were talked to, they mentioned that a guy by the name of 'Evil,' a friend of Manuel's, went with them to the baseball game. When these people in Manuel's car started talking, they told a different version of what happened. They said that Evil shot the victim, and the only thing they differed on was how close Marc was to Evil at the time of the shooting. Some thought they were as close as 25 feet, to some saying it was more like 55 feet. But what everyone agreed on was the fact that Marc didn't have any weapon. There was some suggestion that the person who got the closest to Pete, the shooter, was a person who had taken his shirt off. It was clear that Marc had his shirt on, since the paramedics, when they treated him, had to cut it off of him.

Since the case had occurred in the Downtown area, the case came under the jurisdiction of the DA's Office's Central Bureau. It was given to one of the most experienced trial prosecutors in Central at the time. His name was Tom Rubinson, and he was assigned the case. He had tried innumerable Hardcore Gang cases over his 12-year career with the office. The tough gang cases had taught him that the prosecutor needed to get to the witnesses early in the case, so their statements were recorded and they were tied down as to all the facts.

One of the reasons he was such a good lawyer was that he thoroughly prepared and knew the law pertaining to homicide cases. However, his greatest talent was being able to relate to the jurors. It was as though he could read the jurors' minds as to whether they comprehended what he was telling them. If he noticed some blank looks from the jurors, he would restate the facts or law in straightforward language.

Even though this was factually a simple case, Tom knew that it was imperative that the jurors be able to visualize the crime scene. And there was no question that pandemonium broke out after the shooting. Just imagine thousands of people coming out of the ballgame and fans hearing the sounds of gunshots in the parking lot.

Parents were trying to find a speedy and safe way to get their families protected from the gunfire. The security personnel, on the other hand, didn't know how big an incident was going down. Was it rival gangs having a shootout in the parking lot? Or could it be a madman randomly shooting into the crowd, possibly a terrorist?

The prosecution surmised that the defendant (shooter) was going to claim he shot in Self-Defense. That meant the key to this case was going to be where exactly the victim was standing in relation to the suspects. There were numerous witnesses, and they all saw the event of the shooting slightly differently depending on where they were at that precise moment in time.

However, what made it even more challenging was the fact that the parked vehicles were the anchors on which the witnesses relied to describe where they were standing. Unfortunately, the Expedition was moved when it left the scene. Likewise, the pickup truck that Marc came in was moved from its original location to where it was parked later when the police arrived to take the report. Where the CSI technicians found the expended shell casings would become crucial to the case. Since everyone agreed that the firearm was a semiautomatic handgun, the CSI expert could testify that such a weapon expended the shell casing to the right of the shooter. Generally, the expended casing is propelled four to five feet to the right of the shooter. Therefore, the position of the Expedition was determined to be the parking space next to the two expended shell casings.

The prosecutor recognized he needed to prepare a map of the relevant part of the parking lot and the positions of the vehicles at the exact moment of the shooting. The prosecutor took all the comments made by the witnesses as to where the Ford F150 pickup and Expedition were parked. The pickup was parked facing south, while the Expedition was parked facing north, on the same row some ten spaces apart. With this as the starter, the prosecutor had the CSI staff indicate where the shell casings were found. On the diagram, he had one shell casing marked next to the passenger door on the Expedition and another shell casing found five feet behind the Expedition's rear bumper.

Also on the diagram, the CSI staff marked where the victim's blood was located next to the expended bullet that had been recovered. This location was in the middle of the driveway, less than 15 feet from the rear of the Expedition. The last relevant point on the diagram was the place where the victim was found lying on the pavement. That was marked by the CSI technicians as the place where the victim's clothing was cut off by the paramedic and left at the crime scene.

Now with that diagram completed with all the key points, the prosecutor was ready to meet with all the witnesses to have them explain where they were when the shooting occurred. All the witnesses were in one camp (group) or the other. Marc's (the victim's) friends were supportive of his side, and Manuel's friends were supportive of his group. Very often, witnesses will see things in a manner more favorable to their side.

What is most surprising to police and a prosecutor is how many people in society have no concept of how to read a diagram. The best way to describe a diagram is what a bird flying overhead would see when looking down on a crime scene. Young children have great difficulty looking at a map or two-dimensional diagram and figuring out where they were standing or seating. Often, witnesses cannot orientate themselves to a diagram with north at the top. Some people insist on placing south at the top. Such orientation problems cause great confusion for jurors who are trying to understand the facts of a case by using a diagram.

Prosecutors find some witnesses take considerable time adjusting to the simplest diagram. This isn't caused by the witnesses trying to be untruthful but because they are unfamiliar with how to view a diagram. When a prosecutor finds such people, it is important to have them use photos to describe where they were at the critical time.

When the prosecutor Tom Rubinson talked to each side, he did it individually and was surprised to find that all the witnesses were very similar in their descriptions of where the victim and shooter were at the first and second shots. Then Tom tried to back up each witness as to where the parties were located at the first contact (shouting at each other). This became more problematic, because the moments before the shooting were a fluid situation when the dynamics were changing, since everyone was basically walking toward their respective vehicle. Some of the witnesses had nothing to jog their memories as to what was happening shortly before the shooting.

The prosecutor showed the diagram to each witness and asked them to show where they were standing from when the first words were shouted out to the time of the first shot fired.

After getting input from all the witnesses and using police photos that were taken several hours later, Tom had a good idea as to where the cars were originally parked. Tom used this diagram in his Opening Statement to help the jurors understand the facts of the case. When the witnesses testified, they used the diagram to show the jurors where the witnesses were standing when they saw various events.

Once the jury understood where the vehicles were parked at the time of the shooting, it was time to compare that information with the crime scene evidence that was found by the police detectives and photographed. This case was going to be decided on how close the victim and the suspect were to each other. If they were only a few feet apart, then the Defense could calm **Self-Defense** or even what is considered **'Imperfect Self-Defense.'** (That is when a suspect thinks he has the right to defend himself with deadly force when in fact he doesn't.)

CHAPTER 59. DIVIDE AND CONQUER

Tom understood that there were two components to this case. First, he had to get the witnesses pinned down as to the facts of what happened. Next, since the DA's Office wanted to prosecute both Pete and Manuel for the shooting death of Marc—although Manuel didn't pull the trigger in the shooting, he did contribute to the incident—the question was to what extent he should be punished for his actions.

Prosecuting both Pete and Manuel in the same trial was going to pose problems for the prosecution. The prosecution was relying on Manuel's relatives and friends to testify to the events leading up to the shooting. Those witnesses were the ones who would destroy Pete's claim of **Self-Defense**. In a trial in which Manuel was being prosecuted, those witnesses would naturally be supportive of Manuel. They would be reluctant to provide any testimony that would be harmful to Manuel.

In order to get Manuel out of the trial, Tom, the prosecutor, strategically worked out an offer that Manuel couldn't refuse to accept. It involved permitting him to plead guilty to **Voluntary Manslaughter** and be placed on probation for five years and have a state prison sentence of 12 years hanging over his head if he ever violated the terms of his probation. This meant he would be able to immediately walk out of jail, but he had a heavy sentence hanging over his head. Manuel's attorney quickly recognized the merit of this deal and advised Manuel to plead No Contest to the **Voluntary Manslaughter** charge, which he did.

This was a brilliant strategy, since it left Pete (Evil) being tried alone, and Manuel's relatives who were in the Expedition now had no reason to protect Manuel. Tom's strategy worked well in that Manuel's relatives testified that Marc, the victim, didn't get anywhere close to Pete before Pete fired the gun. As a matter of fact, Manuel's nephew testified that there was a period of 20 to 30 seconds between when Pete got the gun and the time of the shooting. The nephew indicated that they had sufficient time to get in their Expedition and leave. In other words, there was plenty of time for Pete to form the necessary Premeditation and Deliberation for First Degree Murder.

The other thing that hurt Pete was the fact that Alejandra, who was Manuel's niece, had told the police that Pete Marron had laughed about the incident when he had gotten into the car. She said that Pete had said, "That fool, he was scared when I shot him." This statement was contrary to someone who had to shoot someone in **Self-Defense**.

In addition to this, Tom put on evidence that Pete had run away and hid in several places throughout the State of California. After the shooting, the police tried to get Pete to turn himself in. Finally, the police went to the TV show ***America's Most Wanted***, which did an episode about the Dodgers shooting and showed Pete's photo. Calls came in indicating he had moved to Fresno. When they started looking for him up there, they learned he had quickly moved to Rancho Cucamonga. All this evading of the police certainly didn't help Pete when he tried to claim that the shooting was not his fault but was a matter of **Self-Defense**.

The trial was short, and the prosecution did most of the heavy lifting in that Tom called all the relevant witnesses from both sides. Marc's sister and their friend were excellent witnesses, clearly showing that Marc didn't have any weapon and the only weapon was the one used by Pete Marron. The people in Manuel's Expedition supported the position that Pete was the only one with a weapon. Even Manuel's side didn't show that Marc was aggressing toward Pete but they made it seem that Marc was walking away from them.

After the prosecutor finished with his last witness, then it was up to the Defense to decide whether Pete, the defendant, would testify. The U.S. Constitution's Fifth Amendment protects the defendant in that he or she can't be forced to testify. So many people remember that O. J. Simpson didn't take the witness stand and the jury totally acquitted him. The old adage is that a jury doesn't like a defendant who gets up on the witness stand and lies. However, there are times when the type of Defense that the defendant is claiming requires if not mandates that the defendant has to testify before the jury. The jury wants and needs some testimony to support the Defense's theory of the case.

Here, in this case, the Defense was based on what this defendant was thinking from the time he got the gun to the moment when he pulled the trigger. Even though it all occurred over a period of a minute or so, the jury wanted to hear about his thought process. If the defendant had immediately told the police about his fear and explained why he had done what he had done, the defendant might not have had to testify if the prosecution had used that statement in their case in chief. Here, the defendant had run away, and it was months later when he was caught by the police. By that time, he didn't provide the police with any statement when he was caught. In this case, the Defense took a big gamble in not having the defendant testify.

If Pete didn't testify, his attorney would have to argue that the prosecution hadn't proven their case beyond a reasonable doubt. Now the lines had been drawn. The Defense admitted that Pete had shot and killed Marc, but they claimed it wasn't Murder, as charged by the prosecution. What was to follow was just like a law school exam. Every degree and level of homicide had to be discussed. The jury had a broad range of possibilities. Even a third-year law student would have had difficulty following the law involved in this case.

(From author to reader—The next several pages discuss the various legal issues and concepts that were crucial to this case. Some readers may find this material too full of legalese and may want to skip these few pages. The reason I included this legal part of the case is because some readers will be surprised at the final outcome of the case.)

Tom realized that he needed to convey all the various steps the jurors needed to consider regarding the law. First, the jury had to consider if all the elements for Murder had been proven. The first element was that there had to be a killing of a human being. There was no issue regarding that. However, the second element was the issue of whether the killing was unlawful. (Killing someone in Self-Defense would be considered a LAWFUL KILLING.) This was where the issue of Self-Defense came into consideration. Later, Tom would address that issue and conclude that the facts didn't justify a finding of Self-Defense.

The third element was the issue of whether there was 'Malice Aforethought.' Tom argued that when one takes a gun, points it at someone and then pulls the trigger, that is clearly the 'Intent to Kill.' So the elements for Murder had been basically proven up, and the next issue was whether the crime was Second Degree Murder and First Degree Murder. In order to prove First Degree Murder, there has to be proof that there was Premeditation and Deliberation in carrying out the killing.

As to this shooting, the entire incident may have taken less than several minutes—how could there have been sufficient time to prove Premeditated and Deliberate? Most people think Premeditation and Deliberation must require considerable time. There is a belief that it would require sufficient time to plan to do the killing. As to the question of **Premeditation**, all that is required is that it occurs beforehand. As to the **Deliberation**, the law requires that the person has to have spent some time weighing the consideration for and against committing the act.

The courts now instruct the jury that Premeditation and Deliberation can occur in a very short period of time. In other words, it can occur within the period of several seconds, as long as the shooter has the opportunity to reflect on what he or she is about to do and weigh the consequences of his or her action.

In this particular case, the defendant had a very short period of time to consider what he was about to do. Tom realized that he had to educate the jury especially as to the Deliberation. He explained the language the judge would give the jury as part of the jury instructions. Then he gave the jury an example of a practical application of Deliberation. It can occur when a driver stops at an intersection. The driver looks to the left and looks to the right to determine if it is safe to enter the intersection. That is Deliberation on the part of the driver, even though it doesn't take a substantial amount of time. The jurors can relate to this example and realize that Deliberation doesn't require a lengthy period of time.

CHAPTER 60. DEFENSE SELLING SELF-DEFENSE

Of course, the Defense would like the jury to come back with a finding that the killing was done in **Self-Defense**. In order for this defendant, Pete, to be able to utilize it, he needed to convince the jurors that he had the following:

A Reasonable Fear;

That the Danger was Immediate, Apparent, and Imminent

It had to be Instantly Dealt With

This fear must have been the only motivation; and

The threat must not have ended.

Without the defendant testifying, there was little chance that the jury would be able to answer "Yes" to all of these requirements.

Realistically, Pete's attorney knew that his best Defense was called **'Imperfect Self-Defense.'** This is a concept that derives from an appellate case ***People v. Flannel***. It is a modified version of how the old Wild West operated, in which people tended to use guns whenever they felt they were threatened. There were times when the gun shooter overreacted and killed someone instead of using his fists to settle the argument. This **Flannel Defense** was created to protect those who had a 'hair trigger' when it came to using a gun. The courts wanted to create something between Self-Dense and Murder. As to Self-Defense, the defendant would go free; however, if convicted of Murder, he would end up serving 15 to 25 years to Life in prison.

The result of the legal concept of **'Imperfect Self-Defense'** was that when someone overreacted, they didn't get to go free but received the milder punishment under the crime of **Involuntary Manslaughter**. This concept of **'Imperfect Self-Defense'** can be confusing for jurors to comprehend. So Tom knew he had to make sure that the jury understood clearly what facts had to exist in order for this type of Defense to be considered by the jury. He explained to the jury in laymen's terms that this legal concept of **'Imperfect Self-Defense'** was when a person shot or killed someone when he had an unreasonable belief that he had a right to do so.

Both sides realized that the legal concepts in this case were going to be challenging to explain to the jurors. After all the witnesses had testified, it was time for Argument. Both sides vigorously argued their side of the case. The final jury instruction was given, and the jury started their deliberations. The jury was out for three hours, and they came back with a **First-Degree Murder** verdict. They found that the defendant did use a firearm and they found the Special Allegation to be true. What that meant was that 19-year-old Pete would be sentenced to 60 years to Life in state prison. In other words, he wouldn't ever see the life of freedom unless he lived a long life into his 70s.

Why did the jury convict Pete of First Degree Murder? Maybe it was because they could identify with the fact that they could have been at Dodger Stadium and they could have been struck by stray bullet. The feeling may have been that the use of a gun to settle a dispute in this type of setting is so dangerous, subjecting so many innocent people to being hit by flying bullets.

There may have been a feeling that one shouldn't use a firearm at a sport's event. The original concept of the Olympics was that the athletes as well as the spectators were to lay down their weapons some distance away from where the games were held. The athletes were nude, so the other competitors knew that they were unarmed. The Olympics carved out the rule that athletic events were meant as battles between individuals and not to decide who had the best or latest armament. There is the feeling among many that there should be certain free zones where weapons and violence aren't tolerated. This would include churches or any sacred location where arms and violence are off limits.

This Pete Marron case was one that ran the entire gamut of possibilities. The defendant could have walked out a free man if the jury had believed that this was a case of Self-Defense. On the other hand, if the jury found that the facts justified a First-Degree Murder with a firearm being used, then the sentence was 60 years to Life in state prison. This was an extreme range of consequences for a set of facts involving several macho dudes who found themselves in a squabble. When one is in a quarrel, one has to quickly assess the situation as to whether one is at a handicap because of size or numbers involved.

In this situation, Manuel and Pete could easily see that they had confronted dudes who were bigger than they were. The gun was the great equalizer. The pulling of the gun might have ended the confrontation. Most people who are unarmed and see a gun pointed at them will back off and leave. But in this case, Marc wasn't initially deterred by the gun pointed at him. This is when a gun immediately turns from an asset to a liability. The law doesn't permit one to use deadly force when a quarrel escalates. The idea of pointing a gun at someone to end a confrontation may work, but you run the risk of using deadly force when it isn't legally justified. Unfortunately, Pete Marron made the wrong decision, which cost Marc his life but also cost Pete his useful life. For the next half century, Pete will have more than enough time to reflect on grabbing that silver semiautomatic, aiming it and pulling the trigger.

CHAPTER 61. IT HAPPENS AGAIN—DEJA VU

On March 31, 2011, it was opening day between the Dodgers and Giants. The stadium was packed with fans excited to see how the teams would match up for another season. Bryan Stow (42) was a paramedic who had come down from the San Francisco Bay Area to LA to support his dearly beloved Giants. He had donned his Giants jersey and cap, letting all know his allegiance. As usual, there was the typical banter back and forward between the various set of fans in the stadium.

As the game wound down, Bryan Stow went to the parking lot to find a taxi cab to take him and his group back to his hotel. As he stood in the parking lot, two guys came along and hit him from behind. A tussle occurred, and one of the guys struck him so hard Brain went spinning backwards. He lost his balance and fell to the ground, and one of the two guys came over to him and started to kick him in the head as hard as he could with his shoes.

Bryan was a paramedic from Santa Clara in the Bay Area, where he had treated many people who had hit their heads, but now he was the one on the ground with a stream of Dodgers fans walking by. No one realized how serious his injuries were until Bryan didn't get up or even attempt to get up. Eventually Dodgers security came over and checked out the situation and it was decided to call an ambulance. Bryan's head was secured so he could be safely transported to Los Angeles County General Hospital.

There, doctors treated Bryan for a severe fractured skull and damage to the frontal lobe of his brain. He was placed in an induced coma. Eventually, part of his skull was removed to reduce the pressure from the swelling of the brain.

No one was immediately arrested for causing those injuries. The politicians of the City of the Angeles immediately issued rewards to anyone providing information about those who were responsible for this attack. The Mayor and Police Chief gave press conferences seeking the public's help in finding the perpetrators.

After a week, the medical team tried to reduce the coma-inducing medication so the victim could regain consciousness. When they did this, he started suffering seizures, so the neurosurgeons decided to return Stow to a coma for another week. The hospital still listed him as being in critical condition.

The police gave out a description of the two men who attacked Stow. One was described as stocky Latino, 18 to 25, with a shaved head, goatee, and mustache, weighing about 170 pounds, with a distinct mole on his left cheek. The other attacker was a taller Latino or white male, about six feet one inch and 170 pounds, with hazel eyes and short hair. One of the distinctive features was that he had a tattoo on his neck. A forensic artist with the help of witnesses to the attack were able to create composite sketches. Both men were with a woman and a 10-year-old child.

On May 22, 2011, Giovanni Ramirez (31) was arrested for the attack on Bryan Stow. Ramirez's parole agent said that he looked similar to the description given by witnesses to the beating. One of the identifiable features of Ramirez was a large tattoo that wrapped around his neck. His photo was shown to some of the witnesses, who identified him in a photo lineup. Later, a lineup was conducted at the Central County Jail, and Ramirez was picked out as one of the attackers.

The pressure on civic leaders was immense, since Los Angeles didn't want tourists to think it was unsafe to visit LA. The Mayor and Police Chief wanted to assure everyone that it was safe to attend 'America's Favorite Pastime,' baseball, in Los Angeles. Chief Beck was asked by a reporter how certain he was that they had arrested the right person involved in the beating. The Chief responded that he was confident that the Northeast detectives had gotten the right man.

The police were pleased with their investigation, since they had positive identification of the main attacker. The LAPD wanted the DA's Office to file criminal charges against Giovanni Ramirez. There was no question that Giovanni was a bad dude. He had been a longtime gang member and possessed a gun while he was on parole. However, the DA's Office wanted something more before filing criminal charges.

Giovanni was represented by a veteran Defense attorney by the name of Anthony Brooklier. His Defense attorney was telling the DA's Office that the police had the wrong guy. At first it sounded like what all Defense attorneys say—that their client was innocent. However, the daughter of Ramirez appeared in a TV interview saying that he was home with her at the time of the attack. Even Ramirez's mother said that her son didn't like baseball and never went to Dodger Stadium. The Defense attorney said that Giovanni had passed a polygraph test showing he wasn't at the Dodger game. The polygraphist said that he was certain Ramirez wasn't at the baseball game. When he asked Ramirez whether he was at any part of Dodger Stadium, such as the stands, the field, the parking lot or the 'bullpen,' Ramirez stopped the polygraphist and asked him what is a 'bullpen?'

Although every defendant may claim he or she is innocent, few defendants ever give the DA's Office the names of witnesses who can be checked out before even filing the case. As a result, the DA's Office said to the police, "then show us pictures of Ramirez at the Dodger game." There are dozens of cameras at Dodger Stadium, and surely there was at least one with a photo of Ramirez. The detectives went through endless videos from security cameras hoping to find Ramirez somewhere in the ballpark, but nothing was uncovered.

Chief Beck was starting to feel the heat from the questioning whether the LAPD had got the right man. The Chief did something that certainly wasn't popular with the department when he removed the Bryan Stow case from Northeast detectives and transferred it to the Robbery Homicide Division (RHD). This created an enmity within the department between the hardworking local detectives and the Downtown 'hotshot' RHD detectives.

It turned out that move was what was needed to find the real suspects. The emphasis changed from trying to prove Ramirez did it to reviewing all the tips that had earlier come in and following up on them. There were a number of fans who indicated that there were two guys in the stands above the third base area who were harassing Giants fans. This included throwing peanuts at the opposing fans, and later it included throwing beer or soft drinks on people wearing Giants jerseys. What the detectives from RHD did was figure out where the disruptive fans were seated. Then, when that was determined, the detectives worked with the Dodger ticket office. They were able to determine what credit card was used to purchase the tickets for those specific seats.

It came back to a Mr. Sanchez from Rialto. The detectives were able to obtain an address and went there to talk to Donna (Pseudonym). At first there were denials, and eventually, "I was there with my brother Louie Sanchez (29) and my husband Marvin Norwood (30) at the Dodger game." She and the others admitted being at the game but claimed they were not involved in any fight or attack on Bryan Stow. After several versions, Donna stated that she didn't see anything but her brother was drunk and the two guys went after some people. All she knew was that they came running back to her and told her to drive out of the parking lot. She noticed some blood on Norwood's hand.

Then on July 20, 2011, both Louie Sanchez and Marvin Norwood were arrested for the beating of Bryan Stow. The RHD detectives placed both suspects together in an interview room and both detectives stepped out of the room and left the audio-video recorder on. On the tape, Louie Sanchez stated, "I socked him, jumped him and started beating him." He apologized to Norwood for dragging him into the fight. Marvin Norwood responded on the tape, "That happens, bro, I mean, what kind of man would I have been if I hadn't jumped in and tried to help you."

When Chief Beck made the announcement of the arrests, he told the news media that Giovanni Ramirez had had nothing to do with the attack. He stressed it was important to let the public know that the police had arrested him on the basis that witnesses had identified him but there was no other supporting evidence. The Chief stated that other evidence totally vindicated Giovanni.

In June 2012, a preliminary hearing was held over a year after the attack. Donna testified how her brother and husband were involved in something in the Dodger parking lot and came running toward her and told her to drive as fast as she could.

Afterwards, defendant Louie Sanchez pleaded guilty to Mayhem, and he received eight years in state prison. Marvin Norwood pleaded guilty to Assault Likely to Cause Great Bodily Injury and was sentenced to four years in state prison, which meant with credit for time served he would shortly be a free man. In addition, the feds brought charges against both of them for firearms violations.

What was interesting was the Pete Marron case involved the death of Marc, while in the Sanchez/Norwood case, Bryan Stow was not killed but was injured. However, the media made the Sanchez/Norwood case an international case. The question was why the case involving a death wouldn't be the more serious one. The news media showed little to no interest in Marc's case but was constantly showing the disability of Bryan Stow. The Stow situation created so much more publicity.

When the Stow family brought a civil lawsuit against the owner of the Dodgers, it was the news media that made out the owner as being too cheap to have adequate security to protect the fans. Even though the Dodgers had more security staff the night of the incident, the attorney for the Stow family was able to make it appear the Dodgers organization were negligent in protecting people in their parking lot. In the civil trial, the jury awarded the Stow family $18 million from the Dodgers organization for their lack of security.

What else was newsworthy about the Bryan Stow matter was the fact that the police wrongfully arrested Giovanni Ramirez. The question is, how often does the wrong person get arrested for a crime they didn't commit? The answer is that no one knows for sure, since it is quite common for guilty defendants to claim they are innocent. Prosecutors have a dual job of not merely convicting the guilty but also protecting the innocent from being wrongly charged.

In this case, it was the prosecution who put on the brakes, since they wanted some corroboration that Ramirez was truly at the game. Many prosecutors have had the unfortunate situation of charging the wrong person based on faulty eyewitness identification. That is why experienced prosecutors will require some form of corroboration when an entire case rests on only eyewitness identification.

THE KILLING FIELDS OF LOS ANGELES

People vs. Tak Sun Tan, Jason Chan, Indra Lim

CHAPTER 62. LIFE IN CAMBODIA

Leaving Dodgers Stadium, we return to old Route 66, which is a continuation of Sunset Boulevard in this area. We travel only a couple of blocks until we reach Beaudry Avenue, where we veer to the left. As we head up the slight incline with rows of apartment houses on both sides, we are on the outskirts of Chinatown. Unfortunately, this is the site of one of the most gut-wrenching cases ever handled by the DA's Office, as well as one of the most problematic cases to try before a jury. This case involved the robbery murder of Dr. Haing Ngor, one of the most remarkable human beings one would ever meet.

Dr. Ngor was born in Cambodia in 1940, and grew up in humble surroundings. While in school he was a diligent student who wanted to learn about everything. His academic efforts paid off and he succeeded in becoming a prominent doctor in his beloved country. He specialized in obstetrics and gynecology.

Graphics Page

While gaining his medical training, he met and fell in love with Huoy Chang, who was studying to be a schoolteacher. They married and had a happy life together living in Phnom Penh. In the early 1970s, things couldn't have been better for the two of them and their extended family.

However, in April 1975, the Khmer Rouge political party was able to rise to power in Cambodia. It occurred so abruptly that Dr. Haing Ngor was in the middle of an operation when the Khmer Rouge took over the capital of Phnom Penh. He had to leave the patient on the operating table and flee the city. He and his wife escaped to the countryside, where they were designated 'war slaves.' The Khmer Rouge routinely slaughtered all educated people, believing they were the cause of the degeneration of society.

The Khmer Rouge's objective was to impose radical social reforms aimed at creating a purely agrarian-based Communist society. That meant that the city-dwellers were deported to the countryside, where they were forced to work in the fields and live like the other rural peasants. The Khmer Rouge wanted to eliminate anyone suspected of involvement in free-market activities. They suspected capitalists to be anyone who was a professional or anyone who was educated.

At first, Dr. Ngor worked as a cab driver to blend into the masses, but later he was forced to be a laborer in the rice fields. At that time, Pol Pot was the leader of the Khmer Rouge. Although they ruled Cambodia for only four years (1975 to 1979), they are best remembered for the genocide they created. During this period between, 1 ½ and 2 million Cambodians died in the so-called 'Killing Fields.' Many died as result of executions, torture, starvation, lack of medical care and forced labor.

Dr. Ngor personally suffered the harsh conditions. While living in this country encampment, his wife became pregnant. Because of the poor conditions and malnutrition, his wife needed to have a C-section. Dr. Ngor couldn't try to assist in the care of his wife, since the Khmer Rouge guards would learn that he was a doctor. Dr. Ngor was faced with one of the most difficult decisions anyone could ever encounter in one's life. If he tried to help his wife, he certainly would have been executed.

He made the decision to remain silent in hopes things might work out. As a result, his wife and baby died before his eyes. They weren't the only family members that Dr. Ngor lost during the Khmer Rouge reign. He lost his father and several other members of his family to the killing that occurred throughout Cambodia.

Dr. Ngor was able to survive the harsh conditions of starvation and oppressive labor as a field hand. He was tortured several times and even had one of his fingers cut off. Another time they tried to burn him to death. He truly lived in the middle of and survived the 'Killing Fields.'

In 1979, the Khmer Rouge was forced out of power by the Communists from Vietnam. This gave Haing Ngor a chance to escape the cruel conditions. The only family member to survive with him was his six-year-old niece. Her parents had been killed, so he later raised her like a daughter. So he and his niece set out on the long walk to the Laos border. There he started helping other immigrants who needed medical attention.

By 1980, he and his niece had the opportunity to migrate to America, where they ended up in Los Angeles where they eventually settled. Although he had been a successful doctor in Cambodia, he didn't have a license to practice medicine in his new country. He didn't have any easy options but found a job as a counselor for refugees similar to himself at a non-profit agency in the Los Angeles Chinatown Service Center.

CHAPTER 63. KILLING FIELDS MOVIE

Haing Ngor made the most of his life in Los Angeles and came in contact with many immigrants who had endured the atrocities in Cambodia. In 1984, a British film company decided to make a movie about three journalists who survived the carnage committed by the Khmer Rouge regime. The basis of the story was Sydney Schanberg's writings titled ***The Death and Life of Dith Pran***. Sydney Schanberg had received the Pulitzer Prize for his writings about the fall of Phnom Penh during the Khmer Rouge takeover of Cambodia.

But the British filmmakers went to Hollywood to find creative talent for the movie ***The Killing Fields.*** What they needed was someone who could give them insight as to what life was like in those turbulent times. When the moviemakers asked for help learning more about background for the movie, they continually were told to contact a Cambodian immigrant counselor who worked in Chinatown.

When they contacted Haing Ngor, he was more than willing to talk to them about all aspects of the Khmer Rouge years in his beloved country. The film researchers found him to be a wealth of information. He was so passionate in describing what life had really been like. The film crew was faced with the problem of finding an actor to play the role of Dith Pran, the photographer who was the sidekick of the journalist Sydney Schanberg. Someone made an offhanded comment that Haing Ngor would be perfect for the part, since he was the same size as Dith Pran and he had the ideal accent. As the time was fast approaching to start filming, they reviewed their options and found no other Cambodian actor was available to play the part.

Although Dr. Ngor had no experience as an actor, he was a quick learner in being able to play the role of the photographer. He joined the cast and crew and helped to make the movie. In 1984, the film was distributed by Warner Bros. It turned out to be a gigantic success, winning many awards. It won the BAFTA award for Best Film of the year, as well as receiving seven Academy Award nominations. And it was Haing Ngor's performance as Dith Pran that won him the Oscar award for Best Supporting Actor.

Even after the great success he had in *The Killing Fields*, he continued to act in other movies and television programs. Haing felt so blessed in continuing to earn money for his acting. He donated much of his income and royalties and lecturer fees to various charities. He helped to start two refugee organizations and provided medical services to needy Cambodian refugees. Later on, he contributed funds to combating gang violence by providing jobs and counseling for at-risk youths. He never forgot how various charitable organizations had helped him when he was a poor refugee.

Dr. Ngor was not pretentious as to how he lived or conducted himself. He lived a very modest lifestyle. He had a tiny apartment in the Chinatown neighborhood. However, there were two things that might have set him apart from the other apartment dwellers he lived among. He had a large Mercedes-Benz sedan that he enjoyed driving. The other thing of value was his fondness for his $6,000 Rolex watch, which he always wore. For some reason, his car and watch were his pride and joy.

Haing Ngor had an interesting set of values. For example, the evening of the Academy Awards ceremony, he sat in the back of the theater as each nominee's name was read off. Then it was time to announce the winner. The presenter opened the envelope and mumbled the name of the winner. He seemed to have difficulty pronouncing the name of Haing Ngor. It was like a bolt of lightning striking Dr. Ngor. Not expecting to be a winner, Dr. Ngor slowly got up from his seat. It was as if he was experiencing a dream.

People next to him were leaning over to congratulate him for winning. He started walking up to the stage as if in a daze and took the gigantic steps up to the stage. He graciously thanked everyone he could remember to thank. Then there was thunderous applause and he was taken backstage as a winner. He was ecstatic that the film ***The Killing Fields*** was being recognized. He appeared uncomfortable having the attention directed to him. Afterwards he attended a few parties celebrating the various winners. However, he made the necessary appearances and then headed home to get some rest.

The next morning, he was up at 6:30 a.m. as usual and off to work at the Cambodian refugee center. By 8:30 a.m., he was assisting new immigrants to find jobs and places to stay. Less than 12 hours earlier, he was being recognized for his acting ability in the movie ***The Killing Fields***. He couldn't understand all the fuss, since during the filming he didn't think he was acting but merely relating what he had lived through. What he didn't understand was that his performance was so convincing that moviegoers were able to really feel the pain and suffering he was depicting on the big screen.

CHAPTER 64. SHOOTING DURING ROBBERY

It was Sunday, February 25, 1996, and Dr. Ngor had gone to Long Beach to visit a Cambodian couple. They had had an early dinner and talked about old times. It was a pleasant day for all of them. The wife had taken a photo of the two men seated on the floor. Haing was smiling with his Rolex watch on his wrist. Both men had contented looks on their faces as though all was at peace in their world after all they had lived through in Cambodia. Haing left his friends' place around 8:00 in the evening, driving his big Mercedes up the Harbor Freeway.

After an easy 30-minute drive, he was headed through Downtown. As he neared Chinatown, he turned off the freeway and took surface streets to turn onto Cesar Chavez Boulevard (old Route 66) for the short drive to Beaudry Street, where he made a right turn. Then he proceeded up the long alley to his apartment's carport.

Now, at 8:30 p.m., Los Angeles had cooled down, and there was definitely a chill in the air. There were three Cambodian members of the Oriental Lazy Boyz gang who had been snorting up cocaine. They needed more money to buy more 'coke.' Since they didn't have any money, they decided to find someone to rob. They had done some 'chain grabbing' in Chinatown and were continuing into the apartment complexes hoping to find better pickings. They were walking down the alley behind Dr. Ngor's apartment and they noticed a large Mercedes whizzing up the alley. It looked like an expensive car, and they waited for the driver to pull into the carport and park behind the apartment.

What exactly happened next is a little sketchy. The three of them most likely swarmed around the car. They demanded the driver, who was Dr. Ngor, give them money. From the physical evidence, Dr. Ngor's Rolex was taken. There may have been a request for the gold necklace he had around his neck. This becomes the crucial issue in the case. Since the necklace contained a locket with a photo of his wife who had died during childbirth, did he resist when they were demanding the gold chain with the locket?

The prosecution's theory of the case was that the robbers shot Dr. Ngor when he failed to give up this gold chain that held a heart-shaped locket. What we know from the physical evidence is that Dr. Ngor was shot while seated in the driver's seat of his Mercedes. It was a 9 mm caliber gun that was used to shoot him, most likely a Glock handgun.

Then, as Dr. Ngor lay dying, one of the three robbers snatched the chain and locket. Since the shooting created substantial loud noise, the robbers knew they needed to get out of the carport area before neighbors became witnesses. There was no time to go through pockets looking for a wallet or checking out the car for other valuables. If they had looked, they would have found at least $3,000 in cash in the back seat. Also, Dr. Ngor had several hundred dollars tucked in his wallet.

The three robbers were able to run down the alley and found some homies driving toward them. They talked to these homies and asked for a ride out of the area. The robbers escaped with the Rolex watch and the gold chain with the locket. Also still in their possession was the 9 mm Glock handgun that was used to shoot Haing Ngor.

After hearing shots fired, one of Haing's neighbors came running to the carport and found Haing's bloody body lying on the cold concrete floor of the carport. She had the police called, and soon the alley was covered with police cars. Eventually the detectives arrived to take over the investigation. Initially, it appeared to be a possible robbery. However, when they found the victim's wallet untouched and the $3,000 in cash left in the car, the detectives wondered if there could have been another reason for the shooting.

When the media learned the name of the victim, Dr. Haing Ngor, immediately the shooting turned into a possible political-retaliation killing. Dr. Ngor had been very critical of the Cambodian government and Pol Pot, who was still the leader of the

Khmer Rouge in a small portion of Cambodia. Dr. Ngor's killing had some of the earmarks of a political attack in that initially nothing appeared to have been taken. Only later was it learned that his Rolex watch was missing and the gold chain and locket had been taken.

The CSI crew completely dusted Dr. Ngor's Mercedes for latent prints. It was hoped that the killers somehow inadvertently may have touched something. After much reviewing of the various latent prints on the car, nothing was found that could be traced to a suspect.

The Ballistics experts examined the trajectory of the bullet that went through Dr. Ngor and was recovered from under the driver's seat. This made it appear that the shooter was standing immediately outside of the driver's door. This was more consistent with a robbery than a political hit. From all the physical evidence, the police detectives were more inclined to believe that the shooting was the result of a robbery gone bad. The bullets that were recovered were from a Glock 9 mm handgun. The gun used by the robbers was never found. The biggest controversy in the case was whether he refused to give up the locket because it contained the photo of his wife. If this were the only photo of his wife, then the theory had merit, since it was understandable that he wouldn't want to give up such an important remembrance of his wife. On the other hand, if he had other photos of her, then the locket photo might not seem to be so valuable.

It turned out that in Dr. Ngor's bedroom, there was a similar photo of his wife in a large round frame. It is possible that the locket was the original photo and the one in his bedroom was merely a reproduction.

The police detectives were hoping that they would be able to recover the Rolex watch from a pawn shop or from the suspects' house. However, the Rolex was never recovered. It may have acted as a red flag to the thieves and robbers, since one who wears such an expensive watch most likely has other valuables.

As part of the investigation, the detectives scoured the neighborhood to find any witnesses who might have seen someone in the area at the time of the shooting. Three weeks after the shooting, the detectives talked to two possible witnesses. They said that when they heard the shots, they saw **Jason Chan, Indra Lim** and **Tak Sun Tan** come running down the alley. These individuals asked the witnesses to drive them over to Thol's (Pseudonym) house. The detectives videotaped their statements.

The police went to talk to Thol, who was helpful in that he said two weeks before the shooting he saw one of the defendants with a gun like the one used. He went further and stated that Chang and Lim were at his house just before the shooting and they were discussing their plan to commit a robbery later that evening. Again the detectives got him on videotape making these statements.

The detectives knew that Chang, Lim and Tan had been named as possible suspects in the shooting, so they were brought in individually to the station for a talk. What was surprising was that each one of them was willing to talk without an attorney. However, they gave exculpatory statements. They admitted being present at or near the time of the shooting. But they were more than happy to implicate their companions for committing the robbery and shooting. Of course, the detectives were astute enough to have their statements recorded so they could be used later at time of trial.

CHAPTER 65. TRIAL

The DA's Office assigned the case to prosecutor Craig Hum, who had been in the Hardcore Gang Division but transferred to the Major Crimes Division. Convictions in the toughest gang cases were his forte. Craig had the 'can do' attitude even when the sky was falling. He seemed to excel the more obstacles the Defense was throwing at him. When the DA's Office had publicity cases fraught with insolvable problems, Craig's name would come up as the person to assign to prosecute the case. However, the only caveat was the fact that Craig was one of the few prosecutors who opposed the Death Penalty. In other words, the DA's Office couldn't give him a case in which the Office was seeking the Death Penalty. Since the Dr. Ngor case didn't involve Capital Punishment, it was a no-brainer to assign Craig Hum to this case.

The Ngor case had all the elements of a gang case in which the witnesses were gang members who didn't want to testify against their fellow homies. The case needed someone who could deal with gang witnesses who wanted to recant their statements at time of trial. As to other civilian witnesses, they were afraid of retaliation from the Oriental Lazy Boyz gang if they testified.

Although the murder case was relatively straightforward, the prosecution of the case was much more complicated than the facts would suggest. The co-defendants' statements were exculpatory as to the defendant making them; however, the statements mentioned various activities of the co-defendants. Some of those statements implicated those co-defendants. Under the ***Aranda/Burton*** case law, the prosecution can't use a co-defendant's statement if it implicates another defendant. The legal theory is that the defendant talked about doesn't have the right to cross-examine the defendant making the statement.

Therefore, the admissibility of a defendant's statement in a multiple defendant case is limited, unless those statements can be edited in such a way as to eliminate the incriminating part involving the co-defendants. The prosecutor recognized there was no way to edit the statements without changing the meaning of the statements.

Another option was to have three separate trials, which might take over a year. The prosecution was relying on several gang member witnesses. Those witnesses claimed that they had picked up the three defendants just moments after hearing the shooting.

The prosecutor, Craig Hum, was well aware that these witnesses would not be able to withstand three separate trials. Each one of the witnesses was now recanting their statement and deadly afraid of testifying against the Oriental Lazy Boyz gang members. Also, the prosecutor was calling as a witness a fellow gang member to say that he told the police that defendant Chan had in his possession a 9 mm Glock pistol just days before the shooting of Dr. Ngor. To show how petrified this witness was at time of trial, one only needs to review his testimony at the preliminary hearing when he described to the judge what it meant for him if he testifies, "*My life is over. If they want to kill me, go ahead. But I just want to say to all my homies, I am sorry.*"

(The author is aware that the next several pages maybe difficult to follow and comprehend. However, it provides you, the reader, with insight as to what is going on behind the scenes. Not everything is simple and easy to understand, especially in our Criminal Justice System.)

So if Craig wanted to try the case once before one jury, then he would not be able to use any of the defendants' statements regarding being present at the shooting. Craig requested the court to have **a single trial using three separate juries** to listen to the evidence. When it came time to introduce the defendants' statements, only that defendant's jury would hear what he said to the detectives before being arrested. The other two juries would be excluded from hearing that defendant's statements.

The prosecutor persuaded the judge to have **a single trial using three separate juries**—one jury for each defendant. This had been done only once before in the California courts. The single trial with three separate juries was the only way the case could be tried; however, it was not without logistic challenges. This required that there be 48 jurors and alternates seated in the courtroom. Each of the three sets of jurors had to be color-coded so they didn't mix with the other two sets of jurors.

There had to be three sets of exhibits, for each separate jury. Also, the prosecutor had to give three separate Opening Statements and had to make sure he didn't mention any of the evidence that had been presented to the other juries.

The following is part of the prosecution's Opening Statement explaining to the jurors the facts of the case.

What happens is: As Dr. Ngor returns from his friends' house, he comes off Alpine and he turns north into the alley... Dr. Ngor drives north, up the alley, almost to the top, where he turns right and parks his car in the carport of his apartment building. He shuts off his engine, opens his car door, ready to get out and walk to his apartment; but he never makes it, because what Dr. Ngor didn't know is that as he drove up the alley towards his home, he passed the three gang members... These three defendants had just finished smoking the last of their cocaine in the alley. They wanted more, but they needed money. And at that precise moment, Dr. Ngor drives right past them. The defendants see Dr. Ngor pull into the carport and they follow him. And as Dr. Ngor turns off his engine, the three gangsters approach him. They are planning to rob him to get money for more cocaine. And defendant Chan has a nine-millimeter semiautomatic handgun, and he is ready to use it.

The defendants demand Dr. Ngor's watch. He gives it to them, no problem. But then the gangsters see Dr. Ngor's gold chain, the chain with the locket and picture of his wife. This picture that meant so much to Dr. Ngor. The defendants demand the chain. It is a thick gold chain, and gold will bring them plenty of money to buy more cocaine. But Dr. Ngor refuses to give it to them, not this time, not again, and not to these three gangbangers. After all he's been through, Dr. Ngor is not going to give these three gangsters the only thing he had left of his wife. He refuses. So suspect Chan, high on cocaine, shoots him. He aims his gun at Dr. Ngor and he pulls the trigger; the gun fires. First bullet passes through Dr. Ngor's right leg. It misses the bone; it comes out the other side of his leg. It's a non-fatal bullet wound. But the second bullet is much more lethal. Suspect Chan fires his second bullet directly into the side of Dr. Ngor's chest... Dr. Haing Ngor is dying. As Dr. Ngor gasps for breath, the defendants snatch the chain from his neck; they then flee on foot, running down the alley away from the murder scene...

Ladies and gentlemen, Dr. Haing Ngor, who survived so much hardship, who survived torture, who survived the death of his wife and their unborn child, who survived the killing fields of Cambodia, the slaughter of a million of his fellow countrymen, dies on the cold pavement of a carport in Chinatown, gunned down by these gangbangers for a few lousy rocks of cocaine.

This Opening Statement gave the jurors a basic idea what the case was about. The hard part was the trial, in which the prosecutor had to call witnesses who would testify to these facts. Craig was able to have both witnesses testify how they talked to the three defendants in the alley and drove them away. However, they had changed their tune and denied saying anything to the detectives. Craig played the videotape showing them making statements to the detectives. These witnesses still denied making any statements, even as the jury viewed the videos in which they laid out all the facts. It was the strangest situation, in which these hostile witnesses refused to acknowledge the obvious. Some of the jurors must have wondered how a person could deny making such a statement when you can hear their voices making such a statement.

The other witness who had said he had seen defendant Chang with the gun testified he didn't say that, even as the jurors heard him saying it on the tape recording. The prosecutor got as much as he could out of all the hostile witnesses. All three juries heard this testimony all at the same time.

As to each of the statements made by each defendant, they came in only before that defendant's jury. Those statements showed that each of the defendants were present at the time of the shooting. The other thing these statements showed was how many inconsistent statements each of the defendants had made to the detectives. This proved 'consciousness of guilt' on the part of each defendant.

After the prosecutor had rested his 'case in chief,' the Defense started to present evidence. First he claimed that the locket photo wasn't the only photo of the victim's wife. The Defense claimed there was a similar photo on the wall in the victim's bedroom. The question was, what impact would that so-called 'other photo' have on the jury?

It was a major task to keep each set of jurors separated from the other jurors. Also, during the Argument, Craig had to be careful not to make the mistake of mentioning something that was not testified to before that jury. Craig argued, ***"What***

these defendants did was take the life of an unbelievable human being, doctor, Academy Award-winner and great humanitarian. Dr. Haing Ngor survived the Killing Fields of Cambodia, where over one million people died, just to be murdered in the killing streets of Los Angeles."

The Defense argued that the so-called eyewitnesses couldn't be believed, since they had given so many inconsistent stories. The Defense wanted to allude to the possibility that the killer could be someone from the Khmer Rouge. However, the prosecutor objected to any mention of retaliation by the Khmer Rouge on the grounds that this was 'Third Party Culpability' and couldn't be argued by the Defense unless evidence had been specifically presented. Since there was no such evidence introduced, the judge didn't permit the Defense to argue the Khmer Rouge reprisal theory.

Eventually, all three juries had heard both the prosecution and Defense Arguments. Each one of the three juries went to separate jury deliberation rooms. After several days of deliberation, all three juries found their respective defendants guilty of **First Degree Murder**.

At time of sentencing, the judge sentenced **Jason Chan** (20) to Life in Prison Without the Possibility of Parole. He had a lengthy criminal record from age 13. He was the one who had and used the gun. As to **Tak Sun Tan** (21), he received a sentence of 56 years to Life in state prison, because he had a prior robbery conviction. As to the last defendant, Indra Lim (21), he received a sentence of 26 years to Life in state prison.

Each of the defendants appealed their convictions. On appeal, the Defense attorneys claimed that there was **prosecutorial misconduct** when Craig mentioned to the juries the hardships suffered by Dr. Haing Ngor. After examining the entire transcript, the California appellate courts found **no prosecutorial misconduct**. Then the defendants went over to the federal courts and were able to convince a district court judge (Judge Margaret Morrow) to grant a petition for federal habeas relief. In other words, one federal district court judge decided to throw out the convictions of all three Oriental Lazy Boyz gangsters. Since the witnesses had moved out of state in fear of their lives, there was no way this case could ever be retried.

The reason for the reversal of the conviction was over the issue of whether the prosecutor was appealing to the sympathy of the jurors when he stated in his closing Argument the following:

Ladies and gentlemen, these defendants took the life of Dr. Haing Ngor. He was a doctor, he was an actor, he was an incredible man. These defendants tried to rob him of the most precious thing he had, his gold locket, the one thing that meant everything to him. That's what they tried to take. And when he wouldn't give it to them, ladies and gentlemen, these three defendants killed him for it, because to them it meant a few rocks of cocaine, and that's all that mattered.

Ladies and gentlemen, Dr. Haing Ngor survived the Killing Fields of Cambodia where over a million people died just to be murdered in the killing streets of Los Angeles. He was murdered by these defendants, and he was murdered for a few lousy rocks of cocaine.

The prosecutor ended with a call to justice, as he stated:

Dr. Ngor never got justice for what was done to him in Cambodia, but justice is in your hands now, and let's make sure that he gets justice for what was done to him in Los Angeles. Ladies and gentlemen, find the defendants guilty, because that's justice.

The cases were further appealed in the Ninth Circuit Court of Appeals, where three exceedingly experienced justices under the guidance of Justice Stephen Trott stated the following: ***"Because the state court's determination that the prosecutor's statements were proper was not an unreasonable application of clearly established federal law and was not based on an unreasonable determination of the facts, we reverse the district court's decision to grant the petitioner's habeas petitions."***

In other words, **the Justices of the Ninth Circuit Court of Appeals made sure that Justice was finally given to Dr. Haing Ngor.** As a result, the three Oriental Lazy Boyz gangsters didn't get away with the murder of one of the most wonderful, inspiring, humanitarian individuals to ever live and work in our City of the Angels. **JUSTICE WAS FINALLY DONE FOR DR. HAING NGOR.**

THAT WOMAN SHOULD BE DEAD

People vs. Frank Beltran

CHAPTER 66. BELTRAN SHOOTING

After leaving Chinatown, the path of old Route 66 basically follows Figueroa Boulevard up to Colorado Boulevard in Pasadena. From there, its trail becomes a straight arrow following Foothill Boulevard. After 15 miles, the road travels through the City of Azusa, were it veers to the right on a wide old road with the name Alosta Avenue. After a short distance, when approaching the City of Glendora, one notices that the street signs display the name of Route 66. As one travels the genuine 'Mother Highway,' we come to the intersection of Route 66 and Loraine Avenue. There, tucked behind some shrubs and bushes, is one of the last remnants of Route 66—one of the original service stations.

Our next case occurs just up Loraine Avenue, one block from Route 66. On the evening of February 4, 2006, Glendora police Officer O'Gorman received a radio call to go to a residence on Worthy Drive regarding a domestic violence dispute. This officer was patrolling on Route 66 when he received the radio call.

Grapahics Page

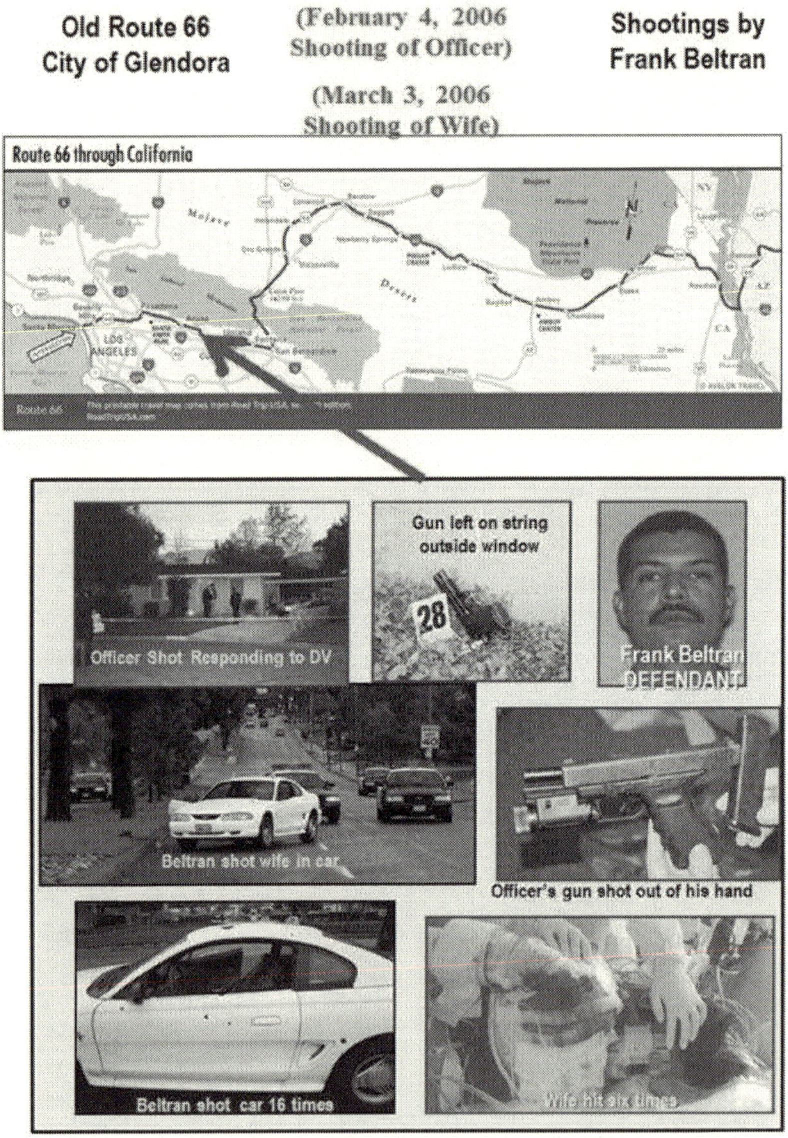

As to domestic violence (DV) police radio calls, they can amount to next to nothing, since the offending party is generally gone by the time the police officer arrives. However, there are the situations when both parties are present and the officer becomes the unwelcome referee between the two warring parties. Responding officers never know what they are getting involved in. Generally, there are no weapons involved, merely pushing and shoving.

When an officer comes in contact with the parties, the first order of business is to separate the parties, so the officer can get an idea as to what needs to be done. The officer knows not to concentrate his or her effort on deciding who started the dispute, since both sides always believe that it was the other party who started it. This is when a backup officer becomes very useful.

Unfortunately, the Glendora officer hadn't received any backup when he arrived at the residence. So the officer approached the front door in a cautious manner. Since the call indicated a possible kidnapping of the wife, the officer removed his gun from the holster and held it down at his side. He was holding a flashlight in his left hand and had his gun out in his right hand. He pushed the doorbell and could faintly hear the chimes ring. Several vehicles were in the driveway and the lights were on inside the house. The officer could hear noise coming from the interior of the house. He couldn't make out whether it was a stereo or TV playing in the background. No one was responding to the doorbell ringing, so the officer, in a loud, firm voice, shouted, "Police officer."

As Officer O'Gorman waited for a response, he could feel the freezing level had dropped. This city was once the heart of the largest orange-growing areas in California. Years earlier, this drop in temperature would have resulted in orange ranchers preparing to light up their smudge pots in order to save their orange crops from freezing. This was a divisive point between the city dwellers and the ranchers. Those living in the city disliked the ranchers for smudging, since it created soot on their drapes and smelled up an entire house for months. Of course, the ranchers felt it was necessary for them to save their orange crops.

Since the citrus groves have gone by the wayside, just like Route 66, Officer O'Gorman didn't have to be concerned with the temperature dropping below freezing. Since he wasn't getting any response from the occupants inside, he thought maybe the police station should call the 'call back number.' As he stood in front of the front door, there was the loud sound of a gunshot. He immediately felt his flashlight go flying out of his hand. He felt the bullet go directly through his hand, forcing him to drop his weapon.

His initial reaction was, where could he find some cover? From his position, he didn't know for certain where the shot had come from. Instantly he used his left hand to pick up his handgun. He moved backward to look for cover and decided to position himself between cars parked in the driveway. He used his radio to call for backup and indicate he had taken fire. He waited in the dark, looking behind him to see if any other units had arrived. Fortunately, Officer O'Gorman had a bulletproof vest with the flashlight to protect the officer from being killed or seriously injured. When the backup officer arrived, she found Officer O'Gorman between the cars in the driveway. She shone the light on O'Gorman's hand and could see the bullet hole. They hunkered down, moving backward out of the range of fire.

While the officers were regrouping, the police station dispatcher was receiving phone calls from frightened residents who were stranded inside their homes. From a small room inside the house, a male called the police dispatcher from his cell phone. He and two other people had run and hid in this room and locked the door. The dispatcher asked what type of emergency it was, and the man said in a muffled voice that he thought it was a 'Home Invasion' and someone had a gun. The dispatcher was trying to get the address where they were calling from. The man only knew they were on Worthy Drive, but had no idea what the address was. The dispatcher tried to get more information, but the people who were hiding inside just happened to be visiting and had no idea what the address was. Eventually, the dispatcher figured out that the callers were at the house where the officer had responded regarding a DV call.

Then all of a sudden shot could be heard on the phone line. The man said, "Shit, he's shooting at us." The dispatcher told the man to get down low so he wouldn't be hit. The situation was chaotic with the gunfire and the dispatcher trying to pry more information from the terrified people hiding inside. The dispatcher told the man that they had units outside the location. Then she asked him whether he could see the police units, to which the man, in a scared voice, said they were hiding in a back room and couldn't see anything in the front of the house.

The man sounded more desperate in that he said the man with the gun was running. He claimed he was afraid that the man was going to come back to kill them. Then the dispatcher asked who the runner with the gun was. He described him as **Frank Beltran**, the ex-husband of the woman who lived there.

At that point, the dispatcher put out the information that they were looking for a Frank Beltran. At that same moment, the Sheriff's Department came on the line with the dispatcher. They asked if the local police needed assistance, and the dispatcher stated that they would like an airship (helicopter) if the Sheriff had one available. The dispatcher stated that one of their officers had been wounded and they wanted to search the area to find the shooter, Frank Beltran. The Sheriff's deputy on the line asked what the main streets were, and the dispatcher said Loraine and Ada. The deputy, trying to get the airship up, asked again for the cross streets. This time the dispatcher said it was Loraine and Route 66, to which the deputy acknowledged he now understood the location. (It's amazing how 'Route 66' still carries considerable name recognition.)

However, when the police were able to get into the house, they found Angelique Beltran, who had been living there with their daughter. Emotionally distraught and scared to death, she related to the police what had occurred between her ex-husband and herself. Earlier in the evening, Frank Beltran, her ex, had talked her into meeting with him to try to work things out between them. She went alone to the Pomona Fairplex to meet Frank. He became very belligerent and demanded to see their daughter. She refused, because she was afraid that he was going take her away from her. He started to pull her hair and punch her. Then he removed some handcuffs and hooked her up. In desperation, she said that she would take him to where he could see his daughter.

They drove together to the Worthy Drive house in Glendora, where the daughter was located. At that point, Frank called a friend to come by and take their daughter away. This was done, and Angelique became irate at him and he pulled a gun and threatened everyone who was there in the house. That was when the other people maneuvered their way to the back room of the house.

Next door neighbors hearing the disturbance called the police to report the incident. That started the chain of events in which Frank Beltran barricaded himself in the house. When the first officer approached the front door, Frank shot directly at him. If it weren't for the bullet hitting the flashlight, he could have been killed or seriously injured. Once the police regrouped, they totally surrounded the house. Before they had the rear of the house covered, Frank was able to escape through the backyard.

Eventually, the police were able to contact the hostages and Angelique. When they checked the backyard, they found that Beltran had taken the gun and tied it to a string and had it dangling outside the back window. It was unclear why he had placed the gun on a string. Most likely he didn't want to be caught with the gun in his possession. And he may have thought that he could later come back and retrieve the gun.

The police started to conduct a massive search for Frank Beltran in the community. However, Frank was able to move himself all the way up to Foothill Boulevard, where he called a relative to come pick him up. Beltran seemed like a cat with nine lives in that he was able to evade the police dragnet.

CHAPTER 67. NO PLACE IS SAFE

Three weeks after the kidnapping of Angelique and the taking of their daughter, she was living in fear that her ex-husband would track her down and kill her. With the help of the courts and the DA's Office, she was relocated. The prosecutors wanted her to be protected so she would be available for court to testify against Frank for an earlier DV case between them. She was given a housing voucher to stay at the 20th Century Motor Lodge in Glendora. This motel was directly on Route 66 and was just east of Loraine Avenue. This was only several blocks from the location of shootout on Worthy Drive. The 20th Century Motor Lodge was well named, since it embodied the architecture and style of another century, especially the heydays of old Route 66. It had served as one of the classier motels, with roomy brick cottages spread over spacious green lawns. In the center of the motel complex was an old-fashioned swimming pool that was a meeting place where tourists gathered to tell stories of their travels on the 'Mother Road.'

Almost next door was the well-known 'Golden Spur Restaurant' with its Western motif. It catered to the tastes of the orange-ranching crowd mixed with the visiting tourists heading for LA. Nifty Nolan owned the restaurant and it projected a homey atmosphere. His manager, Walter Cason, gave it a family orientation that made it a typical Route 66 hangout. (Recently it had a little sprucing up and is still going strong, as though time has stood still within its walls.)

Unfortunately, most of the motels along this stretch of Route 66 have long been torn down. Yet the 20th Century Motor Lodge has struggled to find ways of making money in order to survive. The Witness Protective Program provided a source of steady income for the motel. It wasn't like the good old days when the 'No Vacancy' sign was turned on before 6:00 p.m.

Angelique felt safe living in this motel not because of the nostalgic past but because it was a long distance from West Covina, where they as a married couple had lived. She was driving a sporty white Mustang which was a boast to her self-confidence. She was always fearful that she might have to make a quick escape, and she felt a comfort having her Mustang nearby.

On March 3rd, 2006, during the afternoon she needed to go to the store to shop for food and get some items from the drug store. Angelique got into her Mustang and pulled out the motel's driveway onto Route 66 continuing eastbound. Little did she know that her ex, Frank Beltran, was hiding across the street in the Armstrong Nursery parking lot. As she drove toward the market on Lone Hill Avenue, she noticed in her rearview mirror a car was following her. She didn't recognize the little Chevrolet Cavalier until it came up alongside. When she saw it was her ex, she pulled into the Route 66 Shopping Center parking lot, hoping to lose him.

He rapidly pulled directly behind her. She raced to the other side of the parking lot and exited onto Lone Hill Avenue heading south. This seemed to lose him, at least for the moment. Then, down the block, she was faced with a red signal with traffic backup. By the time she was able to pass through it, again he was behind her. All she could think of was trying to outrun him. It seemed her Mustang would give her the advantage. But fate was against her in that she continually got stuck in traffic. When the signal changed, she raced down Lone Hill to Arrow Highway, which was the next major cross street.

Then she heard gunfire as he started shooting at her while she was trying to drive. She desperately pulled over to the right and stomped on the brakes. She leaned down in her car for protection as more bullets struck her car. She realized that she was like a sitting duck, so she shifted the car into drive and went plowing over the median divider as she headed eastbound on Arrow Highway.

He followed her, and her Mustang struck the curb and she lost control as her Mustang spun around. He came up to the side of her car and continually shot at her on the driver's side. Eventually, she fell down on the front seat as he continued to fire at her. Everyone in this busy intersection was petrified. It seemed like an eternity as bullets were flying in all directions, and then it was silent. No one knew why the shooting had stopped. Had he run out of ammo, or had his gun jammed? He slowly drove away eastbound on Arrow Highway.

The end result was that Angelique's Mustang was struck over a dozen times. At least six of the bullets penetrated her body. When she arrived at the ER, it initially appeared that little could be done to save Angelique. However, a doctor started poking at the various entry wounds and found that they mainly involved her left arm and shoulder. The bullets hadn't penetrated any of her vital organs. It was like working on 'Humpty Dumpty'—where should the doctors begin to put her back together again? To the credit of the ER staff, they didn't give up on Angelique.

After hours of surgery, the medical staff pulled off a miracle in saving Angelique's life. After a lengthy recovery, she lost some functionality in her left arm. She is a walking, talking example of how today's ERs can save lives when they have the right personnel and the right equipment.

CHAPTER 68. TRACKING DOWN THE SHOOTER

The police weren't at a lost for a suspect, since everyone knew that her ex-husband wanted to kill Angelique. But the question was where to find him. Was he still around? Who could be hiding him? Even though he had come within inches of killing Angelique, Frank still had his group of supporters. His claim was that he loved his daughter so much and he didn't want her to be raised by a druggy mother like Angelique. It was well known that Angelique had a sever drug problem. She had tried to clean up, but her addiction was deep rooted. Her ex-husband may have been a slightly better parent, since Frank's parents really tried to care for the little girl.

The Sheriff's Department was in charge of the investigation, and it conducted a search of the area of the shooting in hopes of coming up with witnesses or evidence that could help find Frank Beltran. Late on the night of the shooting, a deputy Sheriff spotted a car parked in the Target parking lot two blocks from where the shooting occurred. What attracted the deputy's attention was the fact that the front right tire was flat. He ran the license plate, which came back to a Chevrolet Cavalier but a different Cavalier, not the one in the parking lot. Then, when the VIN was entered, it came back as stolen from Pomona.

Then the deputy started to do an inventory inspection, during which he found a shell casing on the floor of the car. Then it was compared up to the shell casings from the shooting scene and found to be from the same gun. So the detective had found the car which was used by the shooter, but the question was, where was the shooter, Frank Beltran?

It was March 28, 2006, 25 days after the shooting of Angelique, when the Sheriff received word that Frank Beltran was at a house in Rancho Cucamonga. The authorities went to this large house not knowing what they would find, but the information was Beltran was holding up at this place that contained a large number of weapons. When they arrived, they learned that Beltran was inside but he wasn't going to surrender. The SWAT team was called and took up strategic locations.

No one wanted to engage in a firefight, so negotiators were brought in to talk Frank out. After several hours, Frank walked out and surrendered. When the authorities checked out the upscale house, they found handguns and rifles all over the place. They obtained a search warrant for this house and another house the owner lived in, in the adjacent City of Upland. There they discovered hundreds of weapons and thousands of rounds of ammunition. What it turned out to be was the home of a clandestine arms dealer from Cuba.

It's interesting how some investigations mushrooms into gigantic illegal activities. Here Frank Beltran was wanted merely for Domestic Violence against his wife, but his arrest led to the largest weapons seizure in San Bernardino County history.

Frank Beltran was tried on Attempted Murder charges involving the Glendora officer and his wife. His wife was well enough to testify against him as to him shooting her in the street. The Glendora officer testified that he had been shot at. Frank Beltran testified in his trial, and his justification was that he wanted to protect his little daughter from having to be raised by Angelique, who he considered a 'rotten mother.'

The jury didn't show any mercy for Frank, and after he was convicted, he was sentenced to 15 years to Life in state prison. What was sad about Frank's case was the fact that their daughter was the biggest loser. Although Frank would have been the better parent of the two, the little girl wouldn't have him in her life, at least for the next 15 years.

Putting aside the violent memories of the Frank Beltran case, the fair City of Glendora went on a crusade to resurrect old Route 66. The nostalgia buffs want to turn back the clocks to a more peaceful time. This Beltran case took place in the heart of one of the most sacred stretches of Route 66. Ironically, the Beltran case proves that we can't go back in time since some things have forever changed. Merely changing the name back to 'Historic Route 66' doesn't guarantee that we can return to the GOOD OL' PEACEFUL DAYS.

WHICH WAY DOES THE CREEK FLOW?

People vs. David Mahler

CHAPTER 69. MAHLER CASE

From the City of Glendora, old Route 66 continues eastbound on what is known as Foothill Boulevard. After traveling through Upland and Rancho Cucamonga, you cruise by one of the icons of the 'Mother Road' in Rialto, where many families have spent a night or two at the Wigwam Motel. These old tepees were built of stucco back in 1949 and reflected the glory days of the route. Although they may not be the most comfortable motel rooms, they have been a major attraction for young kids who wanted to play 'Cowboys and Indians' and have the opportunity to sleep like an Indian in a wigwam.

Graphics Page

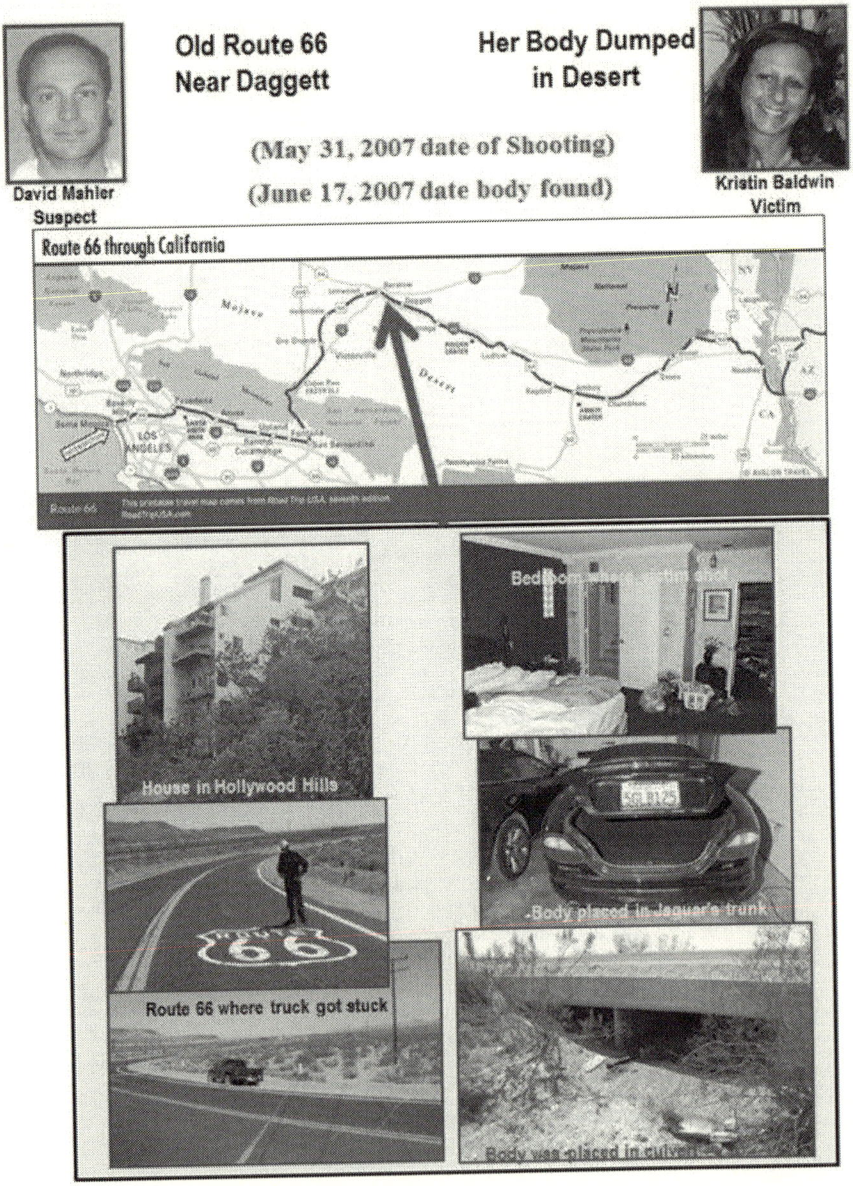

Next, the traveler arrives at the City of San Bernardino, which has seen better days, during its boom years. Then, its claim to fame was having the first McDonald's fast food restaurant. Back in 1940, brothers Richard and Maurice McDonald opened a BBQ eatery with carhops and an extensive menu. By 1948, the McDonald brothers had a better idea for their little restaurant—reducing the size of the menu and concentrating on basics such as hamburgers, malts and sodas. In this way they could provide faster service at a lower price. (A hamburger was a mere 15 cents.) This concept changed the restaurant business forever. This all occurred on the Route 66 business district section that looped through San Bernardino. Later, businessman Ray Kroc purchased the operation and established the new Golden Arches McDonald's in the Chicago area.

Although the City of San Bernardino may have been on the cutting edge of fast food service in the 1940s, its more recent claim to fame is that it was one of three cities in California that declared bankruptcy. Putting aside sadder memories, we head up the Cajon Pass, which was a piece of cake coming from Chicago. But heading eastbound, it contains a steep grade that made it a nightmare for old Fords experiencing 'vapor lock' or Chevys with radiators boiling over. When your car made it to the 4,189-foot summit, there was a sigh of relief. From there on, all one had to do was roll through the town of Victorville and try not to be distracted by stopping at the old Roy Rogers – Dale Evans Museum to visit Roy's favorite stuffed horse, 'Trigger.' (In 2003, the museum was moved to Branson, Missouri, where it remained until 2009, when it finally closed its doors for good. No longer the King of the Cowboys will be saying "Happy trails to you.")

Then it was a relatively straight road through the desert for 30 miles until Barstow appeared on the horizon. The original Route 66 from Barstow east paralleled the railroad tracks of the Atchison, Topeka and Santa Fe Railroad. Barstow is where Route 66 and the railroads share something in common, which is the **Harvey House**. Back in the 1880s, the railroad was trying to improve service for its passengers by building restaurants along its tracks. Fred Harvey established the Harvey Houses, where the passengers could get off the trains to enjoy good home cooking served by friendly Harvey Girls. (This may have been a tamer version of today's Hooters Restaurants.)

The Barstow Harvey House was built around 1910, including a restaurant as well as a hotel for the railroad. Emblazoned over the entrance were the words 'Casa del Desierto,' which meant 'House in the Desert.' Although the Harvey House was built for the railroad passengers, it wasn't long before the Route 66 travelers also used it.

As time went by, the railroads didn't need the Harvey Houses, and they were quietly shuttered. However, the Barstow Harvey House building was revitalized, and in 2001, it became the crown jewel for the true aficionados of Route 66 when it was dedicated as the official Route 66 Museum.

After visiting the Museum, it seems like the visitor has walked down memory lane, getting pumped up on all that nostalgia. Traveling eastward on the main street leads to the original highway. At that point, Route 66 becomes a two-lane road that has its share of dips and gullies. Its official name is the National Trails Highway and it looks and feels like any other old desert road. After several miles, the road comes to a 'T' intersection with Nebo Street. This might appear to be the end of old Route 66.

This nondescript intersection out in nowhere is the last murder crime scene of this book. It all happened on May 31, 2007, around 4:00 a.m., when a dark Jaguar pulled up near this intersection. The driver opened the door and stepped out, scanning the horizon looking for any other souls. It was pitch black for all 360 degrees. The only illumination was the headlights of his car. He could feel a slight desert breeze with a slight whiff of sage as he quickly walked to the trunk, where he reached down to release the trunk latch.

His head looked side to side to see if any headlights were approaching. With a jerk from his hand, the trunk lid popped wide open. He turned his head upward as though he was trying to prevent inhaling the noxious odors emanating from the dead body lying in the trunk. The stench from this three-day-old corpse was more than he could bear.

His confused mind was driving him at that point. His stomach tightened, and he felt the dry heaves racing up his throat. He shook his head, knowing that he didn't have time to waste to barf. His arms went into a robotic mode, reaching under the dead woman's body and slowly lifting her up. Although in life she had been of average weight, he couldn't believe how heavy she seemed to be now. It was like lifting dead weight.

As he attempted to raise her body to clear the back of the trunk, the putrid smell was wavering up the nostril of his nose. Psychologically, he had to reach down within himself to continue. He reflected on the fact that he was a prominent criminal Defense attorney who couldn't be caught with a dead woman's body in his car. At that moment he was being driven by **FEAR**. No way was he going to be caught.

In order to be able to carry on his fine lifestyle, living on top of the Hollywood Hills surround by the most beautiful women, he needed to be sure that this DEAD BODY NEVER WAS FOUND. This anxiety drove him to be able to carry the dead body over to the side of the desert road and drop the corpse into the bottom of a culvert. He climbed down into the ditch and mustered up enough strength to drag and push the body into the three-foot drain pipe. From that location, no one would ever see or find the body.

As he pushed the corpse farther into the drain pipe, a sense of satisfaction came over him. He prided himself on being a great trial lawyer who could always outsmart his opponent. Here he was on his hands and knees doing what was necessary to get away with murder. Then he thought for a moment and remembered that he had better get out of there before someone came along and spotted him in the culvert. With that thought, he dashed up the sides of the gully and slammed the trunk closed and jumped into his Jaguar. His foot hit hard on the accelerator, and the car made a wide U-turn at the intersection of old Route 66. The area was so desolate today, although 50 years ago, this part of the 'Mother Road' would have been crawling with truckers and travelers searching for a better life. The killer peacefully headed back to his home, high above the Sunset Strip.

Now, with the victim's body well covered in this culvert out in nowhere, all the killer had to do was keep his mouth shut and he was home free. Without a dead body, there was little that the police could do to make a case.

Like in so many crimes, a fluke of fate changed everything. Unbeknown to the murderer, there was a flash flood, and the body somehow slightly floated out of the culvert. Some 16 days later, on June 16, 2007, a damsel was driving down Nebo Street approaching the intersection with old Route 66. A pickup truck came toward her crossing over the center line, forcing her to take evasive action by driving onto the shoulder of the highway. This shoulder consisted of soft sand in which her pickup truck quickly became mired down. The more she accelerated, the deeper the truck sank into the sand. Then the realization was that she was stuck in the sand on an isolated desert road. Her immediate reaction was to use her cell phone to call for help. However, where she was located there was no cell phone reception.

Little did she know that she was on the shoulder of old Route 66, on which many years earlier, travelers had had similar problems of becoming stuck in the shoulder or had auto breakdowns. However, one of the extraordinary advantages of traveling old Route 66 years ago was that everyone was considered family. If a person broke down or needed help on Route 66, within minutes someone would stop to see if they could help. For whatever reason, Route 66 exemplified the Golden Rule, which is 'to do unto others as you want them to do to you.'

On that June day, the spirit of old Route 66 was alive and well. It wasn't long before a young man pulled over and asked her if she needed help. As he started to help, another man stopped to help. Both men, one in his 20s and the other in his 30s, jointly agreed what was needed was to find something such as a board or boulder to place under the back tires so she could gain traction.

Since they were in an isolated area, a wooden plank was unlikely, but a flat boulder would be their best bet. Both men as a team walked along the side of the highway and came to a small wash that ran under the highway in a culvert. The one man was intensely looking down into the wash for the appropriate size rocks. All of a sudden, his attention was attracted to a bright flash. He squinted at the light source and noticed that it looked like the face of a watch. This didn't add up for a watch to be in a shallow wash.

In an instant, he mentioned what he had seen to the other man. They were both perplexed by the sighting, so the one jumped down into the wash for a better view to satisfy their curiosity. As he drew closer, he had one of those 'oh shit' moments. He yelled to the other guy to come on down.

They both stood in surprise, not knowing what to say or do. The one went over to examine what appeared to be a dead body. It was a grim sight of a decomposed body that had the appearance of a female with a gold-colored wristwatch on her left hand. The two men climbed out of the wash, and they alerted the Sheriff's Department. Shortly, this old part of Route 66 was turned into a crime scene.

This all became a part of the ***David Mahler*** case, in which a New York criminal attorney moved to Hollywood to live the good life. Unfortunately, his life turned into drugs and prostitutes, with him playing Russian roulette with a young woman whose body was the one found in the culvert. This fascinating case was the basis for the book titled ***Date with the Devil*** by your author and his good friend Don Lasseter.

Several hours later, the coroner's office removed the body. The detectives and the CSI team finished up their crime scene investigation. Then this part of the famous old highway returned to normal, which resembles a deserted highway. This road continued to the City of Daggett, which was well traveled in the peak days of Route 66. However, today it struggles to exist with its post office and grocery store, but most everything else has faded into oblivion.

Route 66 continues through the desert, continuing to use the name National Trails Highway. Today, few people can be seen driving this desolate highway of what used to be Route 66. Maybe a local who is in no hurry or the occasional Route 66 buff who wants to experience a part of America's past will be seen slowly driving down the road. There is nothing to see but desert and more desert. Strewn along the way are the remnants of abandoned buildings such as motels, coffee shops and gas stations that service no one these days. A short mile over is the high-speed superhighway Interstate 40, which sucked the life out of the legendary Route 66.

What is the mystique of old historic Route 66? Why do so many fans have this attachment to the old Mother Highway that today only exists in a person's mind? The answer is that this old highway represents a time in America's history when life was virtuous and peaceful. Crime wasn't rampant, and locking up your house didn't enter a person's mind. The author remembers growing up on Route 66 and how this highway seemed to link the communities together. As the Interstate highway system grew, so did the crime rate. Isn't it ironic that as the legendary Route 66 faded into extinction, a bloody trail of murders followed in its path.

This book reflects how times have changed. Evidence of that is revealed in the **Shootout on the Santa Monica Pier**, where a number of officers and civilians were shot. That was followed by the **'German Tourist'** who was shot and killed next to the pier over a 'robbery gone bad.' This one shooting became an international incident regarding tourism. Before leaving Santa Monica, we remember the **Farmers' Market**, where the dead body count reached ten, caused by an elderly driver.

Continuing down Santa Monica Boulevard, we come to where **Kenneth Hunt the Handyman** liked to kill his old lady clients. Then it's on to the West Hollywood area, where actress **Dominque Dunne** was a victim of Domestic Violence. That one killing propelled her father Dominick Dunne to start writing about the 'rich and famous' murderers. However, not even a Hollywood writer could conceive of a more grotesque mutilation case than that carried out by **Keven Graff**. We travel to **Dodger Stadium**, where it isn't safe to walk to your car in the parking lot without being shot or beaten to death. As we near Chinatown, we learn that the **Killing Fields** are not exclusively in Cambodia.

In the heart of the revitalization of Route 66 in the City of Glendora, a young woman, **Angelique Beltran**, is shot six times by her ex-husband and is left for dead. Although we leave the jurisdiction of Los Angeles County, we still encounter one of its dead bodies placed in a culvert by attorney **David Mahler** off of Route 66 just outside of the desert town of Barstow.

Yes, there are many murder victims who litter the path of old Route 66. We can't blame the Mother Highway for all this crime. But there seems to be no end to the **KILLINGS ON ROUTE 66.**

Made in United States
Orlando, FL
04 November 2026

90205460R00187